Foster Catalogue 2001

D0860780

Die Deutsche Bibliothek –
CIP-Cataloguing-in-Publication-Data
A catalogue record for this
publication is available from
Die Deutsche Bibliothek

Library of Congress
Cataloguing-in-Publication is available

©2001, Foster and Partners, London
and Prestel Verlag, Munich · London
New York

Prestel Verlag
Mandlstrasse 26
80802 Munich
Germany
Tel +49 (089) 381709-0
Fax +49 (089) 381709-35
sales@prestel.de

175 Fifth Ave.
Suite 402
New York NY 10010
USA
Tel +1 (212) 995-2720
Fax +1 (212) 995-2733
sales@prestel-usa.com

4 Bloomsbury Place
London WC1A 2QA
United Kingdom
Tel +44 (020) 7323-5004
Fax +44 (020) 7636-8004
sales@prestel-uk.co.uk

Printed in Spain
ISBN 3-7913-2401-2
D.L. M-26693-2001

Foster Catalogue 2001

Prestel Munich · London · New York

Contents

Architecture and Sustainability Norman Foster

A photograph of our studio at Riverside, taken shortly after we occupied it in 1990, shows only a handful of computers on the desks; today every single workstation has one. Computer screens have already replaced the traditional drawing board and some of the most fundamental aspects of our profession are changing as a result of this technology – in terms of working patterns, social relations and our responses to environmental challenges. For example, many of the 'green' ideas that we explored in early projects are only now being made possible by the new technologies at our disposal.

This book is a survey of almost forty years of work over a period of huge social and technological transformation. The rate of change is increasing rather than diminishing, and that is reflected in the buildings and projects illustrated here. However, it is also possible to trace consistent themes and concerns throughout our work.

Our buildings have always been driven by a belief that the quality of our surroundings directly influences the quality of our lives, whether in the workplace, at home or in the public spaces that make up our cities. This emphasis on the social dimension is an acknowledgement that architecture is generated by people's needs, both spiritual and material. Allied to this is a willingness to challenge accepted responses or solutions.

Looking back I can see that our practice has been inspired by the polarities of analysis and action. This means trying to ask the right questions and having an insatiable curiosity about how things work – whether they are organisations or mechanical systems. And it means never taking anything for granted, always trying to probe deeper. This is due in part to a fascination with enquiry, with going back to first principles to identify whether there is an opportunity to invent, or reinvent, a solution.

The quest for quality embraces the physical performance of buildings. How well will they endure in a volatile world? Will they survive or become obsolete? Does the thinking behind their design anticipate needs that might not have been defined when they were created? Only time will tell, and so we design buildings that are flexible and able to accommodate change.

It is not only individual buildings but also urban design that affects our well-being. A concern for the physical context has produced projects that are sensitive to the culture and climate of their place. For me, the optimum design solution integrates social, technological, aesthetic, economic and environmental concerns. We have applied these priorities to public infrastructure projects worldwide – in airports, railway stations, metros, bridges, telecommunications towers, regional plans and city centres.

The last two decades in particular have witnessed changes in public attitudes to ecology and energy consumption. In many of our projects we have anticipated these trends and have pioneered solutions using totally renewable energy sources which limit the consumption of natural resources and offer dramatic reductions in pollution.

Examples are not confined to buildings – working with industry we have created a new generation of wind turbines, cladding systems that harvest energy, even a solar-assisted electric vehicle.

While we frequently explore the newest technologies to find appropriate solutions, we also seek inspiration from forgotten traditions: using natural ventilation or finding ways to reflect natural light into an interior space, for example.

There are often links between the ecology of a building, which is measurable, and the poetic dimension of architecture, which is more difficult to quantify. For example, at Stansted Airport, if sunlight dapples the floor at a particular time of day it is due to a conscious decision that sunlight should be an essential ingredient of the interiors. It has been thoroughly modelled and explored. It comes out of a passion for the quality of that space and the humanity of the building.

Sustainability is a word that has become fashionable in the last decade. However, sustainability is not a matter of fashion but of survival. Sustainable architecture can be simply defined as doing the most with the least means. The Miesian maxim 'Less is more' is, in ecological terms, exactly the same as the proverbial injunction 'Waste not, want not'.

1, 2. Foster and Partners' studio at Riverside in 1990 and 2000 respectively, before and after the introduction of computers.
3. Hong Kong International Airport – the result of an extensive land reclamation programme.
4. A vertical city – the Millennium Tower proposal for Tokyo.

1   2

3

The United Nations recently warned in its Global Environment Outlook 2000 report of a series of looming environmental crises sparked by increasing water shortages, global warming and pollution. It suggested that these trends can be halted, but only if developed countries reverse their pattern of wasteful consumption of raw materials and energy, reducing levels by as much as 90 per cent.

Environmental issues affect architecture at every level. Buildings consume half the energy used in the developed world, while another quarter is used for transport. Architects cannot solve all the world's ecological problems but we can design buildings to run at a fraction of current energy levels and we can influence transport patterns through urban planning. The location and function of a building, its flexibility and lifespan, its orientation, its form and structure, its heating and ventilation systems and the materials used to construct it all impact upon the amount of energy required to build, run and maintain it and to travel to and from it.

Sustainable architecture is not concerned merely with the design of individual buildings. The planning study we undertook in the mid-1970s for Gomera in the Canary Islands pioneered the exploration of sustainable patterns of tourist development. The client, Fred Olsen, who ran cruises to the Canaries, shared our concern for environmental issues. We investigated the use of alternative energy sources – wind and solar power and methane production from domestic waste – to reduce the island's reliance on imported oil and encourage self-sustaining development. It was a 'green' project long before the green agenda was seriously being discussed.

Similarly, sustainable architecture must address the context of our ever-expanding cities and their infrastructures. Unchecked urban sprawl is one of the chief problems facing the world today. As our cities grow horizontally rather than vertically, swallowing up more and more land, people are forced to travel greater distances between home and work. Between 1900 and 2000 the average distance travelled by an individual per day in Britain increased from 1.5 miles to 25 miles. Today 90 per cent of all shopping trips in Britain are made by car.

There is a direct correlation between urban density and energy consumption – smaller, denser cities promote walking and cycling rather than driving. For example, although Copenhagen and Detroit have populations of roughly equal size and similar climatic conditions, a person in Copenhagen consumes approximately 10 per cent of the energy consumed by his or her counterpart in Detroit. This can largely be accounted for by the greater reliance on cars in Detroit due to its population density of 39.2 people per square kilometre compared to Copenhagen's 122.4 people per square kilometre.

High urban density leads to improved quality of life when housing, work and leisure facilities are all close by. High density – or high-rise – does not automatically mean overcrowding or economic hardship. Significantly, the world's two most densely populated regions, Monaco and Macao, are at opposite ends of the economic spectrum. And in London some of the most expensive areas are also the most densely populated: Mayfair, Kensington and Chelsea have population densities of 35,000 people per square kilometre, ten times higher than those in some of the capital's poorest boroughs.

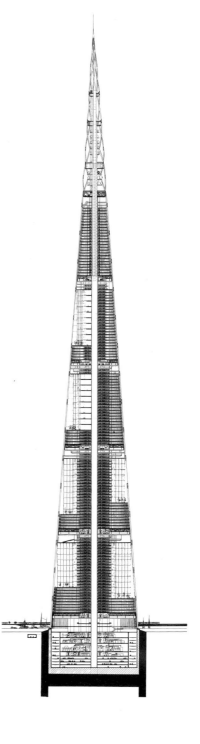

4

The Millennium Tower that we proposed in Tokyo in 1989 takes a traditional horizontal city quarter – housing, shops, restaurants, cinemas, museums, sporting facilities, green spaces and public transport networks – and turns it on its side to create a super-tall building with a multiplicity of uses. It is over 800 metres high with 170 storeys – twice the height of anything so far built – and can house a community of up to 60,000 people. This is 20,000 more than the population of Monaco and yet the building occupies only 0.013 square kilometres of land compared to Monaco's 1.95 square kilometres. It is a virtually self-sufficient, fully self-sustaining community in the sky. This sounds like future fantasy. But we now have all the means at our disposal to create such buildings.

Many cities continue to spread their boundaries because nobody is prepared to make planning decisions at a political level. This is also true of infrastructure, such as transport networks and airports. The new airport at Chek Lap Kok in Hong Kong is an example of how political will can produce a long-term solution to a problem on an unprecedented scale and achieve it quickly. In one-tenth of the time that it has taken London's Heathrow Airport to grow, Hong Kong has overtaken it, realising a greater capacity in a single massive building. By 2040 Chek Lap Kok's planned capacity of 80 million passengers and 375,000 aircraft movements per annum, will be equivalent to those of Heathrow and New York's JFK airports combined.

In Hong Kong, when the time came to select the site for a new airport there was no available land. The site itself had to be created. But far from being an obstacle to development, this became instead the catalyst for the largest construction project of modern times. In 1992, Chek Lap Kok was a compact mountainous island rising out of the sea off the South China coast. An extensive reclamation programme that involved moving 200 million cubic metres of rock, mud and sand reduced the island's 100-metre-high peak to a flat 7 metres above sea level and expanded the island to four times its original size. At 6 kilometres long and 3.5 kilometres wide, it is now as large as the Kowloon peninsula.

The almost universal model of an airport in the Western world is one of incremental, ad hoc growth. Heathrow is still expected to expand on its original site by adding yet more terminal buildings. The end product is a non-finite architecture of individual structures, each in a continuous state of flux, the only limiting factors in this cycle being land and runway capacity. As a result, Heathrow is closer to the 'concrete jungle' of a 1960s new town than to the planned development of Chek Lap Kok.

As architects we are rarely given the opportunity to influence the urban environment on the broadest scale by planning an entire city or neighbourhood, but we can improve the environment at a local level by insisting on the need for mixed-use developments.

Our own studio in Battersea pioneered the reintroduction of mixed-use development in London. Although it has recently become fashionable to advocate the virtues of mixing uses such as living and working in one location, such compact communities are in direct contrast to most of today's planning guidelines, which specify separate zones for residential, commercial or industrial use, or for leisure and culture. The consequences of this approach – social alienation, the need for extensive commuting with all its associated traffic and pollution problems, and the ecological impact of low-density sprawl – are only now beginning to be fully appreciated.

In the past, it was the blighting nature of heavy industry that was responsible for many of these zoning policies. Today, however, 'clean' industries such as microelectronics, and new service-sector offices and studios, are completely compatible with residential areas: workplaces can be combined with housing and retail accommodation to create localised communities. In Duisburg, in the former 'rust belt' of the Ruhr, we have demonstrated that inner cities can be revitalised by introducing these newer industries and locating them alongside housing and schools – even creating more green spaces in the process.

Facing page The Reichstag's cupola is integral to the natural lighting and ventilation strategies for the building as well as forming a landmark for Berlin.
1. Duisburg Microelectronic Park integrates new 'clean' industries into a residential district.

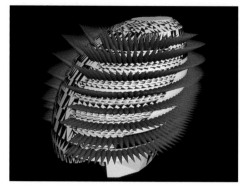

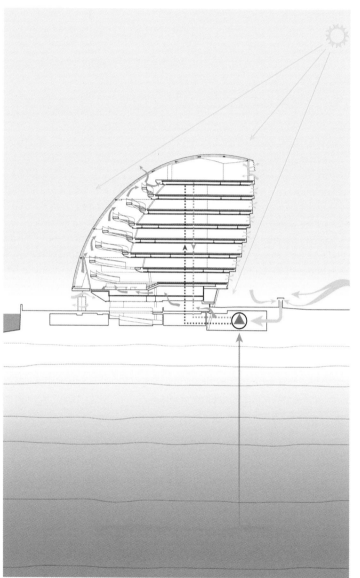

Furthermore, we have shown that such buildings can be ecologically sensitive and strive towards sustainability. In the Duisburg Microelectronic Park buildings we developed the technology to reclaim heat from extracted air and to use that heat to produce chilled water – via an absorption cooling plant – to cool the building in summer.

Adaptability is one of the most important tools in sustainable architecture. Working patterns have become much more flexible over the last two decades. Many people now work from home on a laptop computer, connected to their colleagues via e-mail and fax. In response to technological developments, working patterns will no doubt continue to change. We cannot predict the precise nature of these developments but we can build flexibility into the structure of buildings so that they can continue to be useful as circumstances alter.

For example, the headquarters for Willis Faber & Dumas, completed in the mid-1970s, pioneered the use of raised floors throughout the office accommodation at a time when such floors were exclusive to computer rooms. Raised floors sit above the main structural slab, with a void in-between for channelling electrical and telecommunications cabling. The flexibility inherent in this simple system has huge benefits in environmental terms. Willis Faber was able to undertake extensive computerisation in the 1980s with minimal disruption and was the only large insurance company in Britain that was not forced to commission an entirely new building.

⊕ Heat exchanger

⤴ Natural ventilation

▬ Cellings chilled by
ground water

······· Warm air extracted
via celling is recycled

▬ Cold water from
underground aquifer

We are now installing raised floors for the first time in residential accommodation as part of a mixed-use project in Cologne in Germany, which takes the mixed-use proposition to its logical conclusion. The Gerling Ring project, combines apartments, offices, shops and restaurants within a structure that allows individual units to be easily adapted from offices to apartments should the need arise in future.

Germany's enlightened legislation on working conditions means that all office staff have a right to daylight and access to an openable window. This promotes the design of office buildings with relatively shallow floor-plates, which means that, at a fundamental level, there need be little difference between the basic configuration of an apartment or an office building, except for the provision of bathrooms and kitchens. If, in thirty years' time, there is no longer such a high demand for office space in Cologne, the offices can be converted to apartments in an efficient manner, rather than being wastefully demolished.

Indeed, the constant cycle of demolition and rebuilding puts a huge strain on natural resources and energy usage; in terms of sustainability, demolition should be the option of last resort. In Britain alone, demolition produces a staggering 70 million tonnes of waste material annually.

Construction of new buildings uses approximately 4 per cent of Britain's total energy consumption and generates 40 million tonnes of carbon dioxide each year. Up to 60 per cent of the energy and resources used in construction is spent on the shell and core of a building, so retention of a building's structure through conversion makes sound ecological sense.

Embodied energy is now one of the most important considerations in sustainable architecture. In simple terms, a building embodies the sum of the energy used to make all of its components plus the energy expended in its construction. The longer the building lasts, the greater the return on the investment in its embodied energy will be. This tends to reinforce the argument for the use of high-quality materials that will have a long life. But here the numerical equations for embodied energy become more difficult.

For example, the refinement of aluminium requires such an enormous energy input that it has been dubbed an 'unsustainable' material. But high-quality aluminium can last for decades without maintenance. Lower grade materials, which may appear to be more sustainable, might need to be repaired or replaced in the same period, leading to a greater consumption of energy.

In these terms, sustainability can be equated with durability and the pleasure that people derive from things of quality. Sustainability does not have to mean lack of comfort or amenity.

The shape and alignment of a building can also have a dramatic effect on energy usage. The form of the new headquarters building for the Greater London Authority (GLA) has been generated as a result of scientific analysis, aiming to reduce heat loss and gain through the building's skin, thus lowering its energy needs. Minimising the building's surface area results in maximum efficiency in energy terms. Its form is derived from a sphere, which has 25 per cent less surface area than a cube of the same volume. This pure form has been manipulated to achieve optimum performance, particularly to minimise the surface area exposed to direct sunlight.

This strategy is backed up with a host of passive environmental control systems: the building will be naturally ventilated for most of the year, with openable windows in all office spaces; heat generated by computers, lights and people can be recycled within the building; and cold ground water can be pumped up from the water table through boreholes to cool the building. The combination of these energy-saving systems means that for most of the time the headquarters will require no additional heating and will use only a quarter of the energy consumed by a typical high-specification office building.

3

1, 2. The Greater London Authority Headquarters: natural ventilation and heating strategies combine with a form designed to minimise heat gain.
3. Comparative cross-sections of the Gerling Ring development in Cologne, designed for easy conversion from offices (below) to apartments (above).

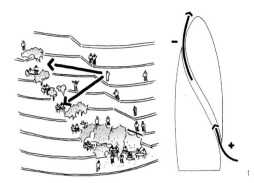

A similar degree of geometric complexity is shared by another project, the London headquarters for Swiss Re – a 41-storey office building in the City of London. The profile of this tall tower can be likened to a cigar – a cylinder that widens as it rises from the ground and then tapers towards its apex. This form responds to the specific demands of the small site: the building appears less bulky than a conventional rectangular block of equivalent floor area; the double curvature of the tower reduces reflections and improves transparency; and the slimming of the building's profile maximises space and daylight penetration at ground level.

The building's environmental strategy focuses on a series of sky gardens which are created by making six triangular incisions into the edges of each circular floor-plate – in plan the floors resemble car wheel hubs with radiating spokes. Each floor is rotated in relation to its neighbour so that the gardens spiral around the building's periphery. The gardens form part of the building's natural ventilation system and will be filled with plants, which help to oxygenate the air.

Swiss Re builds upon an example pioneered at the Commerzbank Headquarters in Frankfurt, which stemmed from a desire to reconcile work and nature within the compass of an office building. This, in turn, recalls earlier projects: for example, Willis Faber, with its turfed roof garden, was an early attempt to bring the 'park' into the office; and at the Hongkong and Shanghai Bank Headquarters we proposed 'gardens in the sky' which unfortunately failed to materialise.

The Commerzbank also gave us the opportunity to design a building that is symbolically and functionally 'green' and responsive to its city-centre location: it is the world's first ecological high-rise tower. It is also one of the tallest towers in Europe – not that that is so significant. What is important is the way in which we developed a strategy that allowed us to integrate such a tall building into the city and to break down its scale. It rises from the centre of a large traditional city block. By rebuilding and preserving the smaller scale of the perimeter buildings we were able to restore the grain of the neighbourhood at street level. The bank is linked to these surroundings by a covered public arcade through the site; this provides a social focus, with cafés and spaces for exhibitions and other events enhancing local amenities.

Thirty years ago, when we were designing the Willis Faber building in another city-centre location, a collaboration with Buckminster Fuller prompted the idea of enclosing the site in a free-form glass skin to create a building with its own microclimate. At the time we lacked the technological expertise to realise the enclosure within the schedule – its complex, double-curved geometry would have made it difficult to build. But today we have digital technologies that allow us to design and build structures such as the GLA and Swiss Re headquarters in a fraction of the time it would have taken in the 1970s.

One such technique is parametric modelling, which was originally developed in the aerospace and automotive industries for designing complex curved forms, and is now having a fundamental effect on the design of buildings. It is a three-dimensional computer modelling process that works like a conventional numerical spreadsheet. It allows any element of a design to be amended, automatically regenerating the model in much the same way that a spreadsheet recalculates numerical changes.

The same technology also allows curved surfaces to be rationalised into flat panels, facilitating economical production of cladding and glazing elements. This has demystified the structure and building components of highly complex geometric forms, ensuring that they are built economically and efficiently.

The Music Centre we are currently designing at Gateshead on Tyneside is a case in point. It is a key element in the cultural regeneration of a derelict riverside area and will provide accommodation for the Regional Music School and three auditoria of varying sizes for performances of classical and popular music. Each auditorium is conceived as a separate enclosure linked by a concourse in the form of a covered 'street' along the water-front. The budget is relatively modest, so we have designed a roof that will shelter the auditoria, the concourse and the music school in the most efficient way possible – closely hugging the buildings beneath.

1. Drawings of the spiralling sky gardens at the Swiss Re Headquarters: their shape encourages the natural flow of air, while the plants they house oxygenate the building.
2. The sky gardens at the Commerzbank – the first ecological high-rise tower.

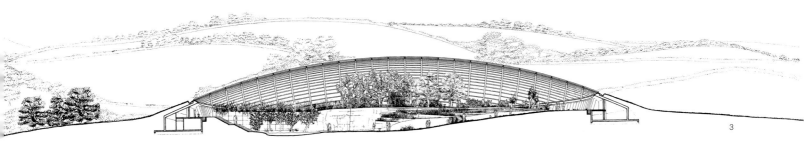

In 'shrink-wrapping' the buildings a free-form shape was generated. However, it was clear that to be an economic reality the roof would have to conform to geometric rules in order to rationalise the manufacture of individual components. We therefore altered the shape of the roof to correspond to the arcs of nine circles to produce a form that was economical and more easily understood, and to articulate its stainless-steel roof surface as a series of mass-producible panels.

Such efficient forms do not necessarily require sophisticated modern materials, however. For example, on a project currently under development, the Chesa Futura in St Moritz in Switzerland, we are using parametric modelling to help design an apartment block which, despite its novel shape, employs traditional timber building techniques.

Timber construction is one of the most environmentally benign forms of building. Wood is an entireiy renewable resource and it absorbs carbon dioxide during its growth cycle. Using timber is especially sustainable if indigenous timber is used so that little or no energy is expended in transportation. In Switzerland, building in timber makes sense for many reasons: it is culturally sympathetic, reflecting local architectural traditions, and it contributes to an established ecology of felling older trees to allow forest regeneration.

Similarly, the Great Glasshouse at the National Botanic Garden of Wales in Carmarthenshire draws lessons from the ecology of its site, in this case to heat and service the building in an energy-efficient way. It is heated in part by a biomass boiler – a modern wood-chip combustion plant – which burns timber trimmings from the gardens and prepared waste supplied by landfill contractors. Compared with the burning of oil, this process emits negligible amounts of sulphur and nitrogen oxides. Furthermore, the carbon dioxide emitted during the combustion process is broadly equivalent to the amount absorbed by the plants during their lifetime, creating a carbon dioxide cycle close to equilibrium.

This environmental approach is continued throughout: rain water from the roof of the Glasshouse is channelled into storage tanks to supply 'grey water' for irrigation and flushing lavatories, while waste from the lavatories is treated in an on-site sewage-treatment plant using natural reed beds. Even the ash created by combustion can be used as a fertiliser. These are systems that work with, rather than against, nature and which have a minimal ecological impact.

Elsewhere, we have been working on other non-polluting forms of energy generation. The wind turbines we developed with the German company Enercon create clean renewable energy, each one producing enough power to supply 1,600 homes. The engineering of the turbine is both innovative and highly efficient.

Unlike most turbines, it has no gearbox; the generator is driven directly by the rotor so that kinetic energy from the wind is converted directly into regulated electric current. Small wings at the tips of the rotor blades – like the 'winglets' on an aircraft wing – reduce aerodynamic noise and enhance the blades' efficiency.

Such sustainable forms of energy generation can be augmented with integrated systems for heating and cooling buildings. For example, the New German Parliament at the Reichstag in Berlin, rather than burning fossil fuels, runs on renewable 'bio-diesel' – refined vegetable oil made from rape or sunflower seeds. Together with increased use of daylight and natural ventilation, this has led to a 94 per cent reduction in the building's carbon dioxide emissions. The building is also able to store and recycle surplus energy using underground reservoirs.

Before the installation of new services the Reichstag consumed enough energy annually to heat 5,000 modern homes. Raising the internal temperature by just one degree on a typical mid-winter's day required a burst of energy sufficient to heat ten houses for a year. Now the Reichstag creates more energy than it consumes, allowing it to act as a local power station supplying heat to other buildings in the government quarter. If a nineteenth-century building can be transformed from an energy-guzzler into a building so efficient that it is a net provider of energy, how much easier is it to design new buildings that make responsible use of precious resources?

3. The Great Glasshouse at the National Botanic Garden of Wales is heated by burning organic waste from the gardens and irrigated by water collected from its roof.
4. The Chesa Futura in St Moritz combines cutting-edge computer modelling techniques with traditional timber construction.

Like the Reichstag, the British Museum in London is a historical building that has been reinvigorated by a contemporary architectural intervention. For nearly 150 years the Museum's Great Court was inaccessible to Londoners and the many visitors to the Museum. The reinvention of this space has not only created an organisational hub at the heart of the Museum that opens up access to the gallery spaces, but has also created a new civic space for London.

Originally an open garden, the courtyard was lost to the public when construction started on the Round Reading Room and its associated book stacks in 1852. The departure of the British Library in 1998 created the opportunity to recapture this magnificent space and enhance the experience of the nearly six million people who visit the Museum each year. Covering an area of 6,100 square metres (equivalent to the turf at Wembley Stadium) the Great Court is the largest enclosed public space in Europe.

Sheltered beneath a unique triangulated glazed canopy, the courtyard is a major new social space. With two cafés and a restaurant, it is possible to eat there from early in the morning until late at night. Newspapers and magazines are on sale at the new bookshop. And for the first time in its history the magnificent Round Reading Room is open to all. To complement the Great Court, the Museum's forecourt has been freed from cars and restored to form a new public plaza. Together they represent a major new amenity for London and a new rendezvous for those who live or work in the neighbourhood.

The Great Court can also be understood in the context of the masterplan we have developed for the environmental improvement of Trafalgar Square, Parliament Square, Whitehall and their environs in central London. The 'World Squares for All' masterplan aims to improve pedestrian access to and enjoyment of the area for Londoners and the thousands of people who visit each year, while enhancing the settings of the area's many historical buildings and monuments. The first phase to be implemented focuses on Trafalgar Square. As part of a comprehensive programme of improvements, the northern side of the square is being closed to traffic and the National Gallery reconnected with the square to create a broad pedestrian plaza in front of the building.

The need to revitalise our cities by improving the urban fabric and achieving a better balance between people and traffic is one of the keys to the future. In the last decade alone, the cities of Barcelona, Berlin, Paris and Amsterdam have shown how the containment of traffic can lead to a better quality of urban life.

Our work in Nîmes showed us how the containment of traffic and provision of new amenities in a city centre can contribute to its economic and cultural revitalisation. The effect of the Carré d'Art, and its related urban works in the Place de la Maison Carrée, has been to transform a whole urban quarter. The square is alive with people, a new outdoor café life has been born, and there is a ripple effect extending well beyond the site.

The Carré d'Art is a compelling demonstration of the way in which an individual project, linked to an enlightened political initiative, can regenerate the wider fabric of a city. A similar objective drives our project in Gateshead, which will help to establish Tyneside as a cultural destination in its own right.

Architecture is both an interior and an exterior experience. The best architecture comes from a synthesis of all of the elements that separately comprise a building: from its relationship to the streetscape or skyline to the structure that holds it up, the services that allow it to work, the ecology of the building, the materials used, the character of the spaces, the use of light and shade, the symbolism of the form and the way in which it signals its presence in the city or the countryside. I think that holds true whether you are creating a landmark or deferring to a historical setting. Successful, sustainable architecture addresses all these things and many more.

If sustainability is to be more than a fleeting fashion, architects in the future must ask themselves some very basic questions. For example, why do we still insist on using greenfield sites when we could build on reclaimed land in our cities? Why do we demolish buildings that could easily be put to new uses? Why do we rely so heavily upon artificial lighting when we can design buildings that are filled with daylight? And why do we rely upon wasteful air-conditioning systems in locations where we can simply open a window?

1. The Carré d'Art in Nîmes sparked the reinvigoration of the surrounding area. *Facing page* The Great Court at the British Museum – a lost urban amenity that has been reclaimed and reinvented.

Selected Projects

Creek Vean House and Retreat
Feock, England 1964–1966

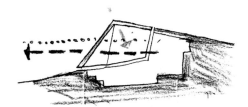

Like other Foster projects, Creek Vean mixes traditional materials – honey-coloured concrete blocks and blue Welsh-slate floors – with industrial components. The structure is open-ended and manifested both internally and externally. Except for the landscaped roof – shades of the later Willis Faber – such a description would fit exactly the Sainsbury Centre of some ten years later, although the departure points in materials, techniques and flexibility are of an opposite extreme.

Built on a steeply sloping site, this private house was designed to exploit classic Cornish views; it looks south towards the broad sweep of the Fal Estuary, west towards a creek and north along a valley. The rooms fan out towards these different views.

The house is organised around two routes. One is external and visually divides the house in two, leading from the road access across a bridge to the front door and down a flight of steps to the waterfront.

The other is internal, in the form of a toplit picture gallery, which at night is floodlit from the outside. It follows the contour line of the site and forges all the living spaces into a continuum, starting at the highest roof terrace and ending as a path to the underground garage.

A small all-weather gazebo 'retreat' is located near the house on a favourite riverside picnic spot with a commanding view of the estuary. A complex, crystalline polyhedron, the glassy structure breaks surface from the slope of the bank and faces towards the sea like the cockpit of a plane or boat. The trapezoid concrete shell, partly sunk into the ground, is splayed outwards on plan to accommodate seating, a small cooker and a sink. Although supplied with electricity and piped water, it is otherwise spartan.

This tiny building established a theme for partially buried glazed structures that would be explored in later projects such as Frankfurt Athletics Stadium, the Crescent Wing extension to the Sainsbury Centre and the Great Glasshouse at Middleton.

Client
Mr and Mrs Marcus
Brumwell
Area
350m²
Team
Anthony Hunt Associates
Hanscomb Partnership

2

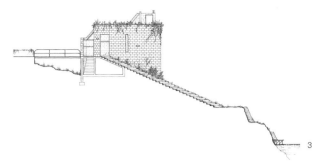

1, 2. Sketch by Norman Foster, and photograph of the Retreat 'cockpit'.
3. Cross-section through Creek Vean House.
4, 5. The landscaped roof and toplit picture gallery.
6. External steps between the house's two wings lead from the entrance down to the waterfront.

Reliance Controls Electronics Factory
Swindon, England 1965–1966

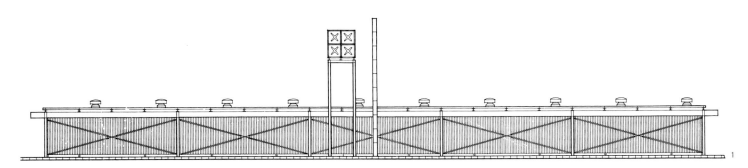

In the 1960s there was still a strong tradition in industrial architecture of the segregated management box and workers' shed, with their overtones of 'us and them', 'clean and dirty', 'back and front'. The Reliance Controls Factory sought to introduce a radical new approach. The result was a democratic pavilion where management and employees shared a single entrance and a single restaurant, a practice unheard of at the time. With the electronics industry then in its infancy, the building was regarded as a light-industrial prototype, its organisation and design implying new democratic standards in the workplace.

The building's emphasis on prefabricated metal components allowed the structure to be built in less than a year at very low cost. The structural steelwork was celebrated both inside and out, with structural members painted white to contrast with the grey, plastic-coated, corrugated-steel cladding.

Wherever possible, elements were designed to do double or even triple duty: for example, the fluorescent lighting was set within the troughs of the corrugated roof decking – a solution which meant that reflectors were unnecessary.

The steel frame enclosed a single open space of 3,200 square metres, within which only the toilets, kitchen and plant room were fixed in place. Much of the rest of the accommodation could be changed at will by moving the non-structural internal partitioning. This latent flexibility paid off when the client, in a sudden production surge, was able, unaided, to increase his production area by a third.

The building was the winner of the first Financial Times Industrial Architecture Award. In its report the jury said: 'Its uncompromising simplicity and unity of general conception and detailed design create an atmosphere that is not only pervasive but notably comfortable to be in. It is refreshing to find something so beautifully direct that it looks like a lost vernacular.'

Completed in 1966, Reliance Controls was the last major project before the break-up of Team 4 and the founding of Foster Associates. The building was demolished in 1991 despite a televised local appeal for its preservation because of its originality and historical importance.

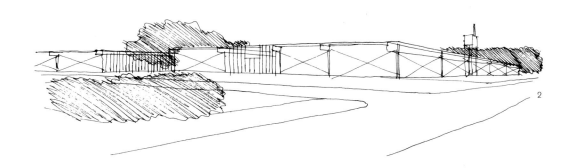

Client
Reliance Controls Ltd
Area
3,200m²
Team
Anthony Hunt Associates
Hanscomb Partnership
G N Haden & Sons Ltd

3

4

1. The south elevation with steel water tower and flue.
2. Norman Foster's early sketch showing how the building might be extended as a series of pavilions.
3. Detail of the exterior showing the diagonal steel bracing.
4. The interior: glass partitions and external glazing created a light, open space.

Fred Olsen Amenity Centre
London, England 1968–1970

Client
Fred Olsen Ltd
Area
2,250m²
Team
Anthony Hunt Associates
G N Haden & Sons Ltd
Hanscomb Partnership
Arthur Aldersley Williams

This project originated from a modest brief to design a canteen and amenity centre for dock workers and a separate administration building at the Fred Olsen Shipping Line berth in Millwall. However, a planning study by the practice generated a radical proposal to bring together white-collar and blue-collar workers in a combined operations and amenity building, which offered the same high standards for everyone. Thus traditional distinctions between 'posh and scruffy', 'us and them' were swept away.

The building was a deep-plan, two-storey structure in which a canteen, rest areas and changing facilities for dockers were located on the ground floor. The first floor contained open-plan administrative offices for clerical and managerial staff. The project was based on a philosophy that the workplace could be a pleasant environment: in addition to the basics, such as showers, it provided facilities for table tennis, billiards and television, and there were art works on the walls from Fred Olsen's own collection.

This democratising process was only made possible by working closely with all the groups involved – unions, middle management in the UK and senior management in Norway. The proof of the exercise was an ongoing pattern of virtually strike-free activity, in sharp contrast to the industrial strife of the London Docks that surrounded this development.

Apart from the democratic nature of the interior, the most revolutionary aspect of the building was its reflective glass curtain wall, specially adapted from an American system developed by Pittsburgh Plate Glass. By day the glazing reflected the activity of the dockside. By night, the glass became transparent to reveal the inner workings of the building in all their detail.

When the company moved its operations to Southampton, the building briefly became home to the London Docklands Development Corporation, before being demolished to make way for wholesale redevelopment.

1

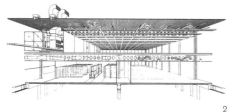

2

1. View of the ground-floor rest area looking out onto the docks.
2. Perspective cross-section showing the deep-plan two-storey structure with services integrated into the roof.
3. The reflective glass curtain wall that faced the dock.

3

Fred Olsen Passenger Terminal
London, England 1969–1970

Client
Fred Olsen Ltd
Area
455m²
Team
Anthony Hunt Associates
Hanscomb Partnership

Fred Olsen Shipping Line's main trade was with the Canary Islands. On the outward journey its ships would carry a mixed cargo, and they would return from the Canaries with bananas. However, in order to get the maximum use from their ships, Olsen combined this trade with cruises, integrating these two apparently contradictory functions in a complementary way.

The Olsen Passenger Terminal resulted from the same planning study that generated the Amenity Centre. The study was concerned in part with the movement of goods and people and ensuring that these activities could carry on harmoniously side by side. Accordingly, the Passenger Terminal can be seen as a set of 'tubes' protecting passengers from the turmoil of the quayside and delivering them to their ship without interfering with loading or unloading on the dock. Like the ships themselves, the terminal separated passengers above from freight below.

Built to an exceptionally tight budget and programme, the building was essentially a covered walkway and ramp fitting tightly around the corner of one of the existing transit sheds. It rested on stanchions, pin-jointed to concrete pads on the quayside and was stayed against the transit shed behind. The tubes were clad in a single skin of ribbed aluminium.

More machine than building, the terminal's many moving parts included a baggage-handling conveyor made from customised agricultural machinery. As in the Amenity Centre, attention to detail and a bright primary colour scheme created a sense of luxury in otherwise bleak surroundings.

1. Exterior view of the 'tubes' that took passengers from the dockside to the ships.
2. The site at Millwall Docks.
3. Aerial view.

IBM Pilot Head Office
Cosham, England 1970–1971

Client
IBM (UK) Ltd
Area
8,400m²
Team
Anthony Hunt Associates
R S Willcox Associates
Hanscomb Partnership
Derek Phillips & Partners
Arthur Aldersley Williams
Adrian Wilder

1

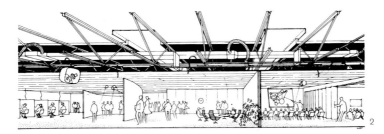

'The building demonstrates', said the assessors for the 1972 RIBA Award, 'that architecture can be produced from a tough commercial situation by the exercise of ingenuity and imagination.'

The 'tough commercial situation' was the requirement to provide accommodation for between 750 and 1,000 employees within eighteen months at a cost comparable to the cheapest temporary structures. The building was to serve as a temporary head office for IBM while a permanent headquarters was built on an adjoining site. Like many expanding companies at the time, IBM relied on a mixture of permanent and temporary accommodation; in some locations as much as half its office space was in 'off-the-peg' structures.

The initial brief was simply to research the available systems and propose a site layout. The response, however, was a report that demonstrated that for the same cost IBM could have a custom-designed permanent building that embraced high architectural and environmental standards. The resulting building is a single-storey, deep-plan structure that groups under one roof a wide variety of functions that would traditionally have sprouted a collection of diverse buildings.

The convention, current in the 1970s, that the computer should have a separate 'shrine' was challenged through the installation of a raised floor on top of the floor-slab, allowing a computer room to be integrated within the office building. With all services located in the roof and wiring carried down hollow steel columns, the interior has been able to respond quickly to growth and change. Initially the building housed offices, computers, amenities and a communications centre. But over the years offices have been reconfigured, the restaurant has been moved and the computer room expanded.

Major internal changes have been facilitated by the ability to insert external doors in lieu of the gasketed glazing panels which otherwise complete the external cladding. The bronze glass reflects the surrounding trees and landscape so that the building merges – almost disappears – into its setting.

Although it was expected to be only a stopgap, the building's ability to respond easily to changing needs has ensured its long-term survival more than thirty years after its completion.

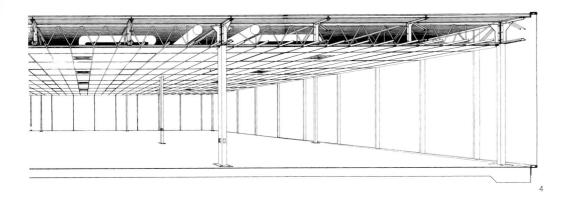

1, 3. Exterior views.
2, 4. Comparative perspective drawings of the practice's 1967 competition scheme for Newport School and the IBM office: both integrate services in the roof to create uninterrupted and flexible spaces.

Willis Faber & Dumas Headquarters
Ipswich, England 1971–1975

Client
Willis Faber & Dumas Ltd
Area
21,000m²
Team
Anthony Hunt Associates
John Taylor & Sons
Davis Belfield & Everest
Sound Research Laboratories
Martin Francis
Adrian Wilder
J A Storey & Partners

1

2

The country headquarters for Willis Faber & Dumas confronted preconceptions about office design. The use of escalators in a three-storey building, the atrium, and the social dimension offered by its swimming pool, roof garden and restaurant, were all conceived in a spirit of democratising the workplace and engendering a sense of community. Orientation throughout the building is immediate, and social contact is encouraged across the company spectrum.

The building's free-form plan responds to the street pattern of Ipswich's mediaeval city centre. Its low-rise construction respects the scale of surrounding buildings and its curved facade reinforces a relationship to the street. Floors are planned on a 14-metre-square structural grid, flexible enough to respond to the piecemeal acquisition of the site and to allow a number of early plan configurations. A necklace of perimeter columns enables the building to flow to the edges of its site like a pancake in a pan.

The sheath-like glass curtain wall, which encloses three storeys without mullions, was developed with the glazing manufacturer Pilkington. It pushed technology to its limits. Panes of solar-tinted glass are suspended from a continuous clamping strip at roof level. Corner patch fittings connect the panes, while internal glass fins provide wind bracing. By day, the glass reflects a faceted collage of buildings and sky; by night it dissolves to reveal the building within.

Conceived before the oil crises of the mid-1970s and heated by natural gas, Willis Faber was a pioneering example of energy-conscious design. Its deep plan and the insulating quilt of its turfed roof ensure good overall thermal performance. Over the years it has attracted as many awards for energy efficiency as it has for its architecture. It also pioneered the use of raised office floors, anticipating the revolution in information technology. When Willis Faber introduced extensive computerisation, it was able to do so with minimal disruption.

Paradoxically, although designed for flexibility, the building has since been given Grade 1 listed status: an honour that means it cannot be changed.

3

4

5

1, 2. Two views of the
building's central atrium
and escalators — a radical
innovation in the context of
an office building.
3. Norman Foster's sketch
highlighting the building's
use of natural light.
4. The turfed roof — both
recreational space and
insulation for the building.
5. The building at night.

Projects with Buckminster Fuller

1971–1983

1. A meeting with Bucky,
seated left.
2. Axonometric drawing
of the subterranean
Samuel Beckett Theatre.
3. Cross-section through
the continuous tensegrity
structure for Knoxville Expo.
4, 5. The model of the
Autonomous House.
6, 7. Perspective drawing
and cross-section through
the Climatroffice.

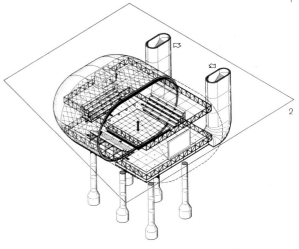

Climatroffice
1971
Team
Fuller & Sadao Inc

Samuel Beckett Theatre
Oxford, England 1971
Client
Oxford University
Team
Fuller & Sadao Inc
Anthony Hunt Associates
Hanscomb Partnership

Knoxville Energy Expo
Knoxville, USA 1978
Client
Knoxville Expo Committee
Team
Fuller & Sadao Inc

Autonomous House
Los Angeles, USA
1982–1983
Client
Richard Buckminster Fuller
Team
Fuller & Sadao Inc

Between 1971 and 1983 the practice designed four projects in collaboration with Buckminster Fuller that were catalysts in the development of an environmentally sensitive approach to design. Norman Foster describes the mindset he shared with 'Bucky' as an 'impatience and an irritation with the ordinary way of doing things'.

Their first joint project, the Samuel Beckett Theatre, was an auditorium buried beneath the quadrangle of St Peter's College, Oxford, 'like a submerged submarine'. The project failed to attract sufficient funding, but it involved research into underground structures which was to inform later projects.

In the 'Climatroffice', undertaken shortly afterwards – during the development of the Willis Faber & Dumas building – a transparent tensegrity structure with its own internal microclimate enclosed landscaped office floors. Purely a research project, it inspired the subsequent urban scheme for the Hammersmith Centre and contributed to the next collaborative venture six years later.

This was a design study for the 1978 International Energy Expo in Knoxville, Tennessee. The proposed scheme was a lozenge-shaped tensegrity structure with a double skin, capable of containing the entire exhibition in a climate-controlled enclosure. It included a wide range of solar heating, cooling and electricity-generating devices to maintain optimum comfort conditions at all times.

The final project was the Autonomous House, a prototype house for Fuller and his wife in Los Angeles (an identical one was to be built in England). Its skin was formed from two concentric five-eighths spheres, the outer one measuring 15 metres in diameter. Structurally, the spheres comprised a series of interlocking frames following segmental lines like the lines of latitude around the Earth. Part opaque and part transparent, the spheres were free to rotate independently in low-friction hydraulic races, allowing the house to be darkened or lightened by means of its rotating action alone. The inner skin supported intermediate floors, which meant that the house could be reoriented to suit the position of the sun or the prevailing wind. Work on the project ceased with Fuller's death in the summer of 1983, but the environmental ideas it embodied resonate in the design of the Reichstag's cupola with its moveable sunshade.

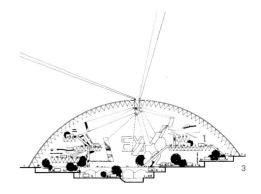

3

4

5

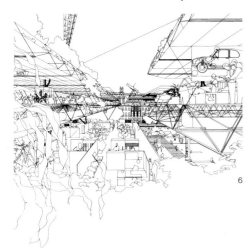

6

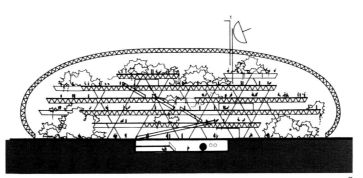

7

29

Sainsbury Centre for Visual Arts
Norwich, England 1974–1978

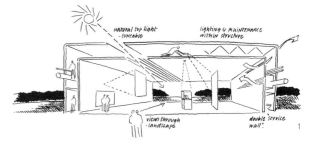

Client
University of East Anglia
Area
6,186m²
Team
Anthony Hunt Associates
Hanscomb Partnership
Tony Pritchard

Much of the practice's early work for industrial clients was concerned with lightweight, steel-framed enclosures, adaptable to growth and change. These early works explored the integration of structure and services and pioneered the development of prefabricated cladding systems. The Sainsbury Centre brought these concerns to a new pitch of refinement.

When Sir Robert and Lady Sainsbury donated their art collection to the University of East Anglia, together with an endowment for a new building, the Sainsbury Centre for Visual Arts was established as an academic and social focus within the campus.

The Sainsburys shared a belief that the study of art should be a pleasurable experience. As a result the Sainsbury Centre is much more than a traditional gallery, where the emphasis is on art in isolation. Here several related activities are integrated within a single space.

Arrival is into a conservatory with a reception area and coffee bar. To one side is a temporary exhibition space; to the other, the Sainsburys' collection of ethnographic and twentieth-century art. Beyond this area, articulated by mezzanines, the University's Faculty of Fine Art, a senior common room and a restaurant are incorporated.

All these activities are grouped within a single, clear-span structure, glazed at both ends, and lit from above. A basement spine provides the necessary storage and workshop facilities.

In order to create this uncluttered internal space, services and ancillaries are housed within the double layer of the walls and roof, which also provides access for lighting installations. Prismatic wall and roof trusses are visible externally at each end and support a flexible system of three different types of cladding panel – glazed, solid and grilled – which can be easily reconfigured in any combination. Internally, the walls and ceiling are lined with motorised aluminium louvres linked to light sensors. The combination of natural and artificial lighting systems provides an almost infinite subtlety of control.

Unusually for an art gallery, the building does not rely on mechanical refrigeration. Because of the considerable volume of the space, warm air is able to rise and be extracted at high level, thereby maintaining user comfort.

A major expansion of the Centre's facilities – the Crescent Wing – was commissioned by Sir Robert and Lady Sainsbury in 1988.

1. Norman Foster's concept sketch showing the integration of structure and services in the double skin of the roof and walls.
2. The open-plan interior.
3. Sir Robert and Lady Sainsbury inspect a mock-up of the display systems.
4. The building at night.
5. Axonometric drawing of the prefabricated cladding system.
Overleaf The building in its landscape setting.

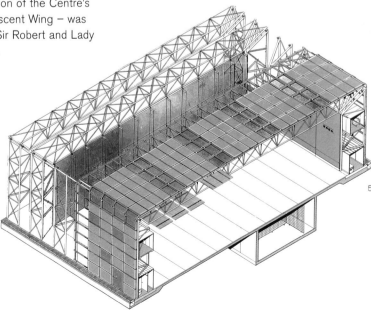

IBM Technical Park

Greenford, England 1975–1980

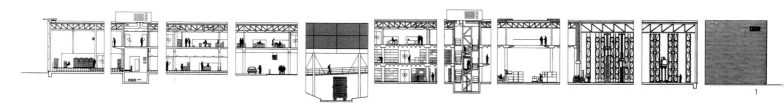

1

IBM Technical Park, built on a reclaimed 16-hectare site six kilometres from Heathrow Airport, sought to give form to new patterns of social and technological change, pursuing high environmental standards, generous landscaping and democracy in the workplace. The development forms IBM's main UK Distribution Centre (UKDC) and incorporates an Installation Support Centre (ISC) which houses its mainframe computers for demonstration purposes.

An initial masterplan identified strategic movement patterns, building zones and a range of future options. Work on the first building, the UKDC, was already under way when, eighteen months into a very tight programme, IBM's American parent company changed the brief and decided to build the ISC. This had to be constructed quickly, for if it could not be completed within a year, there was a risk that IBM would locate the facility elsewhere in Europe.

The solution was a scheme with two distinct elements, delineated at ground level by a service road but linked at high level by offices, which span the road to serve both buildings. A slender pedestrian bridge is suspended below the offices, reinforcing both physical and visual connections.

Activities with widely different spatial and environmental requirements are grouped within enclosures designed around unified structural and component systems, which are flexible for change and growth. Double-height warehousing and loading docks, maintenance and repair centres, small parts storage, offices, staff facilities and an air-conditioned machine hall are all accommodated beneath a common 12-metre roofline. Depending on function, the buildings are sheathed in ribbed aluminium sheet or have free-standing glass curtain walling.

Designed and built on a fast-track programme, the entire building contract was compressed into a 32-week period; steelwork was ordered and foundations laid even before the final disposition of accommodation had been decided, and both buildings were completed on schedule.

2

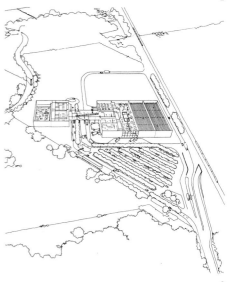

3

1. Cross-sections showing how the structural system can accommodate a range of different activities.
2. Office interior.
3. Aerial perspective of the site.
4. Perspective section of the Factory Systems Study made by the practice in 1969, which informed the design of IBM.
5. Detail of the offices and pedestrian bridge that spans between the two buildings.

Client
IBM (UK) Ltd
Site Area
16 hectares
Building Area
31,800m²
Team
Anthony Hunt Associates
Ove Arup & Partners
Northcroft Neighbour
& Nicholson

Sound Research
Laboratories
Michael Brown Partnership
Freeman Fox & Partners
J A Storey & Partners
John Taylor & Sons
Modern Materials
Management

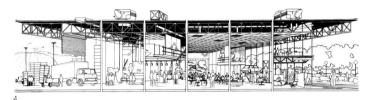

4

5

Regional Planning Study
Gomera, Canary Islands 1975

1

1400

1550

1750

1950

1975

2000

2

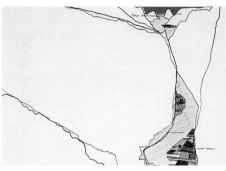

3

4

In the early 1970s, Gomera exhibited all the characteristics of an island in decline. The water supply was dwindling, the road network inadequate, public transport was negligible and, with the exception of one forty-bedroom hotel, there were no facilities for tourists.

Fred Olsen ran cruises to the Canaries and wanted to investigate Gomera's potential as a tourist destination. In response to that brief, this masterplan raised issues of sustainability long before the 'green' agenda was being addressed worldwide. Its aim was to encourage self-sustaining development on the island, based on a combination of indigenous construction techniques and prefabrication. The report stressed gradual change, its proposals in deliberate contrast to the aggressive patterns of commercial exploitation then being implemented throughout the Mediterranean.

Studies of original settlements highlighted a single-aspect dwelling that looked out to the sun and had as much shaded area outside as it had habitable area inside. These ingredients generated a high-density, low-rise solution that responded well to the climate. Its traditional construction techniques addressed the island's surplus labour problems and the high cost of importing materials. At the same time it was suggested that new, clean industries could be established to prefabricate kitchens, bathrooms and the like.

This approach was reinforced by alternative methods of energy generation and water collection. Constant sunshine and steady winds made the island a natural test-bed for solar and wind power, while other systems, such as methane production from domestic waste, were explored to reduce dependence on imported oil. One of the priorities was to improve the water supply. A number of natural systems were proposed, including the construction of a catchment round the upper levels of the island and the use of solar stills.

Existing proposals for a new airport and a ring road around the island were challenged. Instead a series of access roads and funiculars to Gomera's many small bays was proposed. In the same spirit, an island-hopping link by STOL aircraft was suggested. Both alternatives sought to preserve the traditional character of the island whilst recognising the importance of modern communications to its long-term survival.

1. View of the island.
2. The island's past and future as envisaged by the masterplan.
3, 4. Drawings of the landscape as found.
5, 6. Wind turbines were proposed to enable the island to create its own energy.
7–10. Drawings of building developments employing indigenous techniques, labour and materials.

Client
Fred Olsen Ltd

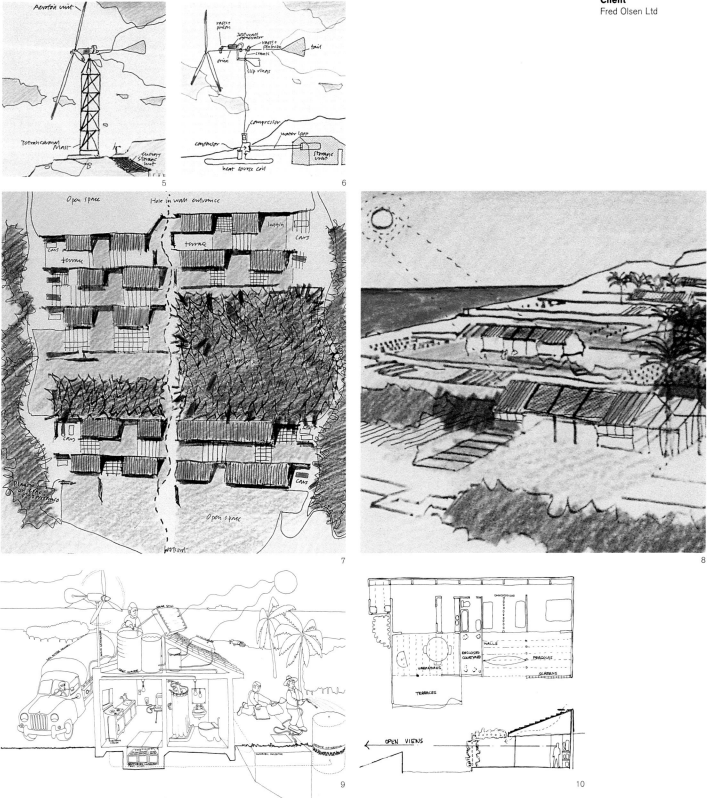

Hammersmith Centre

London, England 1977–1979

This project for a transport interchange, office complex and public space in Hammersmith, West London, has been described as one of the great missed opportunities of post-war urban renewal.

Hammersmith is one of the busiest transport intersections in Europe. The site was virtually an island, with a bus garage and Underground station at its centre and run-down commercial buildings at its perimeter, surrounded on all sides by busy lanes of traffic. The commission originated from London Transport's wish to renew the bus garage and station and create an integrated transport interchange subsidised by speculative office development.

The proposal created wide, toplit pedestrian malls, entered at street level and running beneath the surrounding roads to provide access to the Underground station below or to the bus station, elevated 3 metres above ground level and linked to the road system by shallow ramps. Above all this was a public plaza, equal in size to Trafalgar Square but, enclosed as it was by perimeter buildings, closer in spirit to one of London's garden squares. The whole space was enveloped by a canopy, developing ideas that were explored in the Climatroffice project with Buckminster Fuller.

The lightweight roof produced savings on other elements, which balanced the cost of the roof itself, and the enclosed volume formed a climatic buffer, which offered substantial energy savings. In winter the temperature inside would have been warmer than outside, making it suitable for open-air activities such as ice-skating. Service towers at the 'corners' of the site supported the canopy and were developed as symbolic gateways to the space within.

The scheme hinged on a triangle of forces: it had to sustain itself financially, work operationally as a transport interchange and create something for the community. When the individuals and idealism behind the project disappeared – and with them the community heart of the project – the practice felt it necessary to withdraw.

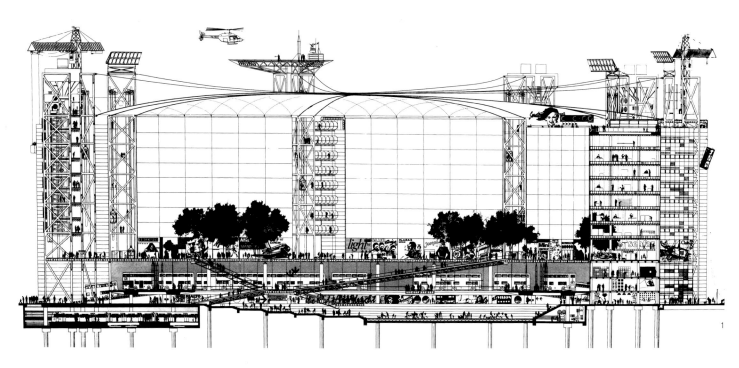

Client
London Transport
Area
2.4 hectares
Team
Ove Arup & Partners
Brown Crozier & Wyatt
Davis Belfield & Everest
Sound Research
Laboratories
J A Storey & Partners
Richard Ellis
Jones Lang Wootton
Shankland Cox Partnership
Coopers & Lybrand

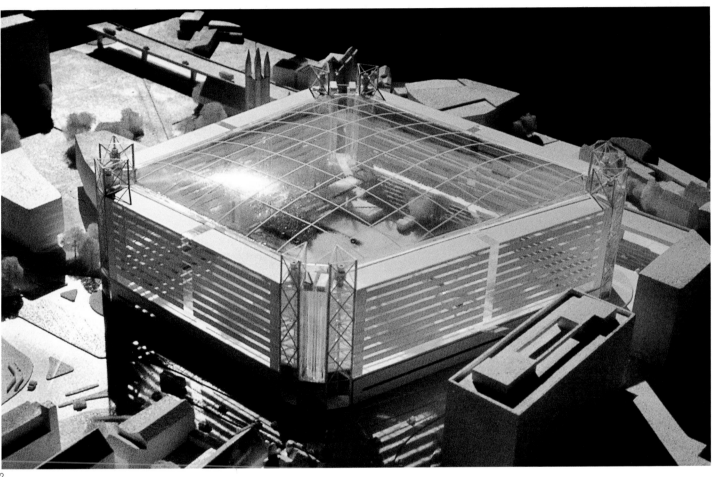

2

1. Cross-section
through the complex
showing the green urban
oasis created at its core.
2. View of the model
looking through the
lightweight roof to
the plaza below.
3. Plan at plaza level.

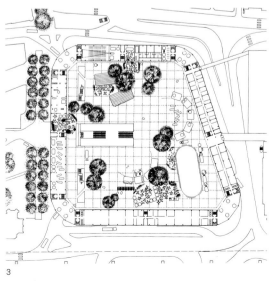

3

Shops

Joseph
London, England 1978
Client
Lynxmead Ltd
Area
95m²
Team
Anthony Hunt Associates

1

1–3. The interior of the
Katharine Hamnett shop,
Norman Foster's sketch
outlining the use of
natural light, and the
arched glass bridge
leading into the space.
4, 5. Sketch and exterior
view of the shops designed
for Cacharel.
6–8. The interior and
exterior of the Esprit shop
on Sloane Street and, 8,
the same interior before
stairs were inserted, as it
was designed for Joseph.

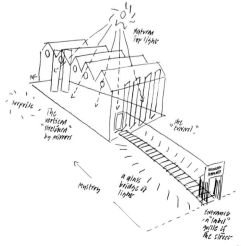

2

3

Katharine Hamnett
London, England 1987
Client
Katharine Hamnett
Aguecheek
Area
500m²
Team
Buro Happold
Yates Associates
Monk Dunstone Associates

Esprit
London, England 1988
Client
Esprit-de-Corp
Area
200m²
Team
Ove Arup & Partners
Davis Belfield & Everest
Anthony Ross Ltd

Cacharel
Europe 1991–1992
Client
Cacharel
Area
80–100m² per shop

4

5

The practice has always approached the design of shop interiors as a spatial rather than a decorative exercise: the drama of a shop is heightened by bold use of light and space rather than through surface elements.

The shop designed in 1978 for Joseph Ettedgui in Sloane Street, London, reflected the understatement of his clothes, displaying them in a minimalist, functional environment. At the time, the design was considered a surprisingly 'masculine' context for the display of women's clothing. By ranging the clothing around the perimeter of a bright, airy space, the display and storage area was maximised, freeing the central area of the shop. Clothing was displayed on a specially designed steel gantry that supported two levels of continuous hanging rails.

When the shop was subsequently refurbished for the American clothing company Esprit, the basement was opened up to provide additional retail space. A generous triangular staircase with treads of thick-float glass linked the two levels and echoed the shop's triangular plan.

For the fashion designer Katharine Hamnett, a former London car repair workshop was converted into a showroom. It was possibly the only fashion store in London without a shop window. The main space was set back from the street, reached via what had been a gloomy tunnel-like approach. This unpromising route was transformed by the insertion of a gently arching bridge of etched glass panels, lit from below, which recreated the theatricality of the catwalk. Inside, the building was stripped back to its shell to reveal a long, triangular skylit space. Changing rooms and storage facilities at the far end of the plan were hidden behind mirrored panels, which added to the sense of drama and emphasised the generous volume.

For its menswear outlets the French retailer Cacharel sought to recreate the feel of a traditional gentleman's outfitters. This theme was suggested by a modular storage and display system consisting of oak-lined cabinets backed with Irish linen. The system is highly flexible and the elements can be easily reconfigured. The project extended to the design of Cacharel's corporate identity and printed elements such as price tags and wrapping paper.

6

7

8

Hongkong and Shanghai Bank Headquarters

Hong Kong 1979–1986

Client
Hongkong and Shanghai
Banking Corporation
Area
99,000m²
Team
Ove Arup & Partners
Roger Preston & Partners
Levett & Bailey
Northcroft Neighbour
& Nicholson

Claude and Danielle
Engle Lighting
Tim Smith Acoustics
Technical Landscapes Ltd
Quickborner Team
Jolyon Drury Consultancy
Corning Glass
Humberside Technical
Services
Project Planning Group
R J Mead & Company

Conceived during a sensitive period in the former colony's history, the Hongkong and Shanghai Bank Headquarters was a statement of confidence, created without compromise: the brief was for nothing less than 'the best bank building in the world'. Through a process of questioning and challenging – including the involvement of a feng shui geomancer – the project addressed the nature of banking in Hong Kong and how it should be expressed in built form. In doing so it virtually reinvented the office tower.

The requirement to build in excess of a million square feet in a short timescale suggested a high degree of prefabrication, including factory-finished modules, while the need to build downwards and upwards simultaneously led to the adoption of a suspension structure, with pairs of steel masts arranged in three bays. The building form is articulated in a stepped profile of individual towers – respectively 29, 36 and 44 storeys high – which create floors of varying width and depth, garden terraces on the roof of each tower, and vigorous east and west elevations.

The 'bridges' that span between the masts define double-height reception areas. These spaces break down the scale of the building both visually and socially, reflecting village-like clusters of space. A unique system of movement through the building combines high-speed lifts to the reception spaces with escalators beyond.

From the outset, the Bank placed a high priority on flexibility. The masted structure allows another radical move, pushing the service cores to the perimeter so as to create deep-plan floors around a ten-storey atrium. Interestingly, over the years, the Bank has been able to reconfigure office layouts with ease, even incorporating a large dealers' room into one floor – a move that could not have been anticipated when the building was designed.

At the top of the building, a mirrored 'sunscoop' reflects sunlight down through the atrium to the floor of a public plaza below. At weekends this sheltered space has become a lively picnic spot. Significantly, it also allowed the Bank to develop the site at a plot ratio of 18:1 when 14:1 was the norm. From here, escalators rise up to the main banking hall. With its glass underbelly, it is literally a shop window for banking.

1

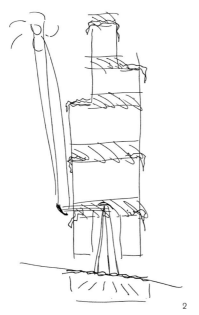

2

3

1. A view of the pedestrian plaza created beneath the Bank – now a popular weekend picnic spot.
2. Norman Foster's concept sketch for the sunscoop that reflects sunlight through the building to the plaza below.
3. The building at night. *Facing page* Looking into the ten-storey atrium.

Renault Distribution Centre
Swindon, England 1980–1982

Client
Renault UK Ltd
Area
25,000m²
Team
Ove Arup & Partners
Davis Belfield & Everest
Tim Smith Acoustics
Technical Landscapes Ltd
Quickborner Team

The Renault Centre has been described as the practice's most 'playful' structure. However, its development owes much to earlier, perhaps more reticent schemes for clients such as Reliance Controls and Fred Olsen, which delivered inexpensive, flexible, egalitarian buildings to tight schedules.

The Centre is the French car manufacturer's main UK distribution facility. In addition to warehousing, it includes a showroom, a training school and workshops, offices and a staff restaurant.

The notion that 'good design pays' has almost become a cliché, but in this case it is quantifiable: on the strength of the design supportive local planners increased their site development limit from 50 to 67 per cent, allowing a floor area of 25,000 square metres. This is housed within a single enclosure supported by tubular masts and arched steel beams. The roof is a continuous PVC membrane pierced by glass panels at each mast, which bring toplight into the interior.

Four bays wide overall, the building is stepped at one end, narrowing to a single, open bay that forms a porte-cochère alongside a double-height 'gallery'. Primarily a showroom – as signified by suspended, brightly coloured car body shells – the gallery has become a popular venue for arts and social events, encouraging wider community involvement in the building.

The structural system achieves the maximum span with the minimum amount of steel and allows a much larger than usual planning module – 24 by 24 metres – which optimises planning flexibility. With an internal clear height of 7.5 metres, the building is able to accommodate a range of uses from industrial warehouse racking to subdivision into office floors.

The primary structure runs outside the perimeter walls, allowing all the elements of the structural skeleton to be expressed, while a neoprene eaves detail, inspired by the tie-down fixings on articulated trucks, allows members connecting the inner and outer rows of masts to pass through. The nautical joints and guy rods and the drilled-out webs of the beams have an almost festive quality; in bright sunshine they cast changing shadow patterns, animating the facade and introducing a human scale.

Significantly, the building's 'Renault yellow' exoskeleton has created such a memorable image that, alone among the company's facilities, it does not carry the Renault logo. In fact it is so closely associated with the brand that Renault has used it as a backdrop in its advertising campaigns.

1

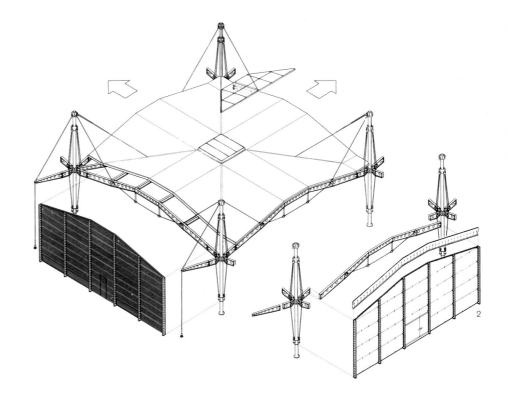

2

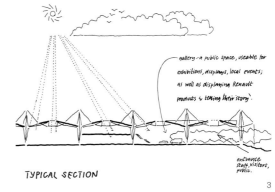

gallery - a public space, useable for exhibitions, displays, local events; as well as displaying Renault products & telling their story'.

entrance staff, visitors, public.

TYPICAL SECTION

3

4

1. View of the showroom.
2. Axonometric drawing
of the prefabricated
structural system.
3. Concept sketch
by Norman Foster.
4. The exterior with its
'Renault yellow' exoskeleton.

Stansted Airport
England 1981–1991

1

2

3

Client
BAA
Area
85,700m
Team
Ove Arup & Partners
BAAC
Beard Dove
Currie & Brown
Claude and Danielle
Engle Lighting
ISVR Consultancy Services
University of Bristol

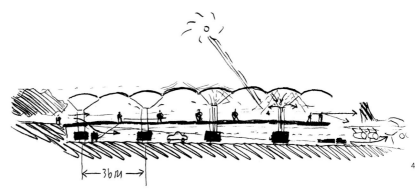

Stansted Airport, which opened in 1991, challenged all the accepted rules of airport terminal design. It went back to the roots of modern air travel and literally stood conventional wisdom on its head.

Early airport terminals were very simple: on one side there was a road and on the other a field where aircraft landed into the wind. The progression from landside to airside was a walk from your car through the terminal to your plane, which was always in view. In contrast to most contemporary airports, there were no orientation problems.

Stansted was an attempt to recapture the clarity of those early airfields, together with some of the lost romance of air travel. Allied to that were strong environmental imperatives: the building had to be discreet in its rural setting and energy efficient.

From the traveller's point of view, movement through the building is straightforward and direct. Stansted has none of the level changes that disfigure most airports. Passengers proceed in a fluid movement from the set-down point to the check-in area, passport control and on to the departure lounges, where they can see the planes. From there, an automated tracked transit system takes them to satellite buildings to board their aircraft.

This degree of clarity was achieved by turning the building 'upside down', banishing the heavy environmental service installations usually found at roof level to an undercroft that runs beneath the entire concourse floor. The undercroft also contains baggage handling and was able to accommodate a mainline railway station which was integrated into the building at a late stage.

All service distribution systems are contained within the 'trunks' of structural 'trees' which rise up from the undercroft through the main concourse floor. These trees support a lightweight roof which is freed simply to keep out rain and let in light. The concourse is entirely daylit on all but the most overcast of days. The constantly changing daylight gives the space a poetic dimension and also has significant energy and economic advantages – running costs are half those of any other British terminal. Further energy savings are made because the building is dug into its site, and this also helps to reduce its impact on the surrounding landscape.

Since its completion Stansted has become a model for airport planners and designers around the world.

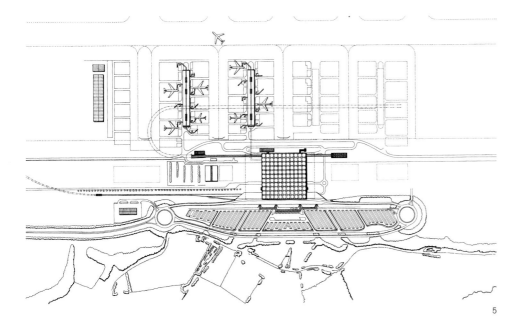

1. View of the concourse.
2. The railway station in the undercroft.
3. The set-down point.
4. Norman Foster's sketch of the environmental concept: a lightweight roof, freed from services, allows natural light to flood the concourse.
5. Site plan.
Overleaf From the landside the aeroplanes are directly visible.

Athletics Stadium
Frankfurt, Germany 1981–1986

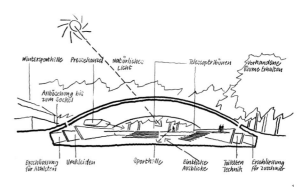

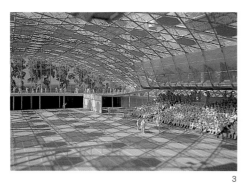

1. Concept sketch by
Norman Foster of the
partially buried structure.
2, 3. Exterior and interior
views of the model.
4. Services formed
an integral part of the
latticed roof, adding an
extra layer of detail.
5. Cross-section through
the stadium.

Client
Stadt Frankfurt-am-Main
Hochbauamt
Area
12,500m²
Team
Ove Arup & Partners
Pettersen & Ahrends
Büro Zitnik
Braun & Schlockermann

The subterranean or partially buried building has been a consistent theme in the practice's work, from Norman Foster's first built project – the tiny 'cockpit' Retreat above the Fal Estuary in Cornwall – to the American Air Museum at Duxford and the Great Glasshouse at the National Botanic Garden of Wales. The proposal for an athletics stadium dug into its site in Frankfurt never came to fruition but the scheme was developed to a high degree of detail.

The brief called for a 200-metre running track with additional lanes for 100-metre and 60-metre sprinters, long-jump and high-jump areas and special stands for discus and shot-putting. Retractable seating for up to 3,000 spectators was also stipulated, along with the usual support facilities.

The site lay in the Waldstadion, a complex of sports buildings on the outskirts of Frankfurt, and was situated between the small Winter Sporthalle and the much larger covered grandstand of the Hauptkampfbahn.

The building's ground-hugging form was inspired by a respect for the heavily wooded surroundings. At the same time the shallow arched roof represented the most cost- and energy-efficient of the many structural alternatives considered.

Externally, the vaulted roof merged with the ground so that the building appeared almost to dissolve into the landscape. Internally, it was a combination of triumphal arch and amphitheatre. Spectators progressed from the entrance at ground level down to their seats around the sports area. At each end the entry level effectively became a public viewing gallery, covered by a large-scale portico.

The arched roof assembly, with its deep lattice structure, continued the practice's research into the refined integration of structure and services. Structural members and all service elements – ducts, lighting and so on – were contained within the roof zone, where they shaped and informed the enclosure, breaking down the scale of the space and creating a filigree of detail within the overarching sweep of the roof.

4

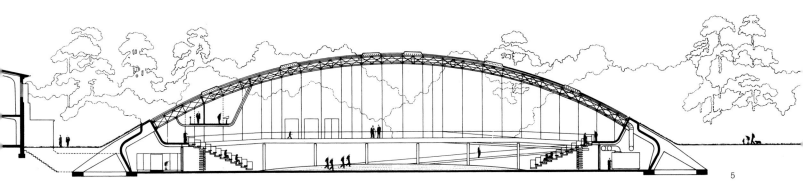

5

BBC Radio Centre

London, England 1982–1985

Client
British Broadcasting Corporation
Area
52,000m²
Team
Ove Arup & Partners
YRM Engineers
Davis Belfield & Everest
Tim Smith Acoustics

The BBC Radio Centre was the brainchild of the then chairman of the BBC, Lord Howard, who held an international competition, which the practice won in 1982. Although the BBC provides public service broadcasting, it is a surprisingly introverted organisation. The practice worked closely with BBC staff to develop a series of strategies to make the Corporation more publicly accessible in its new home.

Located on the site of the Victorian Langham Hotel (acquired by the Corporation some years earlier) at the southern end of Portland Place, opposite Broadcasting House and John Nash's All Souls' Church, the context was highly sensitive – both historically and in terms of urban planning. The BBC also had stringent criteria: the building had to provide technical capacity to allow for every foreseeable broadcasting development; construction could not interfere with broadcasting activities; and the new building had to replace as many of the BBC's scattered London facilities as possible.

The design responded to three contextual problems: the relationship with Cavendish Square to the south-west, the need for a punctuation mark at the southern end of Portland Place, and the juxtaposition with Broadcasting House and All Souls' on the bend of the street. More than a hundred design options were evaluated.

The resulting scheme stepped gradually upwards in keeping with neighbouring buildings. A low elevation faced Cavendish Square, while a cluster of glass lift towers on the north-east elevation formed a climax to Portland Place. A seven-storey glass wall opposite All Souls' marked the main entrance and the glazed atrium that bisected the building diagonally. Lined with shops and cafés and placed on an axis with All Souls', the atrium formed the public heart of the building. Radio facilities were placed on either side of the atrium and below it in three subterranean storeys of sound studios and auditoria.

In 1985, following the appointment of a new chairman with a different vision for the BBC, the scheme was abandoned just as it was to be submitted for planning permission. The BBC subsequently sold the Langham site and relocated staff to White City in West London.

1, 2. Views of the model showing the glazed atrium from above and from within, looking towards All Souls' Church.
3. Sketch by Norman Foster exploring the social dynamic of the surrounding buildings.
Facing page Visualisation looking from the peristyle of All Souls' into the atrium.

Carré d'Art
Nîmes, France 1984–1993

Médiathèques exist in most French towns and cities. Typically they embrace magazines, newspapers and books as well as music, video and cinema. Less common is the inclusion of a gallery for painting and sculpture. In Nîmes, the interaction within the same building of these two cultures – the visual arts and the world of information technology – creates a richer totality.

The urban context of Nîmes was a powerful influence. The site faces the Maison Carrée, a perfectly preserved Roman temple. The challenge was to relate the new to the old, but at the same time to create a building that represents its own age with integrity. The Carré d'Art refers, but does not defer, to the exquisite temple. The Maison Carrée's portico was a reference point – generous, urban and public. So, too, was the vernacular architecture of the region, with its courtyards, terraces and green oases. The Carré d'Art combines these themes in a modern way.

Art galleries are placed on the upper levels to maximise natural toplight, whilst reference areas are located close to the entrance to facilitate easy access. Half the nine-storey structure is dug deep into the ground, keeping the building's profile low and sympathetic to the scale of the surrounding buildings. These lower levels house spaces that do not need light, such as archive storage and a cinema.

At the heart of the project, a roofed courtyard exploits the transparency and lightness of modern materials, especially glass, allowing natural light to permeate all floors. Within the courtyard, cascading staircases link the public levels, culminating in a shaded roof-terrace café overlooking a new public square.

The creation of this urban space was an integral part of the project. Metal railings, parked cars and advertising were removed and the pedestrianised realm in front of the building was extended around the Maison Carrée and linked to the city centre. The geometry follows the Roman grid to recreate tree-lined streets along the building's long edges. This exercise in urban landscaping not only encourages the dialogue between the Carré d'Art and its historical neighbour but has also created a new public forum and a new outdoor café life, which has reinvigorated the centre of Nîmes.

The Carré d'Art shows how a building project allied with an enlightened political initiative can be a powerful catalyst in regenerating the social and physical fabric of a city.

1

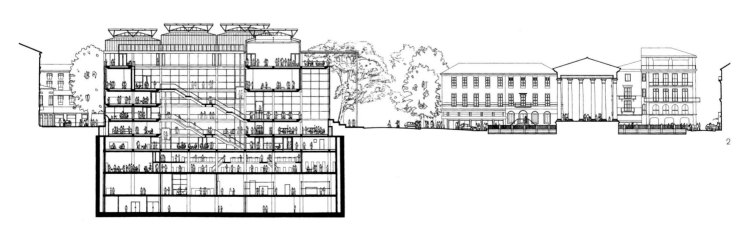

2

Client
Ville de Nîmes
Area
18,000m²
Team
Ove Arup & Partners
OTH
Thorne Wheatley
Claude and Danielle
Engle Lighting
Commins
Jolyon Drury Consultancy
Casso Gaudin
Algoe

3

4

1. The glass staircases
in the covered courtyard.
2. Cross-section showing
how the lower four stories
are dug into the ground.
3. Sketch by Norman Foster.
4, 5. The new urban
square in front of the Carré
d'Art, and the same space
before regeneration.
Overleaf The loggias
of the new building and
the old face each other
across the square.

5

Client
Tecno spa, Italy

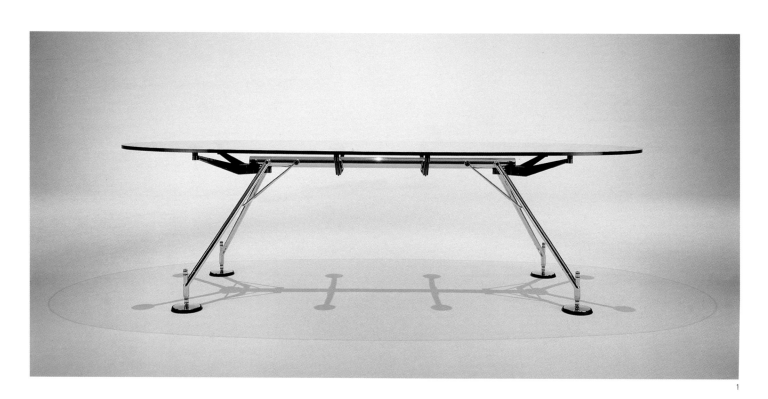

1

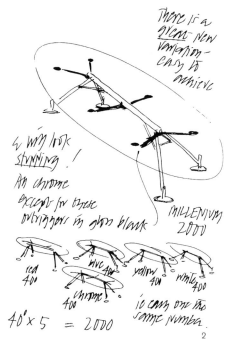

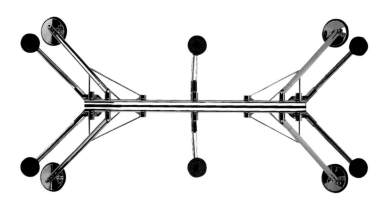

2

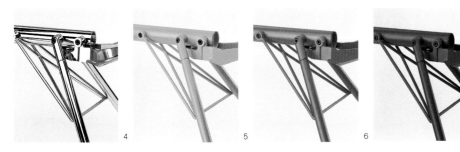

4   5   6   7

Office furniture, like the office itself, must be adaptable to changing patterns of work. The Nomos concept is rooted in an earlier foray into furniture design. In 1981, when the practice expanded into a new studio, no existing furniture system could provide tables that were adjustable for meetings, drafting or display. The outcome was a custom-designed table, made in a small production run by a sympathetic workshop.

Modified versions of this table were used in the reception areas, offices and restaurant of the Renault Distribution Centre in Swindon. The Italian furniture manufacturer Tecno subsequently commissioned the practice to develop the design. Tecno required a system that could optimise floorspace, accommodate cabling, and be easily reconfigured. Launched in 1987, the Nomos range has been in production ever since.

The concept of Nomos (a Greek word meaning 'fair distribution') is based on the relationship between the user and the space he or she occupies. A flexible kit of precision-engineered components can be combined to create miniature environments for individuals or groups, complete with built-in task or background lighting.

The starting point is a spine, to which are added legs, feet, supports, work surfaces and superstructures. A vertebra-like conduit carries cabling. The system can also accommodate shelves, storage, screens and signage. It is designed for unlimited flexibility, but is governed by the ergonomics of the human body, seated or standing.

The table is characterised by its splayed feet – an undercarriage more evocative of motion than the legs of a traditional table but one that ensures stability. Some critics have suggested references to the lunar landing module; another image is the grasshopper with its slim body and gangly legs.

In 1999 Tecno commissioned a new table to mark the millennium. The rectangular and circular-topped versions are established favourites. In the quest for another classic shape, smooth curves were investigated to encourage better eye contact across the table's length, making it feel more friendly. The primary frame is expressed in a vivid palette – red, yellow or blue – with other elements in bright chrome. A more classical option has a chrome frame with the secondary elements in black.

8

1, 2. Photograph and concept sketch by Norman Foster for the Nomos 2000 Table.
3. The table frame seen from above, showing the spine, legs, feet and supports.
4–7. The primary frame in classic chrome and the new 2000 range of colours.
8. The Nomos Desking System seen with Kite! chairs.

Sackler Galleries, Royal Academy of Arts
London, England 1985–1991

Client
Royal Academy of Arts
Area
312m²
Team
Anthony Hunt Associates
James R Briggs
George Sexton Associates
Julian Harrap Architects
Davis Langdon & Everest

The commission for the Sackler Galleries at the Royal Academy of Arts provided the practice with its first opportunity to work within a historical building. The project demonstrates how contemporary interventions can enhance the old by relying on sensitive juxtaposition rather than pastiche.

Although perceived by the visitor as a single entity, the Royal Academy consists of two buildings: the original Palladian house, converted by Lord Burlington in the eighteenth century, and a Victorian gallery behind, linked by a central grand staircase.

The brief required the replacement of the undistinguished nineteenth-century Diploma Galleries at the top of Burlington House. A masterplan was also devised to equip the Royal Academy for increasing numbers of visitors and to improve disabled access. The practice's proposal was to insert a new lift and staircase in a reclaimed lightwell between Burlington House and the Victorian extension.

In the process redundant historical accretions were peeled away, revealing the garden facade of Burlington House for the first time in over a century. Cleaned and repaired, it contrasts strikingly with the Victorian structure and the free-standing new insertions. The new work is demonstratively of its own time, using modern materials for modern ends, but it also enables a rediscovery of the potential of Burlington House and the Victorian galleries, much of which had become inaccessible over time.

The Sackler Galleries achieved new environmental standards, allowing the Academy to meet the exacting criteria set by international exhibitions. They include a glazed reception area incorporating the parapet of the Victorian galleries. Sculpture from the Academy's permanent collection is displayed along this route, most notably Michelangelo's tondo of the Virgin and Child with the Infant St John.

The Royal Academy was the first in a line of projects demonstrating a clear philosophy about contemporary interventions in historical structures, which continues with the Reichstag and the Great Court at the British Museum.

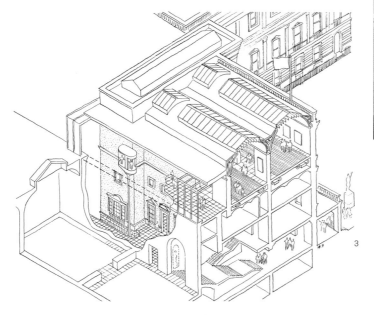

1. A view of one of the new galleries.
2. The entrance to the galleries, with sculpture displayed on the parapet of the Victorian extension.
3. Norman Foster's cutaway drawing of the scheme.
Facing page View of the new glass lift with the rear facade of Burlington House revealed behind.

Televisa Headquarters
Mexico City, Mexico 1986

Client
Televisa SA
Area
75,000m²
Team
Ove Arup & Partners
Roger Preston & Partners
Davis Belfield & Everest
Sordo Madaleno y
Asociados SC

1

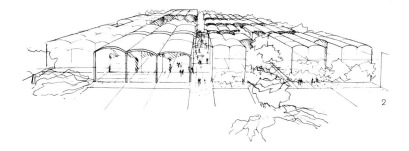

As Mexico's largest national broadcaster, Televisa plays a major role in the country's business and cultural life. It operates four television networks and seven radio stations together with associated activities from dubbing to cable TV, theatre and video.

In 1986 Televisa commissioned a scheme to consolidate its disparate production activities in a single location adjacent to the Azteca Stadium. Bounded by roads on all sides, the site comprised a former landfill area, a disused basalt quarry and a lake. The ambition was to combine a unified television production facility with a major public cultural centre and art gallery.

The design response was inspired by the kasbah, with its pattern of streets, paths and spaces beneath an all-embracing roof. Covering almost the entire site, a roof umbrella enclosed an area of 75,000 square metres. Entrance to the building was through a grove of trees via a bridge across a long reflecting pool. The building opened out onto the lake and the escarpments of the basalt quarry, which defined an open-air public sculpture garden – the heart of the scheme.

In the fast-moving world of broadcast communications, growth and change are givens. With a minimum clear height of 9.8 metres, the structure could be subdivided into three floors of offices, two of storage, or a full-height studio. In response to the broad range of Televisa's activities, some spaces were enclosed, some toplit, and others serviced from an undercroft. Thus it offered the communications industry a radical new building type, combining the specifics of broadcasting with the spatial freedom of the airport concourse.

The building's pre-cast concrete structure was designed to exploit the strength of local industries. It also brought other benefits: its high thermal mass allowed passive systems of environmental control to be explored. Together with the relatively mild climate, this meant that the building could be naturally ventilated rather than air-conditioned. The systems-built structure also offered economy of scale and ease of construction.

Although the scheme was abandoned due to local pollution problems, it inspired a later generation of projects, notably schemes for Stockley Park and Paternoster Square.

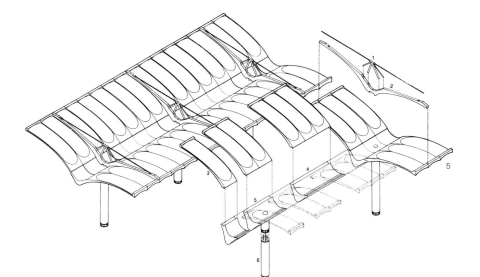

1. View of the model showing the all-embracing roof umbrella, which covered almost the entire site.
2. Norman Foster's concept sketch.
3. Visualisation of the flexible interior space.
4, 5. The pre-cast concrete canopies as seen in the model, and in an axonometric drawing of the roof assembly system.

Riverside Apartments and Studio

London, England 1986–1990

Client
Petmoor Development
Area
13,000m²
Team
Ove Arup & Partners
Roger Preston & Partners
Schumann Smith Ltd
Tim Smith Acoustics
Claude and Danielle
Engle Lighting
Emmer Pfenninger
Partner AG
O & H Construction

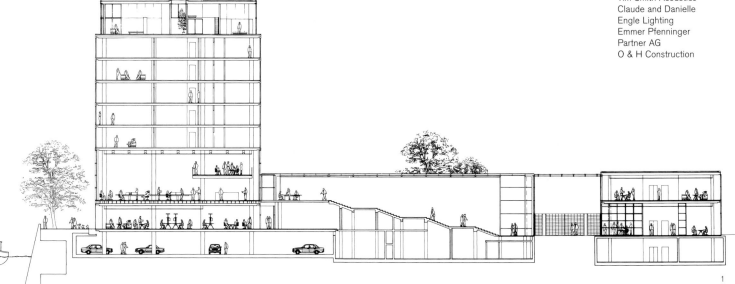

1

Riverside is a pioneering example of a building that combines living and working in one location. There are few contemporary examples of this idea in Britain, and where they exist they break with traditional planning guidelines, which create separate zones for residential, commercial and industrial use.

The site lies on the south bank of the Thames, close to Albert Bridge. As found, it was a scene of urban dereliction. European Community funding was sought to rehabilitate the adjacent dock and in replanning the site a network of pedestrian routes was created. This has made the river accessible to the public as well as forging connections to neighbouring streets, where a new café culture has evolved.

The building has eight storeys, with Foster and Partners' studio occupying the lower three levels, and apartments located on the upper floors. Both office and apartment spaces have spectacular views of the river. A private courtyard provides separate access and security for those who live in the building. At the rear of the site a two-storey pavilion accommodates additional studio space and a print shop.

The main studio, at first-floor level, is entered via steps through a toplit galleried space which contains a bar. The studio is a 60-metre-long, double-height volume with a mezzanine along its southern edge containing meeting and presentation spaces together with a library and image bank. Below the mezzanine is a state-of-the-art model shop. Materials are simple – painted concrete, stretched fabric and a carpet-tiled floor which has removeable panels to allow full access to the cabling beneath.

Everyone in the studio, whatever their job description, has a place at one of the long workbenches; the arrangement is very fluid with no division between design and production. The average age is young – about thirty – and nearly as many languages are spoken. The building is open twenty-four hours a day, seven days a week, and there is a very high level of motivation.

Most offices keep visitors at arm's length. The Foster studio, by contrast, is completely open. Visitors can enjoy the bar – the social focus of the office – while meetings, whether formal or informal, occur in the midst of the creative process itself.

2

1. Cross-section showing the main building on the left, the galleried entrance, and the pavilion to the right.
2. Interior view of one of the apartments.
3, 4. Views of the building from the rejuvenated dock area to the rear and from Chelsea Embankment.

Private Houses

Skybreak House
1965–1966
Client
Mr and Mrs Anthony Jaffé
Area
260m²
Team
Anthony Hunt Associates
Hanscomb Partnership

House in Japan
1987–1992
Client
Confidential
Area
Main house 600m²
Guest house 400m²
Team
Ove Arup & Partners
Roger Preston & Partners
Northcroft Neighbour
& Nicholson
Claude and Danielle
Engle Lighting
Obayashi Corporation

1

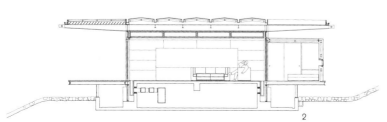

2

3

House in Corsica
1990–1993
Client
Confidential
Area
450m²
Team
Ove Arup & Partners
Roger Preston & Partners
Davis Langdon & Everest

House in Germany
1992–1994
Client
Confidential
Area
750m²
Team
Ove Arup & Partners
Boll und Partners
PFI
Schreiter GmbH
Rawe und Partners
Doktor Berhard Korte
Manfred Krauser

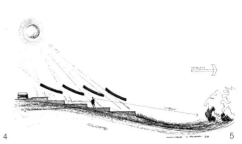

The design of houses poses very different challenges to those of designing the larger-scale building types for which the practice is better known. However, from its earliest days the practice has designed houses for individual clients, such as Creek Vean House and Skybreak House in the mid-1960s. These small projects have explored in microcosm some of the technical and environmental issues that characterise the larger civic schemes.

The private house designed for a stretch of volcanic coastline in Japan combines Western Modernism with Japanese love of harmony and respect for nature. The house floats on a raised deck, positioned to ensure that the entrance lobby and main living room enjoy uninterrupted views out to sea. Services and storage areas are arranged around the perimeter, allowing more flexible use of the central accommodation. Double-height sliding glazed doors lead onto external decks, protected from sunlight by fixed louvres. Internally, the space can be modified by sliding screens, while the quality of toplight through the glazed roof can be controlled by manipulating insulated louvres in the ceiling.

The house on the French island of Corsica was subject to strict planning regulations which required that it be constructed of timber with a shingle tile roof. A single sweeping roof covers the house in a bold and simple gesture, ending in a curved canopy of louvres to provide shade for the south-facing terrace. On the north side the service accommodation is buried into the ground and the landscaping rises to cover its roof.

The two-storey house built in Germany for a young family is dug into the south-facing slope of a hillside. Sheltered by woodland it enjoys fine views across the neighbouring valley. Access from the road leads directly onto a roof terrace. From here a ramp leads down through the house to a lower garden terrace, while exterior steps in the landscape connect all levels. The lowest level is the family domain, centred on the kitchen. The unusual combination of inside and outside circulation enables the house to offer the family and its friends an unusual degree of community, while respecting privacy.

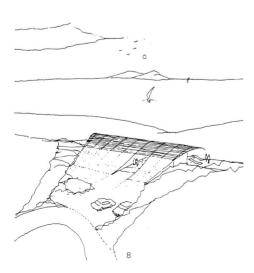

1–3. Interior, cross-section and exterior view of the house in Japan.
4, 5. Interior view and Norman Foster's concept sketch for Skybreak House, completed in 1966.
6, 7. Views of the exterior and kitchen area of the house in Germany.
8, 9. The house in Corsica, as sketched by Norman Foster and seen from the sea.

King's Cross Masterplan
London, England 1987

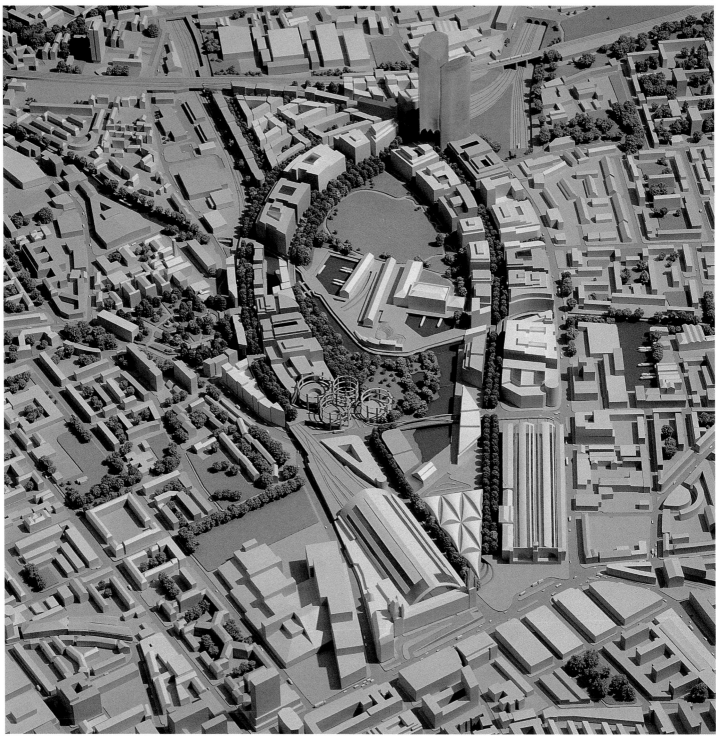

King's Cross Masterplan
London, England 1987

**King's Cross
Masterplan**
1987
Client
London Regeneration
Consortium
Site Area
52 hectares

Team
Ove Arup & Partners
Davis Langdon & Everest
Baker Harris Saunders
Halcrow Fox
Hanna Olins Design Ltd
Julian Harrap Architects
Space Syntax Laboratory
JBB

**St Pancras International
Rail Terminal**
1996–1997
Client
London and Continental
Railways
Length
500m
Team
Ove Arup & Partners

King's Cross, located between the West End and the City of London, represents one of the greatest development challenges in Europe. The masterplan site was the result of rivalry between two nineteenth-century railway companies and ran north from their respective stations: King's Cross and St Pancras. King's Cross is London's largest public-transport interchange with two intercity termini, the Thameslink line, five Underground lines and the North London Line. Its redevelopment was signalled by the advent of the Channel Tunnel and the need for a new international railway terminal.

The site, covering 52 hectares, included several listed buildings alongside housing, a canal and a natural park. The masterplan was an attempt to rediscover a culture of mixed use, encouraging the integration of cleaner industries into residential neighbourhoods and exploring the potential of greener, more ecologically sensitive structures in order to create a sustainable urban community.

Five organisational generators were identified: the preservation of listed buildings, grouped around the historical railway sheds and the canal/road interchange in the centre; the canal itself; the existing road and rail infrastructure; the need to form intelligible new routes through the site; and, at the heart of the development, a new open space in the tradition of London's parks and squares.

The masterplan proposed a pair of towers to the north of the site, designed as linked 'spires', ending the sweep of the park and forming a new London landmark, while the international terminal was placed between King's Cross and St Pancras stations. Responding to the triangular geometry of the site, its vast glass structure was designed to recapture the grandeur of rail travel, evoking a feeling of space, light and airiness. Its daylit concourse featured unimpeded lines of sight, smooth changes in level and reduced walking distances, and housed all the ticketing and retail facilities expected by contemporary travellers.

In 1996 the practice was invited to prepare a more limited masterplan to redevelop St Pancras Station as a European rail terminus. This involved extending the Victorian railway shed to accommodate Eurostar trains and upgrading amenities in and around the station.

3

4

5

6

1, 2. Comparative aerial views of the site and the 1987 masterplan model.
3. Visualisation of the 1987 glass terminal building between King's Cross and St Pancras stations.
4. Model of the 1996 masterplan extending the St Pancras railway shed.
5, 6. Diagrams by Space Syntax showing pedestrian movement through the site before and after implementation of the 1987 masterplan.

Stockley Park Offices
Uxbridge, England 1987–1989

Client
Stanhope Properties
Area
12,000m²
Team
Ove Arup & Partners
Davis Langdon & Everest

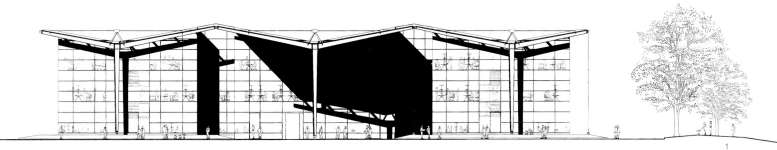

Stockley Park was Britain's first architecturally driven business park. Masterplanned in the 1980s on a site strategically located close to Heathrow Airport and the M4 and M25 motorways, and within forty minutes of central London, it includes buildings by a number of leading British architects.

When the practice first began working for industrial clients in the 1960s, most industrial estates in Britain represented the lowest common denominator in terms of design. The idea of improving the workplace, either by providing better amenities or by eliminating barriers between management and workforce, was seen as unnecessary, if not subversive. Stockley Park demonstrated just how radically ideas had changed over the intervening twenty years.

Set at the southern end of the site, overlooking a lake, this building provides 12,000 square metres of office space. It is designed to house a single tenant but can be easily subdivided to suit multiple occupancy.

The scheme had to fit within design parameters set by Stockley Park's management, which specified pitched roofs, white cladding and sunscreening. Each of the building's three stepped bays are fronted by V-shaped steel 'butterfly' frames, pinned at the ridges and supported on tapering columns. These frames support the roof over each three-storey bay and extend 3 metres over the long elevations to support louvred sunscreens. Between the bays two triple-height atria run the length of the building and carry the primary circulation.

The building is oriented to maximise views across the lake to the east. The main entrance is located in the middle of the three halls on the northern facade, shaded by an overhanging canopy. Plant and services are stacked at the southern side of the building, where they block the heat of the sun. The long east and west elevations are made up of double-glazed units. To reduce solar gain the internal face of the units is stove-enamelled with a white 'frit', which varies in concentration from almost opaque at floor and eaves level to clear between desktop and eye level.

1. North elevation.
2. Looking towards the entrance: each of the building's three bays is defined by a 'butterfly' structural frame.
3. View of the entrance at night: the roof structure extends to form a canopy.

Century Tower

Tokyo, Japan 1987–1991

1

2

Client
Obunsha Corporation
Area
26,590m²
Team
Ove Arup & Partners
Roger Preston & Partners
Northcroft Neighbour
& Nicholson
Claude and Danielle
Engle Lighting
Richard Chaix
Arup Acoustics
Tim Smith Acoustics

Century Tower grew out of the client's belief that the commercial realities of speculative offices could be reconciled with an architecture of distinction. Although it advances ideas first explored in the Hongkong and Shanghai Bank, Century Tower is not a corporate headquarters but a prestige office block with a wide range of amenities, including a museum. The building's main contractor, Obayashi, was an early tenant, as was Japan Airlines, and the upper two floors of the south tower are occupied by the client's office and penthouse.

Located in Bunkyo-ku, in the heart of Tokyo, the building occupies a site subject to complex zoning regulations. The design response was to divide the tower into two blocks, respectively 19 and 21 storeys high, linked by a narrow atrium. The outer form of the two blocks is defined by eccentrically braced frames, responding to seismic engineering requirements in a city where earthquakes and typhoons are very real threats. The floors, spaced at double height with suspended mezzanines between them, form a series of stacked bridges between service cores at either end of each block. This arrangement allows office space to be column-free and to enjoy natural light and views. Narrow bridges span the atrium, enabling tenants to lease entire floors.

Previously it had been prohibited in Japan to combine open office atria with open-access floorspace, due to fire regulations. These were overcome through pioneering use of smoke-activated baffles – reminiscent of the flaps on aircraft wings – which, in the event of fire, descend from the main and mezzanine floors to accelerate air-flow from the atrium into the affected floor. Fans draw smoke across the floor and out of the building to avoid smoke migration.

Century Tower is one of the first of the practice's projects to explore the medium of water. At the foot of the atrium, polished black granite water tables overflow to feed water walls. These frame a staircase that leads to a museum for the client's collection of Oriental antiquities at basement level. The juxtaposition of light and dark and the calming effect of the water prepare the visitor for the cave-like museum with its precisely lit objects. Other facilities include a tea house, a restaurant and a health club and pool sheltered beneath a glazed catenary roof.

Century Tower is the outcome of an exceptional collaboration with the Japanese construction industry, combining lasting values from both East and West.

1. View of the atrium, with bridges linking the two blocks.
2. Exterior view.
3. The health club and pool on the ground floor.
4. Detail of a display case in the museum of Oriental antiquities in the basement.
5. Norman Foster's concept sketch for the eccentrically braced frames that support the tower.

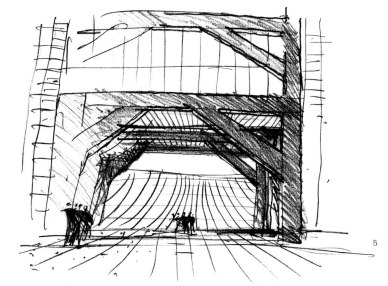

American Air Museum
Duxford, England 1987–1997

1

Client
Imperial War Museum
at Duxford
American Air Museum
in Britain
Area
7,400m²

Team
Ove Arup & Partners
Roger Preston & Partners
Davis Langdon & Everest
Aerospace Structural and
Mechanical Engineering
Hannah Reed and
Associates
Rutherford Consultants

Duxford airfield in Cambridgeshire was a Battle of Britain fighter station. Later, as one of a hundred US Airforce bases in Britain, it was the headquarters of the 78th Fighter Group. Now maintained by the Imperial War Museum, it has the finest collection of American aircraft outside the United States. Nineteen of its thirty-eight aircraft are airworthy and it attracts some 350,000 people to its summer air displays. The centrepiece of the collection is also the largest – a B-52 bomber.

The building to house this collection has three starting points. First, it commemorates the role of the American Air Force in World War II and the thousands of airmen who lost their lives. Second, it provides the optimum enclosure for the B-52 and twenty other aircraft dating from World War I to the Gulf War. Many of these aircraft had suffered through exposure to the elements, and the building creates the right atmospheric conditions in terms of humidity levels and UV protection to ensure their conservation. Third, and equally important, was a desire to exploit the activity of the runway and create a window onto that world.

The dimensions of the B-52 (a 61-metre wingspan and 16-metre-high tail fin) established the building's height and width. The vaulted roof, based on a toroidal geometry, required only five concrete panel types, which were cast on site. A continuous strip of glazing around the base of the vault washes the interior in daylight. The building's drama comes from the single arc of the roof – engineered to support suspended aircraft – and the sweep of the glazed southern wall overlooking the runway. Entry is via a ramp, on axis and at 'nose' level with the B-52. Around and beyond is a panorama of aircraft of every scale. The structure is partly sunk into the ground and its form has been compared to 'blister hangars', which were designed to be invisible from the air.

In 1998 the Museum won the Stirling Prize RIBA Building of the Year Award. The jury wrote: 'The success of this project lies in the resonance between the elegant engineered form of the building and the technically driven shapes of the aeroplanes. The building itself sustains the fascination of these objects.'

1. Looking into the main museum space.
2, 3. The glazed southern wall provides views out onto the runway.
4. Ground-floor plan: a B-52 bomber is aligned to greet visitors as they enter. *Overleaf* Night view.

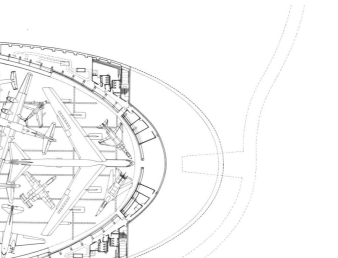

ITN Headquarters

London, England 1988–1990

The design for ITN's central London headquarters set out to challenge preconceived ideas about the business of gathering and disseminating news. The project also advanced the practice's environmental expertise, reconciled the constraints of a speculative office building with the requirements of its key tenant, and demonstrated that a building can be sensitive to its context and still generate a memorable image.

The site, on Gray's Inn Road, had been vacated by Times Newspapers following its move to new premises at Wapping. It included a vast basement, where the old newspaper printing presses had been located, which was dark and apparently unusable. The scheme utilised the full potential of the site by situating television studios in the two basement levels and creating a full-height atrium, soaring through the building's ten storeys, to draw daylight and diffused sunlight down into the office and basement. The atrium is also the focus of the building's circulation, acting as both a physical and social heart.

Because of the high heat loads generated by television lighting and equipment and computers, the building typically produces surplus heat. Its double-layer glazed climate wall has an unusually wide cavity of 350mm, creating a blanket of air that insulates both thermally and acoustically. Air is circulated to exhaust surplus heat and the return air collects at the base of the double-glazed wall, where it is drawn up through the cavity.

The floor-to-floor height throughout the building is 4 metres – greater than usually specified in an office building. This, in combination with raised floors containing the cabling required for news broadcasting, allows 'hot studios' to be located anywhere within the office floors, close to production teams. Almost all ITN's news bulletins throughout the day are broadcast from the office floors, using the newsrooms or the atrium as a backdrop.

This arrangement has proved so flexible that the customised studios, created for ITN's sole use, are now profitably leased to the television industry at large. A further benefit is that the public can share some of the excitement of the news-gathering process. This interaction is further encouraged through balconies in the atrium, which allow visitors to view all levels without impeding operations.

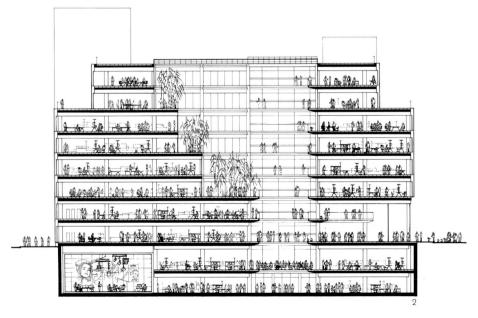

1. The Gray's Inn Road elevation.
2. Cross-section through the atrium - the physical and social heart of the building.
3. A news bulletin being broadcast from a 'hot studio' on an office floor.
4. View of the atrium with mobile sculpture by Ben Johnson.

Client
Independent Television News
Stanhope Properties
Area
41,000m²
Team
Ove Arup & Partners
Roger Preston & Partners
Davis Langdon & Everest
Close Morton Associates
Sandy Brown Associates

3

4

Seating

Kite! Chair
1987–1997
Client
Tecno spa, Italy

Airline Seating System
1997–1999
Client
Vitra AG, Switzerland

1

2

3

A900 Seating and Table
1997–1999
Client
Thonet, Germany

4

In developing designs for chairs and seating the practice has typically developed a 'kit-of-parts' approach whereby a small number of finely crafted components can be assembled into a large number of products. This allows machining processes to be reduced to a minimum and results in a more cost-efficient manufacturing process.

The A900 range of seating for Thonet – whose name has been synonymous with furniture manufacture since the 1830s – was developed in response to the need for a family of chairs that could be used throughout a building, in both interior and exterior spaces. The frame components, produced by three different aluminium extrusions and two castings, can generate a total of nine individual products. This modular flexibility, together with a varied choice of materials, allows the range to be specified in almost any situation.

Airline is a seating system developed with Vitra for use in public areas. The key criteria were that it should be flexible and cost-effective, have a light and non-institutional look, and be comfortable and yet capable of withstanding the rigours of public use. It was also important that the seating be easy to transport and install.

The system is based on extruded and cast aluminium components refined to their minimum thickness and weight. The spine is a central beam – which requires no machining – to which individual components can be simply attached. This allows for a variety of configurations complemented by a choice of materials for both seat and back, including plywood, aluminium and upholstery. The system offers a range of seating positions from upright and short-sit to a more relaxed arrangement for longer usage.

Conceived to accompany the Nomos range of desks and tables, the Kite! Chair quickly assumed an identity of its own. Like a kite, it comprises an efficiently engineered frame over which soft fabrics can be stretched. By specifying different colour and fabric combinations the mood and appearance of the chair can be changed dramatically. It is fabricated on a robotised production line, using welded sheet metal components.

5

6

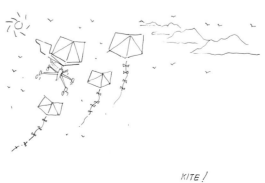

KITE !

7

1–3. Thonet A900 Seating in use on the roof terrace of the Reichstag, during the design process, and as a finished product.
4, 5. Vitra Airline Seating visualised at Stansted Airport and in one of many possible configurations.
6, 7. The Kite! Chair in some of its numerous colour combinations and Norman Foster's concept sketch.

Crescent Wing, Sainsbury Centre for Visual Arts
Norwich, England 1988–1991

1. Exterior view of
the Crescent Wing
and Sainsbury Centre.
2. The curving circulation
zone behind the
sweeping glazed frontage.
3. Sketch by Norman
Foster showing how the
new wing fans out from
the rectilinear geometry
of the original building.
4. A view of the new
conservation facilities.
5. Detail of the
Reserve Collection.

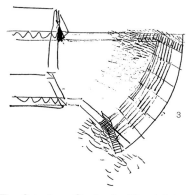

Client
University of East Anglia
Area
3,000m²
Team
Anthony Hunt Associates
Roger Preston & Partners
Henry Riley
George Sexton Associates
Acoustic Design Ltd

The Sainsbury Centre for Visual Arts at the University of East Anglia was completed in 1978. In addition to housing Sir Robert and Lady Sainsbury's collection of modern and ethnographic art, it combines two exhibition galleries, the Faculty of Fine Arts, a common room and a public restaurant beneath a large single-span roof, and provides storage and workshop facilities in the basement.

The opportunity to extend the building arose in 1988 with a major new gift from the Sainsburys to provide additional facilities. The brief included extended space for the display of the reserve collection, together with facilities for curatorial preparation and conservation and a gallery for exhibitions and conferences, giving the Centre far greater flexibility in its programming.

The original building was conceived as a modular, open-ended structure capable of future linear extension, and the first expansion studies explored ways of extending the Centre itself. However, the Sainsburys saw the building as a finite object, perfect in itself, and they encouraged the practice to investigate alternative ways to provide the new accommodation.

The most logical course was to add space below ground, at basement level. To the east and south of the existing building the ground falls away towards a lake. This slope allows the extended basement to emerge naturally into the open, with a glazed frontage onto the lake. The building was modified to accommodate study collections and work-shops in a rectangular continuation of the basement. Cellular offices fan out to the south-east in the form of a glazed crescent incised into the grassy bank. Behind the glass a naturally lit circulation zone gives access to offices.

The exterior gives little hint of what lies underneath. Approaching from the original building, a level grass lawn punctuated by rooflights and a narrow ramp disappearing beneath the turf provide a clue; but only from the lake is the full extent of the wing apparent in the great inclined sweep of fritted glass.

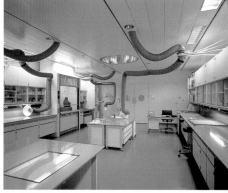

4

5

Communications Infrastructure

Torre de Collserola
Barcelona, Spain
1988–1992
Client
Torre de Collserola SA
Area
Tower platforms 5,800m²
Height 288m
Team
Ove Arup & Partners
Davis Langdon & Everest
MC-2
BMT Fluid Mechanics Ltd
Oxford University Wind
Tunnel Laboratory

Telecommunications Facility
Santiago de Compostela,
Spain 1994
Client
Concello de Santiago
de Compostela
Area
4,100m²
Team
Ove Arup & Partners
Davis Langdon & Everest

In anticipation of the communications requirements of the 1992 Olympic Games, Barcelona was facing an explosion of transmission masts on the neighbouring Tibidabo mountainside. Sensing the environmental impact this would have, Mayor Pasqual Maragall decided that the communications infrastructure for the region should be coordinated. He convinced the three primary players – national and Catalan television and Telefonica – to build a shared telecommunications tower. The competition brief posed the problem as a balancing act between operational requirements and the desire for a monumental technological symbol. The solution reinvents the telecommunications tower from first principles.

A conventional reinforced-concrete tower would have required a shaft with a 25-metre-diameter base in order to achieve the 288-metre height required. Following an analysis of precedents, including bridges and shipbuilding techniques, a new structural concept emerged: a hybrid concrete and steel-braced tube, with a base diameter of only 4.5 metres, which dramatically minimises the tower's impact on the mountainside.

In order to meet a programme of just 24 months the construction of shaft, equipment decks and mast were overlapped. As the shaft was poured, the steel-framed decks and public viewing platform were assembled on the ground ready to be jacked, inch by inch, into position. In a final flourish, the steel radio mast was telescoped up inside the hollow shaft.

The equipment decks are suspended from the shaft by three primary trusses and braced by Kevlar cables, which are transparent to broadcasting signals. Equipment is installed by lift, and a crane at the top of the mast hoists antennae into place. Inherent flexibility ensures that the tower is able to respond to a rapidly evolving telecommunications future.

In 1994 the success of the Torre de Collserola inspired a scheme for a telecoms facility for Santiago de Compostela, also in Spain. The Mayor of Santiago had what he perceived to be a similar problem. Instinctively, however, a tower seemed to be the wrong solution: it risked competition with the spires of the Cathedral, which have characterised Santiago's skyline for centuries. Technical analysis turned the problem on its side, suggesting a low-lying platform – a 'horizontal tower' – that would provide the city with a fitting contemporary symbol.

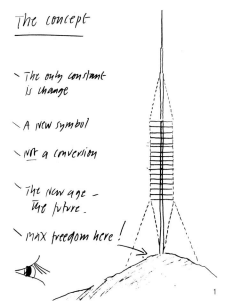

1, 2. Norman Foster's concept sketch, and view of the Torre de Collserola on its mountainside site. 3, 4. View of the model and concept sketch for the 'horizontal tower' at Santiago de Compostela. *Facing page* View of the Barcelona tower from below: the curved triangle of the decks maximises space, stability and aerodynamic efficiency.

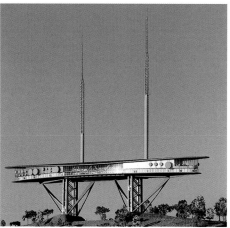

Metro System
Bilbao, Spain 1988–1995 and 1997–2004

A metro system is an excellent demonstration of how the built environment influences the quality of our lives. The building of tunnels for trains is usually seen in isolation from the provision of spaces for people – even though they are part of a continuous experience for the traveller, starting and ending at street level. The Bilbao Metro is unusual in that it was conceived as a totality: architectural, engineering and construction skills were integrated within a shared vision.

The Metro serves the one million inhabitants of Bilbao. The city has a strong tradition of technology; most of the elements were made locally and Spanish engineers who had pioneered mobile gantries for the aerospace industry exploited this technology to erect the prefabricated concrete panels lining the Metro's tunnels. The curved forms of these spaces are expressive of the enormous forces they are designed to withstand.

Many subway systems are difficult to negotiate, relying on signage systems. In Bilbao the architecture itself is legible. Routes in and out – via escalators or glass lifts – lead as directly as possible through tunnels to cavernous stations. These are large enough to accommodate mezzanines and staircases above the trains – the experience of moving through a single grand volume is dramatic, while the concept offers flexibility for future change and makes the spaces clearly legible.

The lightweight elements – mezzanines, stairs, ticket barriers – are designed to be maintenance-free. All services are confined to plugs at the ends of the station caverns. Ventilation ducts and electrical cables run below the platforms, and trains are powered from an overhead source.

The curved glassy structures – or 'Fosteritos' – that announce this network at street level are as unique to Bilbao as the Art Nouveau Metro entrances are to Paris. Their shape is evocative of inclined movement, generated by the profile of the tunnels themselves. They admit natural light by day, and are illuminated at night, forming welcoming beacons in the streetscape.

An addition to the network, Line 2, is extending the system into the Left Bank of the River Nervion. The practice is designing eight of the ten stations on the new line, which is a vital part of the regeneration of the city's former industrial suburbs. Steep hills make it impossible to use escalators to access the new stations, so banks of large-capacity lifts have been designed, grouped in threes to create iconic and easily recognisable entrances. Line 2 will be completed in 2004.

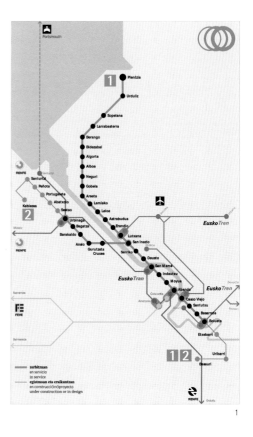

1

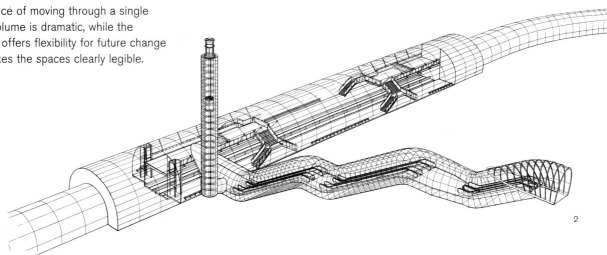

2

Line One
1988–1995
Client
Basque Government
IMEBISA
Length
61km
Team
Sener
TYPSA
Saitec
Ove Arup & Partners
Büro Aicher
Weiss Design Asociados

Line Two
1997–2004
Client
Basque Government
IMEBISA
Length
20.5km
Team
Sener
TYPSA
Atelier Weidner
IMEBISA

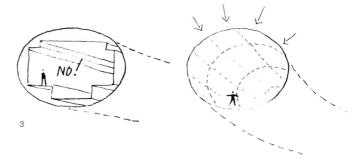

3

4

1. Map of the network showing the original line and its new extension.
2. Axonometric drawing of a typical station showing the direct route from platform to street.
3. Concept sketch for the expressed structure of the tunnels.
4. A 'Fosterito' at night.
5, 6. Interior views of two different stations at platform level.

5

6

Microelectronic Park
Duisburg, Germany 1988–1996

1. Aerial view of the model showing the three completed buildings and a proposed second phase of the Microelectronic Centre.
2–4. The Microelectronic Centre: atrium and front and rear of the building.
5. The Telematic Centre.
6–8. Views of a conference room and the exterior of the Business Promotion Centre, and diagram of its cooling system.

Telematic Centre
1988–1993
Client
GTT
Kaiser Bautechnik
Area
3,500m²
Team
Ingenieur Büro Dr Meyer
Kaiser Bautechnik
ROM
Oskar Anders GmbH

Microelectronic Centre
1988–1996
Client
GTT
Area
12,000m²
Team
Ingenieur Büro Dr Meyer
Kaiser Bautechnik
Ebert Ingenieur
Emmer Pfenninger
Partner AG
ITA GmbH
Höhler & Partner

Business Promotion Centre
1990–1993
Client
GTT
Kaiser Bautechnik
Area
4,000m²
Team
Ingenieur Büro Dr Meyer
Kaiser Bautechnik
Roger Preston & Partners
Oskar Anders GmbH

5

Given the trend towards clean and quiet manufacturing industries, the potential exists to create new kinds of neighbourhoods which integrate places to live, work and play. In 1988 a masterplan was established to integrate new technology companies – which are replacing the old heavy industries of the Ruhr heartland – within a residential district of Duisburg. The first of the practice's German projects to be realised, Duisburg brought with it new attitudes towards energy and ecology that would inform a range of schemes developed during the 1990s.

The masterplan creates a landscaped public park and three new buildings. The focal point of the development is the Telematic Centre. Circular in form, with offices arranged around a full-height atrium, it houses the management centre for the entire complex and provides space for small and medium-sized companies. The forum at the heart of the building provides a public space for exhibitions, conferences and musical performances, together with a restaurant and bar.

The largest building on the site, the Microelectronic Centre, provides multi-use flexible accommodation, such as laboratories, production areas, classrooms, offices and meeting rooms. Within an overall climatic envelope, three fingers of accommodation are articulated by two glazed atria, which create a sheltered buffer zone for exhibitions and cafés. A variety of passive cooling and shading devices is employed to minimise energy consumption.

The Business Promotion Centre takes this strategy a stage further. Its multi-layered outer skin is so thermally efficient that no heating is required, even in the coldest winter. And the building generates and harvests its own energy, burning natural gas to produce electricity by means of a cogenerator. The by-product of this process – heat that would normally be wasted – passes through an absorption cooling plant to produce chilled water. Instead of conventional air-conditioning, dramatic temperature drops are achieved by distributing this water through miniaturised pipes embedded in the structure in a system similar to the fins on a car radiator. This is not only an ecologically responsible solution: the developer makes a significant annual profit from energy management.

6

7

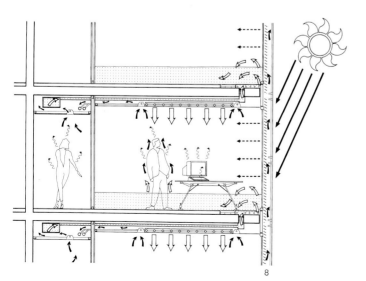

8

Millennium Tower
Tokyo, Japan 1989

Client
Obayashi Corporation
Area
1,040,000m²
Height
840m
Team
Obayashi Corporation

Tokyo is among the 'megacities' forecast to exceed populations of fifteen million by 2020. The Millennium Tower scheme challenges assumptions about such future cities. It presents a timely solution to the social challenges of urban expansion on this scale and to the particular problems of Tokyo, with its acute land shortages. Commissioned by the Obayashi Corporation, it provides 1.04 million square metres of commercial development, stands 170 storeys high and is the world's tallest projected building.

Rising out of Tokyo Bay, two kilometres offshore, the tower is capable of housing a community of up to 60,000 people, generating its own energy and processing its own waste. With its own transportation system, this vertical city quarter would be self-sustaining and virtually self-sufficient.

The lower levels accommodate offices, light manufacturing and 'clean' industries such as consumer electronics. Above are apartments, while the topmost section houses communications systems and wind and solar generators, interspersed with restaurants and viewing platforms to exploit the spectacular views.

A high-speed 'metro' system – with cars designed to carry 160 people – tracks both vertically and horizontally, moving through the building at twice the rate of conventional express lifts. Cars stop at intermediate 'sky centres' at every thirtieth floor; from there, individual journeys may be completed via lifts or escalators. This continuous cycle reduces travel times – an important factor in a vertical city, no less than a horizontal one. The five-storey sky centres have different principal functions – one might include a hotel, another a department store. Each is articulated with mezzanines, terraces and gardens to encourage a sense of place.

Developed in response to the hurricane-strength wind forces and earthquakes for which the region is notorious, the tower's conical structure, with its helical steel cage, is inherently stable. It provides decreasing wind resistance towards the top – where it is completely open – and increasing width and strength towards the base to provide earthquake resistance.

The project demonstrates that high-density or high-rise living does not mean overcrowding or hardship; it can lead to an improved quality of life, where housing, work and leisure facilities are all close at hand.

1

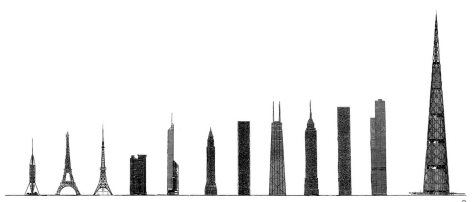

2

1. Model of the 170-storey tower.
2. Comparison of the Millennium Tower to some of the world's tallest buildings.
Facing page Visualisation showing the tower in Tokyo Bay.

Cranfield University Library
Cranfield, England 1989–1992

1

1. The building at night.
2. View of the atrium.
3. Book stacks on
the upper level.
4. Cross-section showing
the four barrel-vaulted
bays of the Library, which
extend at the sides to
form covered walkways.

2

Client
Cranfield University
Area
3,000m²
Team
Ove Arup & Partners
Roger Preston & Partners
Davis Langdon & Everest
George Sexton Associates

Cranfield University was founded in 1946 as a school for aeronautical engineers. Today it is one of Britain's leading technical education and research establishments, incorporating a wide range of postgraduate studies, and is a major foreign currency earner for research contracts.

The new Library provides a much-needed focus for the campus. Built on a square plan, it consists of four barrel-vaulted, steel-framed bays, one of which forms a broad central atrium – the hub of the Library – linking all three floors. The overhanging roof provides sheltered walkways along the sides of the building, while at the front it extends to create a vaulted entrance canopy.

The building reformulates the concept of the library in the information age: it is the reverse of the closed book stacks and forbidding screens and security barriers of traditional libraries. Seven kilometres of open bookshelves are located on the upper levels, freeing the ground-floor entrance area for social uses, focused around a coffee bar.

Library systems are designed to adapt easily to advances in information technology, and a perimeter desking system allows students to plug in their own computers or laptops and have instant access to the University's computer networks and electronic databases.

Maximum use is made of glare-free natural light and views. Rooflights at the apex of each vault bring natural light to the atrium and upper floors. Daylight is evenly distributed across the ceiling by gull-wing deflectors and can be supplemented by indirect lighting from continuous fluorescent tubes. External shading to the glass facades minimises heat gain during the summer months and allows comfortable conditions to be maintained through a ventilation-only system. The complete range of building services is controlled through a comprehensive building and energy management system.

Using a restrained palette of high-quality materials, the Library was built within costs no greater than those of a traditional brick building. Commentators have noted its evocation of a classical temple, complete with peristyle and portico, which is perhaps appropriate given the symbolic role it plays at the heart of the campus.

3

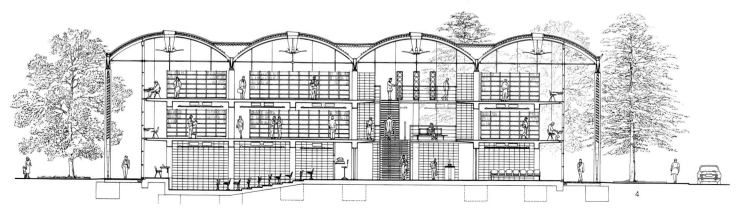

4

Shinagawa Mixed-Use Development

Tokyo, Japan 1990

Shinagawa Mixed-Use Development

1

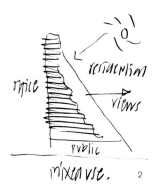

Client
Obunsha Corporation
Area
31,500m²
Team
Ove Arup & Partners
Obayashi Corporation

The Shinagawa project reflected Tokyo's dense urban fabric and its integrated mix of residential and business buildings. This mixed-use scheme was proposed as part of the regeneration of a derelict waterfront site in the Shinagawa district of Tokyo Harbour. Uniquely, it combined office accommodation and a radio station with apartments above a triple-height public realm containing shops, restaurants and cafés, providing a lively social environment for this new city district and a rare public space in a highly congested city.

The site was an elongated sliver of land, bound by the waterfront on one side and railway lines and a highway on the other. Stringent planning regulations regarding setbacks and light angles limited the potential for a pure office development but, by including residential and retail accommodation, the floor area could be increased by 25 per cent, thus enhancing the commercial viability of the project.

The building's distinctive shape was generated by positioning the radio station's transmitter mast at its apex, thus defining an overall height of 28 storeys. The mast surmounted a structural core which housed lifts and services.

Apartments with stepped roof terraces cascaded down the southern elevation, benefiting from sunlight and views in three directions. The basement provided two levels of car-parking and a triple-height sound-proofed recording studio for the radio station. At the heart of the building, facing east and west, was flexible accommodation for the radio station. The whole of the third floor contained recording studios and production offices. The remaining floors provided lettable office space for other commercial tenants.

The proposed structure was extremely efficient, accommodating three storeys of apartments within the height of two storeys of offices. The building's glazed envelope was subtly modulated to cater for the differing floor heights, adding to the animation of the facades, while its stepped profile was softened by a sweeping curve of metal louvres, providing passive shading for the apartments. It created a dramatic silhouette that would have given Tokyo a distinctive new landmark.

1. View of the model.
2. Norman Foster's concept sketch.
3. Cross-section showing the differing floor heights of the offices at the building's centre and the apartments ranged down its south facade.

95

Faculty of Law, University of Cambridge
Cambridge, England 1990–1995

Cambridge University has the largest law school in Britain, with 800 undergraduates and 200 postgraduate students. The Law Faculty is a place with traditions, but it is also forward-looking. The Faculty building provides state-of-the-art facilities for teaching and research, comprising the Squire Law Library, five auditoria, seminar rooms, common rooms and administrative offices.

The building sits at the heart of the Sidgwick site, the focus of humanities education at Cambridge, close to the Institute of Criminology and University Library. Its neighbours include James Stirling's History Faculty, and it is surrounded by lawns and mature trees.

This low, green garden context is the essence of Cambridge. The challenge, therefore, was to preserve the natural setting and to minimise the building's apparent size. The rectangular plan is cut on the diagonal in response to the geometry of the History Faculty and pedestrian routes across the site. It has a relatively small footprint, yet provides 8,500 square metres of accommodation without exceeding four storeys. This was achieved by burying the auditoria below ground, while the curving glass of the north facade helps the building to recede visually.

A full-height atrium forms the focus of the building. It links the different levels visually, creating a feeling of spaciousness, and draws daylight into the lower floors. Natural lighting is used to dramatic effect, especially in the Library, which occupies the upper three terraced floors and enjoys uninterrupted views of the gardens. The curving north facade is entirely glazed; the south, west and east facades are part glazed and incorporate devices to exclude solar gain and glare.

The building is highly energy-efficient. Its partially buried structure and exposed concrete frame combine to give it high thermal mass, making it slow to respond to outside temperature changes. Together with high insulation values, this allows the use of mechanically assisted natural ventilation throughout – only the lecture theatres require seasonal cooling. A lighting management system reduces energy consumption, while heat recovery coils, linked to the air extract, reclaim waste heat.

Interestingly, the building's environmental performance was put to the test during its first summer, one of the hottest on record. Happily, it performed extremely well.

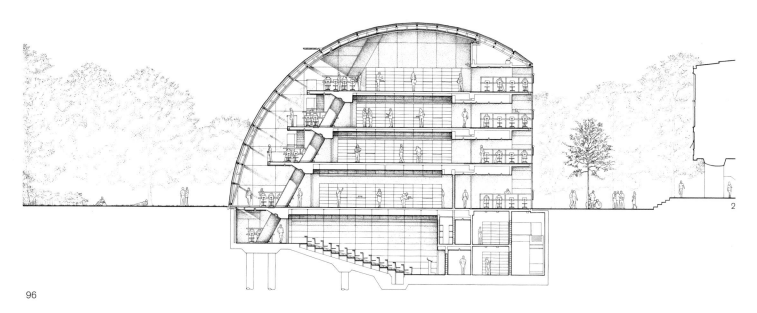

Client
University of Cambridge
Area
8,500m²
Team
Anthony Hunt Associates
YRM Engineers
Davis Langdon & Everest
Sandy Brown Associates
Emmer Pfenninger
Partner AG
Cambridge Landscape
Architects
Ove Arup & Partners
Halcrow Fox

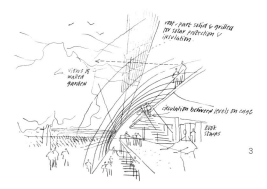

3

5

4

1. View of the north facade: its curved form minimises the building's impact on the landscape.
2. Cross-section showing the terracing of the floors.
3. Concept sketch by Norman Foster.
4, 5. Views of the atrium along the inside of the north facade.

Sagrera Masterplan
Barcelona, Spain 1991

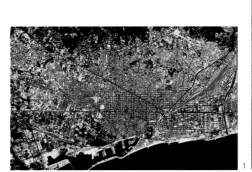

The massive urban renewal programme carried out prior to the 1992 Olympics transformed Barcelona into one of Europe's most dynamic cities. The development of a new railway terminus and transport interchange at Sagrera, in the largely industrial northern quarter of Barcelona, formed the heart of an ambitious masterplan for this last remaining redevelopment site in the city centre.

The Sagrera Masterplan site amounted to approximately three per cent of the land area within Barcelona's new inner ring road. A linear swathe of former railway and industrial land, it stretched alongside the Rec Comtal – a watercourse dating from Roman times – running south from Placa de les Glories to the new ring road interchange at Trinitat.

The masterplan focused on the Rec Comtal and a new 6-kilometre-long landscaped park along its banks. The development proposed a balanced mix of housing, offices, shops, hotels, educational facilities and underground parking to help regenerate the area and to knit it into the wider fabric of the city.

Located at the southern end of the site, the station was a state-of-the-art hub for Barcelona's road and rail transport networks. It was designed to facilitate transfers between local suburban rail routes, and to provide a central bus station, links to the metro system and connections with the airport. It was also envisaged as the principal interchange between French TGV trains and Spain's high-speed network. A twenty-first-century building in the spirit of the traditional railway terminus, it was centred around a vast, light-filled central hall. Planned amenities included computerised baggage check-in and multi-lingual information centres, giving it a quality of service found only at the world's most modern airports.

Community participation was an important ingredient in the planning process. Local consultation informed all phases of the project and the views of residents, schools, businesses and other groups were solicited. To encourage a rich social mix, new public buildings – health centres, libraries, civic centres – were provided on both a local and city scale, and one-third of the residential units were designated as low-cost housing. In Sagrera, Barcelona would have found a vibrant new core.

Client
The Travelstead Group
Area
230 hectares
Team
Ove Arup & Partners
Davis Langdon & Everest
Desvigne & Dalnoky
Cantor Seinuk
CMS Collaborative

1. Aerial view of the site.
2. The masterplan model being assembled in the Foster studio.
3. Aerial view of the model showing the Rec Comtal waterway, a focal point for surrounding development.

3

99

Lycée Albert Camus
Fréjus, France 1991–1993

Client
Ville de Fréjus
Area
14,500m²
Team
Ove Arup & Partners
Roger Preston & Partners
Davis Langdon & Everest
Desvigne & Dalnoky
Claude and Danielle
Engle Lighting
Sandy Brown Associates

1

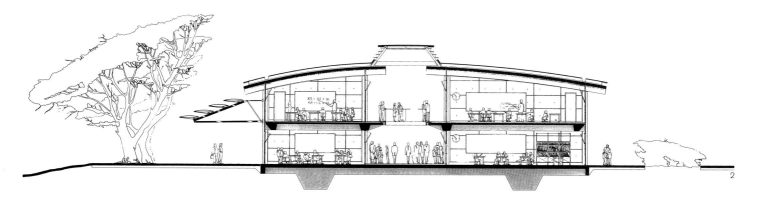

The French lycée polyvalent system offers a partly vocational education to young people in their last three years of schooling. The Lycée Albert Camus is the second school of this type for the rapidly expanding town of Fréjus on the Côte d'Azur.

The school's linear plan form is a response to its site and to a low-energy concept for the Mediterranean climate. The aim throughout was to keep active building services to a minimum. Interestingly, the most effective ecological diagram is also the natural social diagram. The linear central 'street' at the heart of the school, which is essential to the natural air circulation system, is also a central circulation space for people. The street is bisected by an entrance hall. Conceived as a 'village square' this space has its own café and casual seating, and acts as a focal point for the students.

Fresh air is pulled through the street, while the layering of the roof, with a light metal shield protecting the heavy concrete vaults from the sun, also encourages a cooling flow of air – a technique found in traditional Arabic architecture. The solar chimney effect allows warm air to rise through ventilation louvres, whilst brise-soleil along the southern elevation provide a broad band of dappled shade.

The structure is configured to contain two floors of classrooms alongside double-height reception spaces. The building is oriented to separate the public entrance side on the north from the more private southern edge with its magnificent views of the sea and fine trees which provide pools of shade.

Materials were chosen in response to the climate and to exploit local construction expertise. The exposed concrete frame, comprising simple repetitive elements, continues the French tradition of high-quality in-situ concrete as well as facilitating economical and rapid construction. Its high thermal mass allows it to act as a 'heat sink', slowing the rate of temperature change within the building. It is an important factor in enabling the whole structure to be cooled naturally without mechanical refrigeration.

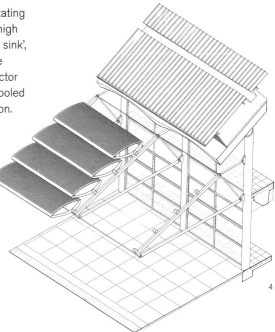

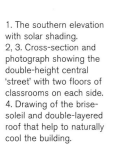

1. The southern elevation with solar shading.
2, 3. Cross-section and photograph showing the double-height central 'street' with two floors of classrooms on each side.
4. Drawing of the brise-soleil and double-layered roof that help to naturally cool the building.

Commerzbank Headquarters
Frankfurt, Germany 1991–1997

Client
Commerzbank AG
Area
100,000m²
Team
Ove Arup & Partners
Krebs & Kiefer
Roger Preston & Partners

Pettersen & Ahrends
Schad & Holzel
Jappsen & Stangier
Davis Langdon & Everest
Quickborner Team
Ingenieur Büro Schalm
Lichtdesign
Sommerland

At 53 storeys, the Commerzbank is the world's first ecological office tower and the tallest building in Europe. The outcome of a limited international competition, the project explores the nature of the office environment, developing new ideas for its ecology and working patterns.

Central to this concept is a reliance on natural systems of lighting and ventilation. Every office in the tower is daylit and has openable windows. External conditions permitting, this allows occupants to control their own environment for most of the year. This strategy results in energy consumption levels equivalent to half those of conventional office towers.

The plan form is triangular, comprising three 'petals' – the office floors – and a 'stem' formed by a full-height central atrium. Pairs of vertical masts enclose services and circulation cores in the corners of the plan and support eight-storey Vierendeel beams, which in turn support clear-span office floors.

Four-storey gardens are set at different levels on each of the three sides of the tower, forming a spiral of gardens around the building. As a result, on any level only two sides of the tower are filled with offices. The gardens become the visual and social focus for village-like clusters of offices. They play an ecological role, bringing daylight and fresh air into the central atrium, which acts as a natural ventilation chimney up the building for the inward-facing offices.

The gardens are also places to relax during refreshment breaks, bringing richness and humanity to the workplace, and from the outside they give the building a sense of transparency and lightness. Depending on their orientation, planting is from one of three regions: North America, Asia or the Mediterranean.

The tower has a distinctive presence on the Frankfurt skyline but it is also anchored into the lower-scale city fabric. It rises from the centre of a city block alongside the original Commerzbank building. Through restoration and sensitive rebuilding of the perimeter structures, the traditional scale of this block has been reinforced. The development at street level provides shops, car-parking, apartments and a banking hall, and forges links between the Commerzbank and the broader community. At the heart of the scheme a public galleria with restaurants, cafés and spaces for social and cultural events forms a popular new route cutting across the site.

On the day the Commerzbank opened, the Financial Times adopted it as the symbol of Frankfurt, just as it features Big Ben and the Eiffel Tower as symbols of London and Paris.

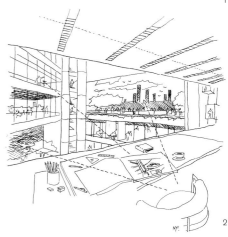

1. One of the sky gardens.
2. Norman Foster's sketch showing sight lines from an atrium office into the sky gardens and out to the city.
3. The café in the public galleria at the tower's base.
Facing page View of the tower from a nearby square.
Overleaf The tower's distinctive profile on the Frankfurt skyline.

102

Furniture

Airport Desking System
1989–1991
Client
BAA
Stansted Airport Ltd

Tabula Table System
1992–1993
Client
Tecno spa, Italy

Library Storage System
1994–1996
Client
Acerbis International

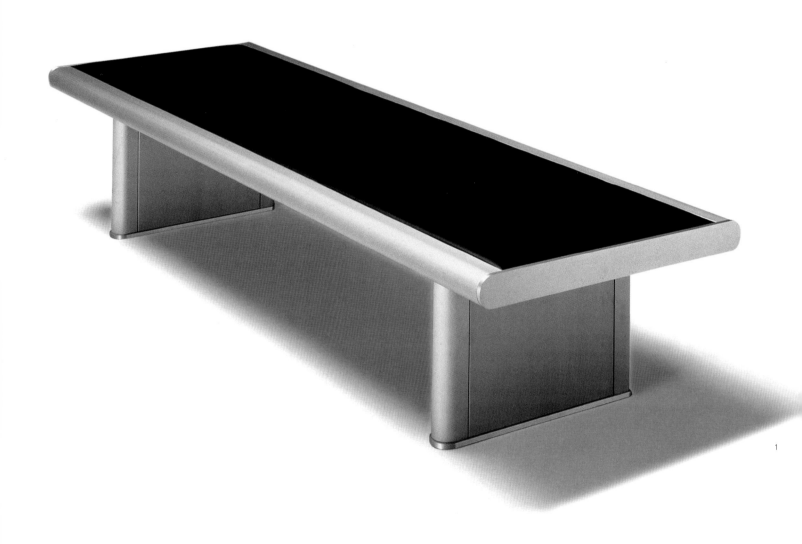

1

1, 2. The Tabula Table
and the Tabula Bench as
used in the Carré d'Art.
3–5. The Library Storage
System in use and in
Norman Foster's sketch.
6, 7. The Airport Desking
System at Stansted Airport,
shown under development
and in use.

2

From its earliest days the practice has designed furniture systems and fixtures in order to give greater cohesion to particular building projects. Often proprietary products have been neither suitable nor flexible enough for a defined need, and so new designs have been developed. The design of furniture systems has now become a discrete activity within the practice and products are developed for major manufacturers, unrelated to specific building commissions.

The Airport Desking System developed for check-in, security and customs at Stansted Airport reflects the approach adopted for the design of the terminal itself. It is based upon the belief that the internal environment should be as calm in its feel as possible. The level of natural light in the concourse influenced the choice of colours, while the choice of materials was developed through a programme of research to provide a tough group of objects capable of withstanding the expected levels of passenger activity within the airport.

The Library Storage System was first developed within the context of the Cambridge Law Faculty Library. It answered specific requirements for library equipment where no adequate solutions were found to exist. The key design criteria were ease of assembly, the ability to integrate a multitude of accessories, and durability. A neutral palette of materials has made the system suitable for a variety of architectural contexts. The system is self-supported on side panels and is consequently very flexible. Accessories include computer shelves and CD and video racks, together with drawers and sliding doors for the domestic market.

The Tabula Table System was initially developed for the Carré d'Art in Nîmes to suit many different purposes, including library reading tables, conservation tables, display cases and shop vitrines. The structure is composed of two aluminium extrusions, one for the legs and one for the rim of the tabletop. By shortening the length of the leg extrusion the Tabula System can also be adapted into a bench. The top is hollow and can be used for routing cables for desktop computer terminals or integrated lighting systems. The inherent flexibility of the Tabula system means that tables of almost any dimensions can be produced to suit any context; and because the tabletop is not structural, but simply slots into the frame, any surface material can be specified.

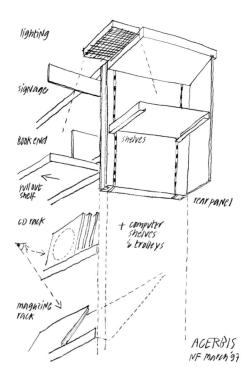

Canary Wharf Underground Station
London, England 1991–1999

1

Client
Jubilee Line Extension
Project (JLEP)
Area
31,500m^2
Team
Posford Duvivier
Jubilee Line Extension
Project
Ove Arup & Partners
Claude and Danielle
Engle Lighting
Davis Langdon & Everest
De Leau Chadwick

The Jubilee Line extension is one of the greatest acts of architectural patronage of recent years, comprising eleven new stations by as many architects. The practice's station at Canary Wharf is by far the largest of these – when the development of the area is complete, it will be used by more people at peak times than Oxford Circus, currently London's busiest Underground destination.

The station is built within the hollow of the former West India Dock using cut-and-cover construction techniques. At 300 metres in length, it is as long as Canary Wharf Tower is tall. The roof of the station is laid out as a leafy landscaped park, creating Canary Wharf's principal public recreation space. The only visible station elements are the swelling glass canopies that cover its three entrances.

Glowing with light at night-time, by day these structures draw daylight deep into the station concourse. By concentrating natural light dramatically at these points, orientation is enhanced, minimising the need for directional signage. Twenty banks of escalators transport passengers in and out of the station. Administrative offices, kiosks and other amenities are sited along the flanks of the ticket hall, which leaves the main concourse free, creating a sense of clarity and calm.

Due to the volume of station traffic, the guiding design principles were durability and ease of maintenance. The result is a simple palette of hard-wearing materials: fair-faced concrete, stainless steel and glass. This robust aesthetic is most pronounced at platform level where the concrete diaphragm tunnel walls are left exposed.

The station introduces many security innovations: glazed lifts enhance passenger security and deter vandalism; access to the tracks is blocked by platform-edge screens, which open in alignment with the doors of the trains. Servicing is also enhanced: cabling runs beneath platforms or behind walls, with access via maintenance gangways, allowing the station to be maintained entirely from behind the scenes.

2

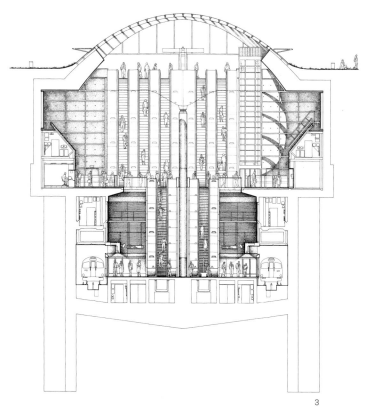

1. View of the main passenger concourse.
2. Aerial view of one of the glass entrance canopies.
3. Cross-section showing the direct route from entrance to platform.
Overleaf The canopies radiate light, clearly indicating the access points to the station.

3

Inner Harbour Masterplan
Duisburg, Germany 1991–2001

Steiger Schwanentor
1993–1994
Client
LEG, Düsseldorf
Pier length
62m
Promenade length
300m
Team
Hans KolbeckIngenieur
Büro Klement

Hafenforum
1995–1996
Client
THS, Essen
Area
1,150m²
Team
Architekturbüro Dieter
Müller
Ingenieur Büro Cosanne
THS
Glamo GmbH

1

2

3

Canals
1996–1998
Client
IDE, Duisburg
Area
175m long
10m wide
Team
ABDOU GmbH
TUV
Ingenieur Büro R Knoke
B-Plan

Housing
1997–2001
Client
THS, Essen
Area
7,000m²
Team
Ingenieur Büro Cosanne
Ingenieur Büro Dr Meyer

In 1991 the practice won an international competition to masterplan Duisburg Inner Harbour – the largest inland harbour in the world. The scheme, set on an 89-hectare site, aims to connect the inner city with the water's edge and with areas north of the harbour. It includes new construction and selective refurbishment to provide residential, social and cultural accommodation together with commercial and light-industrial buildings.

The Steiger Schwanentor, a jetty which provides mooring facilities for sightseeing boats, was the first project to be completed. A pontoon and ramp system allows disabled access to boats. The four steel pontoons are linked to the bank by hinged steel ramps which can accommodate a variation in water levels of up to 7.4 metres. To complement these, a pedestrian promenade, developed along the western part of the harbour, introduces trees, lighting and balustrades.

Further east, the practice has converted an old grain warehouse into the 'Hafenforum' – offices for the Inner Harbour Development Company. Work on a dam and new canals has also been completed, and a major new housing scheme is under construction.

The 97-metre-long cofferdam, which supports a road deck, encloses a 600-metre boating lake. The water level is maintained at the previous high-water mark, making it more accessible from the quayside. The dam forms a physical link across the harbour, stimulating future development. One such project is Euro Gate, situated on the harbour's northern banks. Designed to draw visitors to the area, the complex will be a focal point of the harbour redevelopment.

South of the lake, three new canals penetrate a housing area, bringing the buildings into contact with the water's edge. The canals are fed by rain water run-off from surrounding streets and by ground water, using pumps powered by photovoltaic panels. Water is filtered through reed beds at the head of the canal, before being discharged into the lake.

Housing has already been constructed along the first canal and the practice is currently completing a new terraced housing block that includes low-cost apartments.

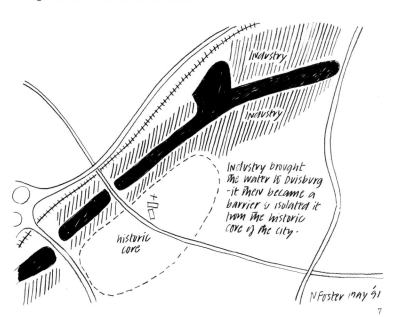

1. Aerial view of the masterplan model.
2. The Steiger Schwanentor.
3. One of the new canals created on the site.
4. A model of Euro Gate.
5. The Hafenforum.
6. Sketch study by Norman Foster for a new terraced housing block.
7. Norman Foster's concept sketch for the reintegration of the harbour area.

Wilhelminapier Masterplan and World Port Centre
Rotterdam, The Netherlands 1991–2010

The practice began working in Rotterdam in the early 1990s, creating a masterplan for the Wilhelminapier, part of the Kop van Zuid redevelopment of the dock area south of the city centre. The scheme is revitalising the city's waterfront and helping to knit the dock area into the broader fabric of the city.

The masterplan challenged the assumption that this historical area should be cleared of buildings prior to redevelopment; instead it has worked within the existing street pattern and retained some viable buildings. This has allowed for phased implementation and ensured that the area has remained active during the redevelopment process. Two Foster buildings have so far been completed within the masterplan framework: the Marine Simulator Centre and the World Port Centre.

Completed in 1993, the Marine Simulator Centre comprises two parts. A new building houses a complex piece of equipment with a 360-degree screen and moving platform, used to teach sailing techniques. This is linked to the converted 1950s Holland-America Line building, where there are four smaller 250-degree simulators alongside classrooms and offices.

The 32-storey World Port Centre stands at the head of a zone earmarked for dense high-rise development, where it enjoys spectacular views across the River Maas. It provides 48,000 square metres of office accommodation and is home to the Rotterdam Harbour Authority.

The building is configured as twin towers, of different heights, with a dramatic curved facade to the west. The two towers are linked by a glazed lift lobby, which rises through the full height of the building, creating a vertical axis on the north and south facades. A conference facility caps the summit of the tallest tower.

Horizontally banded windows on the office floors allow panoramic views, while light-shelves around the circumference of the building act both as sunshades – reducing solar gain – and as light-scoops, reflecting daylight into the office floors. This system, together with high-performance glazing and daylight-controlled lighting, achieves significant reductions in energy consumption. Absorption cooling, using waste heat from the district heating system, contributes to the building's internal climate control, further reducing running costs.

2

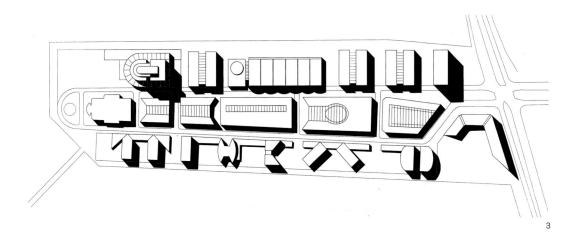

1, 3. Aerial view and site plan of the Wilhelminapier.
2. The World Port Centre illuminated at night.
4, 5. Interior views of the Marine Simulator Centre: one of the simulators in use and the 11-metre-diameter drum which houses the 360-degree simulator.

3

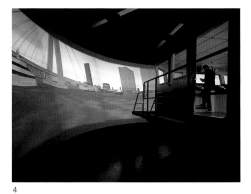

4

Wilhelminapier Masterplan
1991–2010
Client
City of Rotterdam
Laing Management (UK)
SAE (France)
MBO (Amsterdam)
Area
357,000m²
Team
Ove Arup & Partners
Davis Langdon & Everest
Laing Management Europe
Wilma Bouw
Jones Lang Wootton

Marine Simulator Centre
1992–1993
Client
Marine Safety International
Area
3,000m²
Team
ABMA Dirks & Partners
Ingenieurs Buro ir
J Zonneveld BV
Raadgevend Technisch
Buro van Heugten

World Port Centre
1995–2000
Client
ING Vastgoed Ontwikkeling
BV, Den Haag
Area
48,000m²
Team
Adviesbureau Peutz
Aronsohn Raaogevende
Ingenieurs
Bureau Bouwkunde
Bureaubouw Coordinatie
Nederland
Hiensch Engineering BV

5

Motoryacht
1991–1993

Client
Confidential
Length
58.5m
Team
Gerhard Gilgenost
Dr Lurssen Werft

4

1

2

The design of most sea-going vessels – from floating gin palaces to cross-Channel ferries – tends to split responsibilities, with a naval architect working on the exterior and hull, while the superstructure and interior are completed by a designer. The result is often top-heavy and unseaworthy-looking, with interiors that are the reverse of shipshape.

The design for this 58.5-metre private yacht draws inspiration from naval vessels, in which functional efficiency takes precedence over styling. Hull and superstructure are a semi-monococque construction of welded skin, frames and longitudinal stiffeners. The yacht has the largest aluminium hull so far built. Its design minimises the superstructure volume, emphasising exterior deck spaces while maintaining clean lines. The interior focuses on high-quality craftsmanship and appropriate materials. Equally comfortable accommodation is provided for passengers and crew alike.

The yacht has transatlantic and worldwide cruising capabilities and has been built to German Lloyds certification and ABS standards. It is powered by two MTU diesel engines rated at 4,800 horsepower. Its design speed is 30 knots, although 34 knots was achieved during sea trials.

1. The yacht at sea.
2. View of the interior.
3. Side elevation.
4. Side view of a sailboat, commissioned by the same client; with a 51.7-metre hull – only 6 metres shorter than that of the motoryacht – it explored similar design themes within the discipline of a very different hull form.

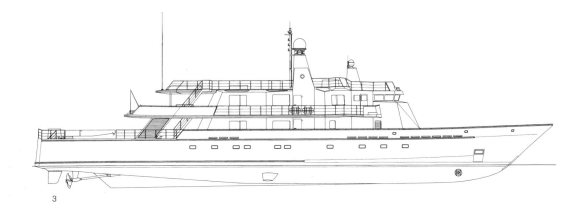

3

Solar-Electric Vehicle
London, England 1992–1994

Client
Sir Robert and Lady
Sainsbury
Royal Botanic Gardens,
Kew
Size
7.2m long
2.5m high
2.3m wide
Team
Transport Research
Laboratory

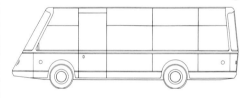

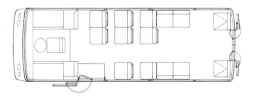

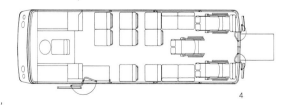

Alternative forms of transport are often explored within environments such as parks, away from the pressures of the highway. This prototype electric vehicle stems from a commission from Sir Robert and Lady Sainsbury. Impressed by the miniature train service at Versailles, they proposed something similar for Kew.

The vehicle is based on a modified standard chassis with a tubular steel superstructure and fibreglass body panels. The windows wrap over the roof to create a feeling of transparency and openness. Capable of carrying eighteen passengers, its air-cushion suspension allows it to 'kneel' to the side or rear to facilitate wheelchair access. Powered by both a 10-horsepower electric motor and roof-mounted photovoltaic cells, it has a range of 12 kilometres and a top speed of 24 kilometres per hour.

Modified versions have been proposed for a new generation of hybrid-powered taxis and minibuses, which could solve many inner-city transport problems.

1–3. The vehicle shown from the exterior, 'kneeling' to take on wheelchair users, and in use.
4. Elevation and plans showing accommodation for wheelchair users at the rear of the vehicle.

Addition to Joslyn Art Museum
Omaha, USA 1992–1994

Client
Joslyn Art Museum
Area
5,800m²
Team
Henningson Durham
and Richardson
Davis Langdon & Everest
Claude and Danielle
Engle Lighting
R F Mahoney and Associates

The museum, gallery complex or cultural centre has the power to become a very strong social focus in the community. In extending the Joslyn Art Museum and addressing its external spaces so that they could work for outdoor events, the practice aimed not only to bring the old building and its environment back to life but to create something that was more than the sum of its parts.

Completed in 1931, the Joslyn is one of the finest Art Deco buildings in America. The brief for a new wing called for over 5,000 square metres of gallery and workshop space, together with limited refurbishment of the existing building.

The Joslyn is unusual in combining art and music in one complex. A 1,200-seat concert hall is flanked on each side by two narrow floors of art galleries. Analysis showed that the main entrance, with its classical portico reached by a majestic, if forbidding, flight of stone steps, was being underused. Most visitors entered the building by a side door next to the car-park. The challenge was to reemphasise the public front of the Museum and design a new wing that did not detract from the simplicity of the original concept.

The new wing adopts a solid rectangular form with similar proportions to the Museum and little articulation. It is clad in matching pink Etowah Fleuri marble from the Georgian quarry that supplied the original building. Linking the new and old wings, and set back from both, a glass atrium forms a new social space, providing restaurant facilities and a secondary public entrance. On the main level of the new wing are temporary exhibition galleries, lit from above by indirect, controlled daylight. The floor below comprises storage vaults, workshops, cloakrooms, a kitchen and a restaurant servery.

At the front of the Museum, the original access road and car-park were reinstated to reinforce the principal axis and encourage use of the original entrance. An open-air amphitheatre for summer concerts was planned to broaden the range of the Joslyn's activities and give it a yet stronger community attraction.

1. View of the new galleries.
2. Picnickers gather for an open-air performance on the Museum's main steps at an annual jazz festival.
3. Norman Foster's sketch showing the new wing and reestablished main entrance.
Facing page The glass atrium that links the new wing and the old.

Agiplan Headquarters
Mülheim, Germany 1992–1996

Client
Agiplan
Area
5,100m²
Team
Ingenieur Büro Dr Meyer
RPK
Rüping Consult MDA Bysh

This addition to the headquarters of Agiplan, a Europe-wide engineering and consulting company, allows many previously scattered departments to be brought together in Mülheim. It is one of several projects by the practice which contribute to the revitalisation of the Ruhr area.

The 5,100-square-metre addition extends a building designed by Agiplan's founder in the 1970s. The new wing provides offices, flexible exhibition spaces and a library. Its four storeys are centred on an atrium, which links the old building and the new. Bridges span the atrium on the upper floors and glazed lifts and stairs connect all levels. Forming an open circulation zone at the heart of the building, the atrium encourages social interaction and provides a focal point for the offices, library, information centre, gallery and conference spaces that surround it.

The facade of the old wing, which now forms one side of the atrium, has been replaced by glass balustrades mirroring those of the new addition; in the process, its radical pre-cast concrete structure has been exposed.

The open-plan office areas on either side of the atrium receive daylight from the central space, while cellular offices along the north facade are naturally ventilated and daylit by a glass-panel facade with integral sunshading.

1. The new extension, to the left, linked to the original headquarters by a glass atrium.
2. Cross-section showing how the new building corresponds to the old.

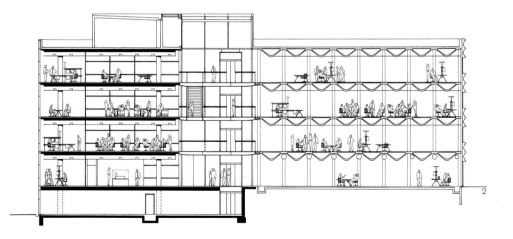

Electricité de France Regional Headquarters

Bordeaux, France 1992–1996

Client
Electricité de France
Area
7,000m²
Team
Ove Arup & Partners
SERETE
MDA France
Kaiser Bautechnik

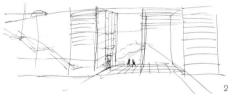

When Electricité de France, the leading French utility company, commissioned new regional offices, it sought a building that would embrace the efficient use of electricity for all its energy needs. The resulting headquarters uses approximately half the energy typically consumed by buildings of similar size in France, and pursues the quest for more ecological concepts allied with a philosophy of social integration.

Bringing together for the first time all the company's previously disparate departments, the three-storey, 7,000-square-metre building has a highly efficient envelope which minimises heat gain and loss. To prevent solar gain the elevations are fitted with bleached cedarwood louvres, positioned to provide shade without obscuring views. Internal heat gain is reduced by restricting the use of heavy heat-producing equipment such as photocopiers to a central air-conditioned zone.

The high thermal mass of the building's exposed concrete frame and floor-slabs helps to maintain comfortable interior temperatures, even on hot summer days. Natural ventilation and lighting are used where possible – a feature that both reduces energy consumption and improves working conditions. At night, the windows on the east and west elevations open automatically, drawing in air to cool the concrete soffit. Extra cooling is provided by chilling the floors, which can also be heated in the winter. The building also reuses its own waste energy: the water-based heating and cooling system is run by an electric pump powered by the central exhaust stack.

The landscaping responds to the geometry and scale of the nearby Château Raba as well as to the warm climate of Bordeaux. A long avenue of indigenous trees provides an imposing yet sheltered entrance to the building. Added drama is provided by the use of strong colour: vivid yellow in the circulation zones and ultramarine on the facades, visible behind the cedar louvres.

1. The building's louvred exterior seen at night.
2. Norman Foster's sketch of the shaded entrance area that cuts through the building.
3. View of the entrance showing the hints of ultramarine on the facades.

Design Centre
Essen, Germany 1992–1997

Zeche Zollverein near Essen is a redundant early-twentieth-century coal-mining complex designed on a colossal scale. Once the largest shaft system in the Ruhr area, it was decommissioned in 1986 when coal production became uneconomic. In an imaginative leap of faith it was decided to reuse the site as a cultural centre and to transform the old powerhouse – a masterpiece of industrial archaeology – into the home of a design centre for the promotion of contemporary design in Germany and abroad.

The powerhouse forms the centrepiece of an extraordinary group of buildings which share a vocabulary of brown- and red-painted exposed-steel I-beams, with an infill of industrial glazing and red brick. These magnificent structures, with their towering chimneys and vast halls, are the cathedrals of the industrial age. The powerhouse has an inner hall of colossal proportions, as impressive as any Gothic edifice. The challenge was to adapt this heroic building without fundamentally altering its character.

The building's facade was restored and a number of later additions removed to reveal its original form. Inside, the heavy industrial feel of the building was conserved. One of the five original boilers was preserved as an example of 1930s technology. The remaining boilers were hollowed out to house independently supported galleries, which are articulated as 'boxes within a box', their lightness juxtaposed with the heaviness of the original fabric. A simple concrete cube contains further exhibition space as well as conference rooms. Visitors enter via the dramatic central hall where the rusty steel structure and exposed brick walls are visible.

The Design Centre's temporary and permanent exhibitions – everything from cars to electrical appliances – are constantly updated, requiring highly flexible galleries. The different exhibition areas and the interaction of old and new architecture create a varied backdrop for the location of exhibits, while the changing nature of the exhibitions themselves adds a further dynamic element to this relationship.

1

2

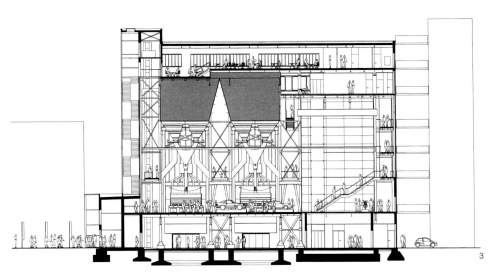

3

1, 2. The facade of the powerhouse as it was originally and after restoration. The chimney was removed for structural reasons.
3. Cross-section showing the preserved industrial machinery.
4–6. Views of the interior: the new exhibition spaces form discrete areas within the existing steel structure.

Client
Bauhütte Zeche Zollverein
Schacht XII GmbH
Area
5,000m²
Team
Ove Arup & Partners
Weber Hamelmann Surmann
Ingenieur Büro G Hoffmann
Stredich & Partners
Büro Böll

4

5

6

Hong Kong International Airport, Chek Lap Kok
Hong Kong 1992–1998

1

2

Client
Hong Kong Airport Authority
Area
516,000m²
Team
BAA
Mott Connell Ltd
Ove Arup & Partners
Fisher Marantz Renfro Stone
O'Brien Kreitzberg
& Associates Ltd
Wilbur Smith Associates

Chek Lap Kok became Hong Kong's sole airport in July 1998. Lying at the hub of a region reaching across Asia and Australasia, it is one of the world's largest airports. By 2040 it will handle 80 million passengers per annum – the same amount as Heathrow and New York's JFK airports combined.

It is among the most ambitious construction projects of modern times. The land on which it stands was once a mountainous island. In a major reclamation programme, its 100-metre peak was brought down to 7 metres above sea level and the island was expanded to four times its original area – equal to the size of the Kowloon peninsula.

Chek Lap Kok extends a concept pioneered at Stansted Airport, a model since adopted for airports worldwide. It is characterised by a lightweight roof – free of service installations – natural lighting and integration of baggage handling, environmental services and transportation beneath the main concourse. With its uncluttered spaces, bathed in light, it forms a spectacular gateway to the city.

Equally important is the clarity of its user-friendly planning. The design accentuates natural orientation both within the building and beyond: users are aware of the land and the water, and can see the aircraft. The building's Y-shaped plan form was written into the design brief. The vaulted roof is a unifying element. The direction of the vaults remains constant, regardless of the divergent directions that the 'prongs' take, so that the roof is itself an aid to orientation.

Departing travellers alight at the Ground Transportation Centre at the eastern end of the terminal. Once through passport control, passengers enter the East Hall – the largest single airport retail space in the world. If the airport is a city, this is its market square. Beyond this space, the terminal narrows to a long concourse from which the 38 boarding gates are accessed.

From Chek Lap Kok, mainland road and rail links cross a causeway to Lantau to the south and continue across two new bridges. The entire journey between city and airport can be completed in twenty minutes.

3

4

The roof is developed out of one simple vault module
The height and width varies according to needs
The structure orders and lights the spaces.

The grain and angle of the structure
provides instant orientation
Both inside the building and also from the outside.

1, 2. The check-in area at the eastern end of the terminal.
3. Aerial view showing the Y-shaped plan form.
4. The road-level set-down point.
5. Norman Foster's concept sketch defining the directional roof vaulting.
Overleaf Extensive glazing fills the airport with natural light and allows clear views of the land, the water and the aeroplanes.

Shopping Centres

The first integrated shopping centres designed by the practice in the early 1970s explored the idea of the shopping centre as a retail and leisure destination in its own right. Functioning almost round the clock, they were envisaged as powerful magnets in their respective communities.

Similarly, the mixed-use Al Faisaliah Complex in Riyadh is spearheading the commercial development of a brand new business district in the city. The provision of high-quality retail and leisure facilities is an essential part of the scheme, aiming to attract other developers to the area. The three-storey shopping mall provides 45,000 square metres of retail space. Two large department stores, including a branch of Harvey Nichols, run through all three levels and form anchors at either end of a long mall. Between them, a variety of smaller shops is arranged on both sides of a central atrium, which draws natural light into the shops and allows dramatic views down the length of the mall.

The shopping centre integrated within Stansted Airport was among the first to address the question of how, as a fundamental part of the architectural concept, large-scale shopping facilities could be incorporated within the airport concourse. In moving through the airport the traveller experiences two architectural orders. The primary order is the lattice-shelled roof, supported on the outstretched branches of tree-like structural columns. The smaller, secondary, order is the system of free-standing enclosures, such as shops, banks and bars, that inhabit the space. This arrangement is highly flexible – shop units can easily be re-sited when required – and maintains clarity of movement from landside to airside.

Hong Kong International Airport, Chek Lap Kok, takes this idea to the ultimate degree. Its shopping centre is the largest single airport retail space in the world, covering an area the size of the old airport terminal at Kai Tak. It offers a powerful illustration of the way that shopping has become an essential part of the airport experience and, interestingly, it is the only shopping centre in Hong Kong with 100 per cent occupancy.

1. Stansted Airport's shops were integrated into the design concept of the airport as a whole.
2. View along the shopping mall at the Al Faisaliah Complex in Riyadh.
3. The world's largest single airport shopping space, at Hong Kong International Airport.

**Stansted Airport
Shopping Centre**
England 1981–1991
Client
BAA
Area
40,000m^2

**Chek Lap Kok
Shopping Centre**
Hong Kong 1992–1998
Client
Hong Kong Airport
Authority
Area
30,000m^2

**Al Faisaliah Shopping
Centre**
Riyadh, Saudia Arabia
1993–2000
Client
King Faisal Foundation
Area
45,000m^2

HACTL Superterminal, Chek Lap Kok
Hong Kong 1992–1998

Client
Hong Kong Air
Cargo Terminal Ltd
Ove Arup & Partners
Area
260,000m²
Team
Levett & Bailey

1

2

The Hong Kong Air Cargo Terminal (HACTL), Superterminal 1, at Hong Kong International Airport is the largest and most technologically advanced single cargo terminal in the world. It reinforces Hong Kong's status as a major centre for international commerce and communications in South-East Asia.

Superterminal 1 consists of two buildings: the Express Centre, a two-storey express cargo and courier facility; and the Cargo Terminal, a seven-storey cargo-handling facility. Together, these two buildings have the capacity to handle 2.5 million tonnes of cargo annually – more than two-and-a-half times the capacity of the nearest rival, Heathrow Airport.

The Express Centre provides express cargo and courier operators with their own sorting facilities. It can process 200,000 tonnes of cargo a year. Specialist facilities allow the Centre to handle anything from livestock to precious items, including diamonds, cash and gold bullion.

The Cargo Terminal is an enormous building, 200 metres wide by 290 metres long. It has two container storage racking systems, each 250 metres long and 45 metres high, and two bulk storage racking systems – the largest combined racking system ever built. The container racking lines the perimeter of the building, visible from the runway through fully glazed walls which allow the building to glow at night. The bulk storage racking systems are located in a concrete enclosure at the heart of the building where cargo can be stored for up to two months. Both systems are fully automated.

Accommodation at each end of the building includes the HACTL offices, airline offices, a customer service hall and a canteen capable of serving 600 people at one sitting. Employees and their families have an unprecedented range of facilities. The Terminal incorporates a sports centre with squash courts, badminton courts and a sports hall. It also has the largest roof garden in the world, with swimming pools and tennis courts, giving the building an extraordinary social focus.

1. Cross-section through
the Express Centre and
Cargo Terminal.
2. View of the interior
of the Cargo Terminal
showing the container
storage racking.
3. Aerial view of
the Superterminal.

3

Kowloon-Canton Railway Terminal

Hong Kong 1992–1998

Client
Kowloon-Canton
Railway Corporation
Area
45,000m²
Team
Ove Arup & Partners
WT Partnership

1

The opening up of China and the return of Hong Kong to Chinese rule have resulted in an exponential rise in rail passenger traffic between Hong Kong and the mainland. To meet this demand, the Hung Hom terminal on the Kowloon-Canton Railway (KCR) has been refurbished and doubled in size to allow vastly increased numbers of people to flow through it comfortably and efficiently. The extension increases its capacity from 50 million to an anticipated 87 million domestic and international travellers by 2014.

The original station, built over a twenty-year period from the 1970s, was on three levels, with tracks at street level, public walkways at mid-level and a crowded concourse on a raised podium. The new terminal clarifies circulation by creating three separate zones – international departures, international arrivals and domestic travel.

The raised podium is dedicated to international travel, with its more complex processes, allowing domestic passengers – the daily commuters – uninterrupted use of the mid-level. This provides easy access to the platforms and reduces the need to change levels, greatly increasing speed and efficiency of movement. Platforms, walkways and concourses are linked by a series of atria that bring natural light down to platform level, while lighting, signage and floor and wall finishes have all been improved.

The station has been expanded to the east through the creation of a pavilion with a striking, lightweight wave-form roof. Linear north-facing rooflights and a full-height glazed curtain wall admit maximum light to all levels of the station with minimum solar gain, reducing the building's energy requirements and greatly improving the feel of its spaces.

1. The new station pavilion at night with its wave-form roof lit from below.

New German Parliament, Reichstag
Berlin, Germany 1992–1999

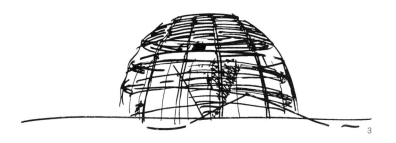

1. View into the
plenary chamber.
2. Detail of the exterior.
3. Norman Foster's concept
sketch for the cupola.
4. Testing the lighting concept
with a large-scale model of
the cupola and chamber.
5. North-south cross-section.
Overleaf The interior of
the cupola with 'light sculptor'
and helical public ramps.

4

Client
Bundesrepublik
Deutschland
Area
61,166m²
Team
Kuehn Bauer und Partner
Davis Langdon & Everest
Kaiser Bautechnik
Fischer Energie und
Haustechnik

IKP Professor Dr Georg
Plenge
Müller BBM GmbH
Claude and Danielle
Engle Lighting
Leonhardt Andrä und
Partner
Planungsgruppe Karnasch-
Hackstein
Acanthus
Amstein & Walthert

In 1992 Foster and Partners was one of fourteen non-German practices invited to enter the competition to rebuild the Reichstag. The practice won the competition after a second stage in 1993 and the reconstruction began following Christo's 'Wrapped Reichstag' in July 1995.

The building's transformation is rooted in four issues: the Bundestag's significance as a democratic forum, a commitment to public accessibility, a sensitivity to history, and a rigorous environmental agenda.

As found, the Reichstag was mutilated by war and insensitive rebuilding; surviving nineteenth-century interiors were concealed beneath a plasterboard lining. Peeling away these layers revealed striking imprints of the past, including graffiti left by Soviet soldiers. These scars are preserved and historical layers articulated; the Reichstag has become a 'living museum' of German history.

The reconstruction takes cues from the old Reichstag; for example, the original piano nobile and courtyards have been reinstated. In other respects it is a complete departure: within its masonry shell it is transparent, opening up the interior to light and views and placing its activities on view. Public and politicians enter together through the reopened formal entrance. The public realm continues on the roof in the terrace restaurant and the cupola – a new Berlin landmark – where helical ramps lead to an observation platform, allowing the people to ascend above the heads of their political representatives in the chamber below.

The building's energy strategy is radical. It uses renewable bio-fuel – vegetable oil – which, when burned in a cogenerator to produce electricity, is far cleaner than fossil fuels. The result is a 94 per cent reduction in carbon dioxide emissions. Surplus heat is stored as hot water in an aquifer 300 metres below ground. The water can be pumped up to heat the building or to drive an absorption cooling plant to produce chilled water. This, too, can be similarly stored below ground. The Reichstag's modest energy requirements allow it to perform as a power station for the new government quarter.

The Reichstag's cupola is also crucial to its lighting and ventilation strategies. At its core a 'light sculptor' reflects horizon light into the chamber, with a moveable sun-shield blocking solar gain and glare. As night falls, this process is reversed. The cupola becomes a beacon, signalling the strength and vigour of the German democratic process.

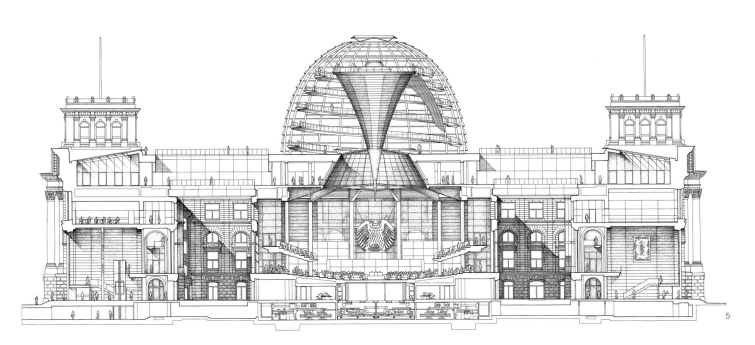

5

Tower Place

London, England 1992–2002

Client
Tishman Speyer
Properties Ltd
Marsh & McLennan
Companies Inc
Area
42,000m²
Team
Ove Arup & Partners
E C Harris
Claude and Danielle
Engle Lighting
Townshend Landscape
Architects
MACE

1. Visualisation of the
offices, seen from the
south across the Thames.
2, 3. Two views of the
model: looking towards
the atrium and from above.
4. Site plan showing how
the building responds to
the mediaeval street plan.

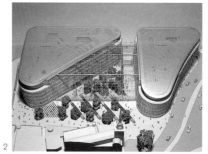

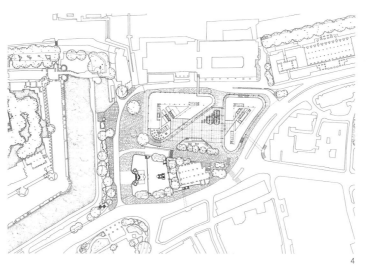

The low-rise, deep-plan, energy-conscious office building with flexible, full-access floors and improved circulation is a typology pioneered by the practice in the early 1970s in the design of the Willis Faber & Dumas Headquarters in Ipswich. Nearly thirty years after Willis Faber's completion, the practice is replacing obsolete 1960s office towers with lower-rise structures for progressive developers. Although each is particular to its site, the design specifications are remarkably similar to those of Willis Faber. What was once avant-garde has entered the mainstream.

The City of London has traditionally been characterised by relatively small-scale buildings laid out on an essentially mediaeval street plan. These seven-storey offices in Tower Place, close to the Tower of London, replace an insensitive sixteen-storey office development that obstructed important view corridors between Greenwich and St Paul's Cathedral and between the Monument and the Tower. The new buildings help to restore the site's traditional urban grain. Historical views are reinstated and a new public plaza with trees and water is created in front of All Hallows Church.

The development provides 42,000 square metres of office space in two blocks, broadly triangular in plan, which are linked by one of the largest glazed atriums in Europe. The engineering of the atrium's glass walls is highly advanced: rows of glass panels are hung like curtains from tension cables stretched between the two buildings. They terminate one storey above ground level, creating an open space through which the public can move freely. This new space incorporates two designated City Walkways, inviting pedestrians to use it as a sheltered thoroughfare. The opening at ground level and a ventilation slot at the junction of the roof and the walls will encourage airflow through the space, counteracting possible heat gain through the glass.

The offices enjoy superb views out towards All Hallows Church, the Tower and Tower Bridge. The stone and glass facades are designed to allow maximum daylight penetration, while blade-like aluminium louvres provide solar shading and add a shifting textural layer to the facades.

Musée de Préhistoire des Gorges du Verdon
Quinson, France 1992–2001

Client
Département Alpes de
Hautes Provence
Area
4,500m²
Team
Bruno Chiambretto
Olivier Sabran
SEV Ingenierie
Davis Langdon & Everest

1

2

The Gorges du Verdon in Haute Provence
form an exceptional archaeological site, rich
in traces of Stone Age life, to which this
Museum is devoted.

The mediaeval village of Quinson is
characterised by traditional stone buildings
and drystone walls. The building responds
to this context, using local materials in their
simplest, most expressive form. A significant
part of the Museum is folded into the landscape, and it blends on one side into an
existing drystone wall which extends
outwards to draw in visitors.

The building is multi-functional, including
areas for academic study alongside a
reference library and research laboratories.
A children's teaching area reinforces the
building's social and educational programme.
An auditorium, capable of seating 100 people
for lectures, can be used independently for
village events.

The triple-height entrance hall is
designed to be refreshing and cool on
a hot day – reminiscent of the caves the
museum celebrates. From here a curved
ramp leads up to the first floor to begin the
circular route around the Museum display.
Here ambient light levels are kept to a
minimum, and light is focused on the objects
rather than the space. The centrepiece of
the exhibition is a reconstruction of a cave
in the Gorges du Verdon that is inaccessible
to the public. This is supplemented by
dioramas showing hunting, fishing and
other scenes from Stone Age life.

1. Aerial view of the
Museum and the village
of Quinson.
2. Ground-floor plan:
research, archive and
office areas fan out from
the entrance hall along the
north side of the building.

Millau Viaduct
Gorge du Tarn, France 1993–2005

Client
Department of Transport
and Public Works of France
Length
2.5km
Team
Chapelet-Defol-Mousseigne
Ove Arup & Partners

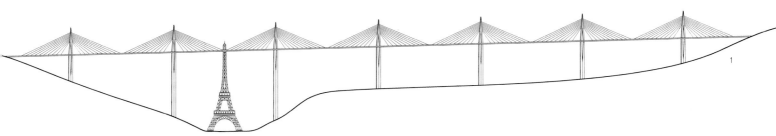

Bridges are often considered to belong to the engineer's realm rather than the architect's. But the architecture of infrastructure has a powerful impact on the environment. The Millau Viaduct, designed in collaboration with engineers, illustrates how the architect can play an integral role in bridge design.

Located in southern France, the bridge will connect the motorway from Paris to Barcelona at the point where it meets the River Tarn, which runs through a wide gorge between two plateaux.

A reading of the topography suggested two possible approaches: to celebrate the act of crossing the river, the geological generator of the landscape; or to articulate the challenge of spanning the 2.5 kilometres from one plateau to the other in the most economical manner.

The structural solution follows from the latter philosophical standpoint. The bridge has the optimum span between cable-stayed columns. It is delicate, transparent, and uses the minimum material, which makes it less costly to construct. Each of its sections spans 350 metres and its columns range in height from 75 metres to 235 metres, with the masts rising a further 90 metres above the road deck. To accommodate the expansion and contraction of the concrete deck, each column splits into two thinner, more flexible columns below the roadway, forming an A-frame above deck level. This structure creates a dramatic silhouette – and crucially, it makes the minimum intervention in the landscape.

2

3

1. Sectional elevation: the bridge's tallest columns are higher than the Eiffel Tower.
2. Visualisation of the viaduct spanning the Gorge du Tarn.
3. View of the model of the competition scheme, which was rationalised during subsequent design development.

Energy Infrastructure

Installations for energy production and distribution have a tremendous visual impact on the environment, and their design requires great sensitivity to the landscape.

The E66 wind turbine, developed with the German power company Enercon, addresses this issue and continues the practice's long-standing interest in developing non-polluting forms of energy generation. With an individual power rating of 1.8 megawatts, each turbine can generate enough clean, renewable energy to supply up to 1,500 homes.

The design approach is holistic: rotor spinner, ring generator, nacelle and tower are all formed with natural paraboloid geometries. The tapering of the 100-metre tower improves the transition of dynamic loads to ground level. In comparison with smaller turbines of equivalent power output, the E66 occupies less ground area and its rotor blades, with a diameter of 66 metres, revolve at a lower rate, creating a visually calming effect. All of these features enhance integration within the landscape.

Variable rotor speed and blade-pitch adjustment ensure that power yield is maximised, while winglets at the blade tips reduce aerodynamic noise and improve efficiency. The rotor blades are constructed in lightweight glass fibre and epoxy composite, while the tower is made up of prefabricated tubular steel modules, facilitating transport and rapid assembly. The largest installation of the turbines to date is located at Europe's highest-yield wind farm in Holtriem, Germany.

1. Detail of the nacelle
and internal mechanism
of the E66 Wind Turbine.
2. The lightweight rotor
blades, which can rotate
at variable speeds to
increase efficiency.
3. The E66 in use at
Holtriem wind farm in
Germany.

E66 Wind Turbine
1993
Client
Enercon GmbH
Height
100m
Team
Engineering by Enercon

Pylons for ENEL
Italy 1999–2000
Client
ENEL
Height
72m (typical)
Team
Ove Arup & Partners
Davis Langdon & Everest

Another environmentally sensitive solution, for a high-voltage power pylon – which won joint first place in a competition held by ENEL, the Italian national electricity company – is being installed throughout Italy. It abandons the conventional 'Christmas tree' configuration, in which cables are supported on arms sprouting at intervals from a mast, and suggests a more streamlined approach.

The pylon is formed from two curved armatures, which rise from the ground and meet to create an A-frame before diverging again to form two arms. The arms work structurally as cantilevers, sharing the loads from the transmission cables.

Designed for mass production, the pylon is efficient in terms of materials, manufacture and installation. Constructed from carbon steel, which is hot-dip galvanised to provide anti-corrosion protection, each pylon is prefabricated to facilitate transportation and installation in remote sites, where the individual elements can be bolted together without the need for on-site welding.

4

4. Visualisation of the ENEL pylons in situ.
5. Detail of the triangulated lattice structure.
6. Elevation: a simple triangle replaces the traditional 'Christmas-tree' arrangement commonly used to support the cables.

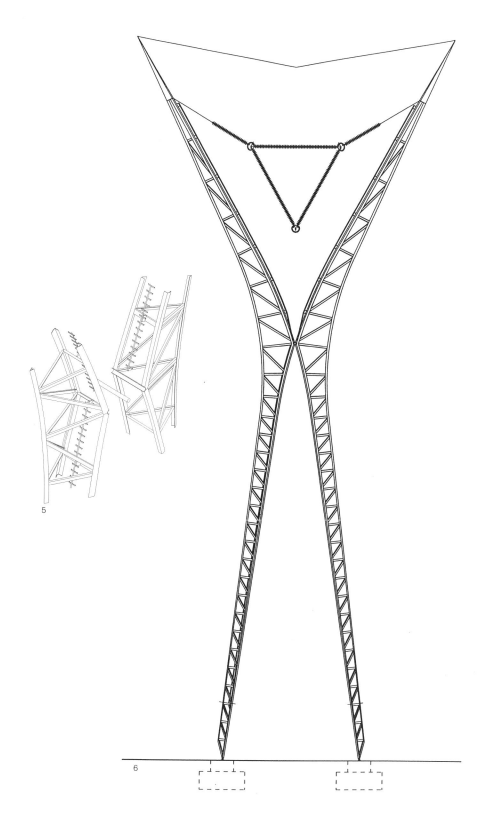
5

6

141

Congress Centre
Valencia, Spain 1993–1998

Client
City of Valencia
Area
16,000m²
Team
Ove Arup & Partners
Roger Preston & Partners
Davis Langdon & Everest
Arup Acoustics
Theatre Projects
Consultants
Ingenieria Diez Cisneros
Claude and Danielle
Engle Lighting

1

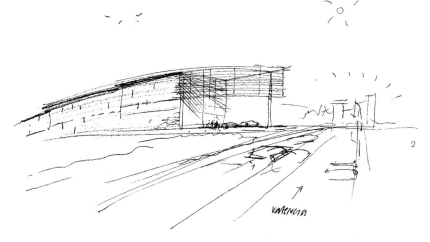

2

VALENCIA

It is paradoxical that as communications technology makes it easier to work in isolation, the demand for new kinds of forum for face-to-face discussion should be growing. Conventions are an international industry, and congress centres are important assets for cities keen to compete in a world market.

Valencia's Congress Centre is a leading European conference venue. It combines state-of-the-art facilities with an architectural celebration of this historical Mediterranean city, as well as heralding arrival in Valencia from the north-west.

The Centre provides three auditoria, seating 250, 468 and 1,463 people respectively. The smallest of these can be subdivided into two. In plan, the building forms a convex lens or 'eye', defined by two arcing facades of unequal length. The auditoria and nine seminar rooms fan out from the tighter curve of the western edge, while the public areas – including the broad, linear foyer – run along the eastern facade.

The Centre responds to the climate and to the quality of light and shade, water and green spaces, found in the city. The foyer looks out onto shady trees and gently curving asymmetrical pools. Fresh air is cooled as it passes over these pools and is drawn into the foyer, minimising the need for mechanical air conditioning.

Reflected sunlight is balanced by shading from brise-soleil so that natural illumination in the foyer is even and finely veiled. Except in the auditoria, daylight is drawn deep into the plan, in some places entering gently, in others forming fine piercing rays.

Following principles rooted in indigenous regional architecture, the roof consists of two layers: an outer metal shield floats above a heavy concrete shell, encouraging a cooling flow of air in between, thus optimising the building's passive thermal performance. The roof sweeps through 180 metres in a single line, surging forward at its peak to create a canopy above the entrance which provides shelter from the sun.

Completed to a tight budget, the Centre combines local skills, materials and construction techniques with the minimum of imported systems. In that sense, as well as in its environmental stance, it is truly a Valencian building – based in tradition but forward-looking.

1. The building at night.
2. Norman Foster's concept sketch of the Centre as seen from the motorway on arrival in Valencia.
3. The foyer that runs along the eastern facade.
4. View of the stairs leading to the auditoria.
5. View of the largest auditorium.

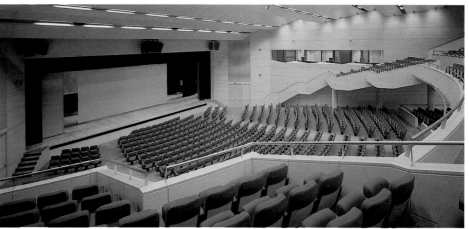

British Library of Political and Economic Science
London School of Economics, England 1993–2001

Client
London School of
Economics
Area
20,000m^2
Team
Adams Kara Taylor
Oscar Faber
Davis Langdon & Everest
Bovis Lend Lease
Schal Construction
Management
Jeremy Gardner
Partnership

1

2

3

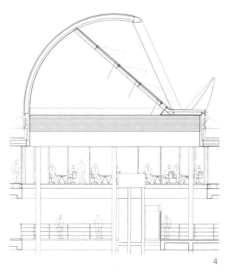

4

The London School of Economics and Political Science has the world's largest and most important social sciences library. The redevelopment of the library building safeguards the future of the school's four million books by improving environmental standards, and provides 500 extra student workplaces and new accommodation for the school's Research Centre.

Built in 1914, the Lionel Robbins building was converted into a library in 1973. The renovation retains the basic building fabric and maintains the integrity of the facades, although the windows have been replaced.

A central atrium has been created by removing the facades of an internal lightwell and extending the floor-plates to encircle a cylindrical space. This increases the floor area, improves circulation and introduces daylight into the heart of the building. The atrium has been driven through to the basement and houses a helical ramp and a pair of glass lifts, which provide the main vertical circulation through the building.

A dome caps the atrium. It has a glazed section cut at an angle to admit north light, allowing maximum daylight penetration without problems of glare and solar gain. The dome also assists natural ventilation: air drawn in through windows at the perimeter of the library rises as it warms and escapes through vents in the dome's glazing.

Book-shelves radiate from the atrium to create clearly defined passageways, and quiet study areas are positioned at the perimeter of each floor. A new fifth floor accommodates the Research Centre, which has its own entrance.

1–3. The circular atrium with its helical ramps.
4. Cross-section through the dome showing the glazed cutaway section that draws light into the building.

ARAG Headquarters
Düsseldorf, Germany 1993–2001

Client
ARAG (Allgemeine
Rechtsschutzversicherung AG)
Area
38,000m²
Team
Rhode Kellermann
Wawrowsky
Schüßler Plan

DS-Plan
Schmidt Reuter Partner
Büro Stefan Schiller
Dinnebier Licht GmbH
Höhler & Partner
Hochtief AG
Josef Gartner & Co
Quickborner Team
Weber Klein Maas

1

The ARAG building is the latest in a family of office towers that push environmental design to new limits. Situated at a major gateway into Düsseldorf, it is the headquarters for one of Germany's leading insurance companies.

The 30-storey building has a high-performance, double-skin glazed facade. A protective outer layer forms a weather shield and sun filter; an inner layer, with openable windows, allows the building to breathe. Maximum use is made of daylight, and the construction allows passive cooling with night storage so that air conditioning will rarely be needed.

Office floors are simple and open in feel. Cellular offices and meeting rooms ring the perimeter while group meeting spaces occupy the centre of the lens-shaped plan. To create the maximum usable floor area, lift shafts are pushed to the corners, with glass lifts allowing panoramic views across the city.

Double-height 'sky gardens' punctuate the building at every eighth floor. Planted with 'meadows' of tall grasses and wild flowers, the gardens provide informal meeting areas and relaxation spaces. Open access between office floors and the gardens encourages a friendly atmosphere as well as improving communication between staff.

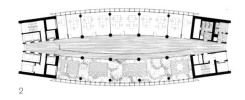

2

1. The tower illuminated
for Christmas 2000.
2. Typical garden-level plan.
3. Exterior view: double-
height sky gardens every
eighth floor punctuate the
glazed facade.

3

Offices in the City of London
London, England

Holborn Place
1993–2000
Client
Paul Hamlyn Ventures
Ltd/Gemini Commercial
Investments Ltd
Area
41,000m²

Team
The Yolles Partnership Ltd
Hilson Moran
Partnership Ltd
Schatunowski Brooks
Emmer Pfenninger
Partner AG
AYH Partnership
Jolyon Drury Consultancy
Bovis Construction

1

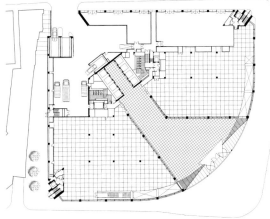

2

100 Wood Street
1997–2000
Client
Helical Bar
Area
20,405m²
Team
Waterman Partnership
Roger Preston & Partners
Gleeds
Emmer Pfenninger
Partner AG
Lerch Bates &
Associates Ltd

50 Finsbury Square
1997–2000
Client
Standard Life Investments
Area
17,000m²
Team
Waterman Partnership
Roger Preston & Partners
Gardiner & Theobald
Büro Happold
Lerch Bates &
Associates Ltd

3

The City of London and its environs are characterised by relatively small-scale buildings laid out on an essentially mediaeval street plan. Designing infill buildings in this context is a delicate balancing act between commercial requirements, the need for flexibility, and respect for the area's historical character and traditional materials.

The site at 100 Wood Street posed the challenge of articulating the transition between Gresham Street and London Wall – two streets that express the traditional and modern aspects of the City respectively. Regulations required that the eaves should not be higher than Wren's St Alban's Church tower, which stands in the middle of Wood Street, and that the Wood Street elevation had to be classically articulated as base, middle and attic. In response the facade has a pattern of alternating glass and stone cladding, sympathetic to both neighbouring stone buildings and the glass facades of London Wall. A pedestrian right-of-way cuts through the site and leads to the churchyard of St Mary Staining at the rear of the building. Here the building's facade is fully glazed and a conical section is scooped from its mass to maximise sunlight reaching the church grounds.

The demolition of two buildings on Finsbury Square at the northern edge of the City created a prominent gateway site to which strict planning constraints applied. These included the requirement for a stone building, to respect neighbouring structures. The new building has a stone-clad structural frame which wraps around a glazed skin. This exoskeleton is punctuated by two key spaces: a double-height entrance lobby and a high-level terrace with commanding views over the square. The trapezoidal plan of the central atrium is complemented by the profile of its roof, which sweeps away from the adjacent building to avoid taking its light.

The Mirror Group's departure from Holborn Circus – located pivotally between the City and the West End – presented the opportunity to replace its 1960s tower with a lower structure, restoring the strategic view of St Paul's Cathedral from Primrose Hill. The office floors look into a full-height glazed atrium that opens out onto Holborn Circus through a dramatic curving glass facade, while a glass floor at the entrance admits daylight to the basement. At street level the building welcomes the working community with shops, cafés and bars.

4

5

1, 2. Holborn Place: exterior view looking through the curved glass facade of the atrium, and the plan at ground level.
3, 4. 100 Wood Street: chequerboard cladding faces the historical Wren church to the front, while curved glazing brings light to a churchyard at the rear.
5. 50 Finsbury Square: exterior view.

Al Faisaliah Complex
Riyadh, Saudi Arabia 1993–2000

Client
King Faisal Foundation
Area
240,000m²
Team
Buro Happold
Lerch Bates &
Associates Ltd
LMN
Sandy Brown Associates
WET Design
Rosewood Hotels
and Resorts
Brian Clarke
Di Leonardo International

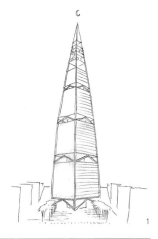

The Al Faisaliah Complex in Riyadh plays a key part in the city's urban development. The 240,000-square-metre complex includes Saudi Arabia's first skyscraper – a distinctive 267-metre-high office tower – alongside a five-star hotel, a banqueting and conference centre, luxury apartments and a three-storey retail mall. The scheme carefully balances cost-effectiveness, flexibility and architectural interest to produce buildings which are efficient in services, planning and operation, easily maintained and responsive to the Middle Eastern climate.

The office tower is square in plan, designed around a compact central core, and tapers to a point, with four main corner columns defining its unique silhouette. Observation decks at stages up the building correspond with giant K-braces, which transfer loads to the corner columns. The building is clad in silver-anodised aluminium panels with cantilevered sunshading devices which minimise glare, allowing the use of non-reflective, energy-efficient glass. These layered facades provide maximum control over the internal environment.

Above its 30 floors of office space, the tower houses the highest restaurant in Saudi Arabia, set within a golden glass sphere 200 metres above ground level. The observation deck below the globe provides a breathtaking panorama of Riyadh and the surrounding landscape. At its pinnacle, the tower narrows to a brightly lit lantern, topped by a stainless-steel finial.

The tower is set back from the King Fahd Highway to create a landscaped plaza. Beneath this is a banqueting hall which can accommodate activities ranging from Islamic wedding ceremonies for up to 2,000 people to conferences for up to 3,400. A high degree of flexibility is achieved by a unique long-span arch system, which provides a column-free space 57 metres wide and 81 metres long, with a moveable partition system that can divide the hall into a maximum of sixteen separate rooms.

A five-storey lobby at the tower's base forms a link between the hotel to the north and the apartments and shopping mall to the south. A spectacular coloured-glass wall in the lobby by the artist Brian Clarke has a desert theme interspersed with images representing natural regional and environmental features.

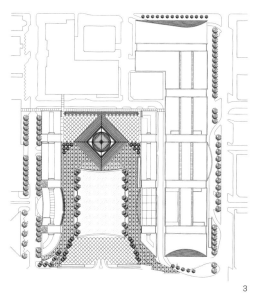

1. An early design sketch by Norman Foster.
2. The entrance lobby, with stained-glass wall by Brian Clarke.
3. Site plan of the complex showing the landscaped plaza.
Facing page Exterior view of the tower – Saudi Arabia's first skyscraper.

Forth Valley Community Care Village
Larbert, Scotland 1993–1995

Client
Central Scotland
Healthcare NHS Trust
Area
1,500m²
Team
Ove Arup & Partners
Davis Langdon & Everest
HED

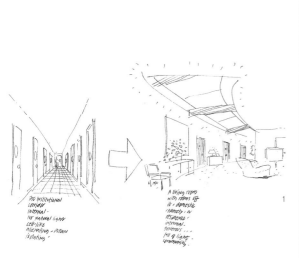

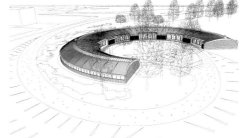

When mentally ill people require constant support their residential needs echo those of any member of the community: a degree of privacy, a feeling of enclosure and access to nature.

The Community Care Village is part of a masterplan for an informal campus in the grounds of Bellsdyke Hospital. It accommodates long-term patients in a crescent of seven houses, each for six people. An open-plan 'family' space with sitting and dining areas constitutes the social heart of each house. The bedrooms, by contrast, are highly personalised spaces, looking out onto trees, where patients can be completely private. The curved form of the building, both in plan and section, and its intimate scale, are part of a deliberate attempt to avoid hard, aggressive forms.

The arrangement of the small dwellings, each with its own front door, around a sunny 'village green', provides a healthier and happier environment than an institutional building with a hostile corridor in the middle. It is protective, allowing supervising staff to move easily from one unit to the next, but it engenders a sense of community that would otherwise be lacking.

1. Norman Foster's concept sketch contrasting institutional and personalised space.
2, 3. Exterior views: six-person units are arranged around a green, balancing community and privacy.
4. Drawing of the curved crescent form.

Faculty of Management, Robert Gordon University
Aberdeen, Scotland 1994–1998

Client
Robert Gordon University
Area
12,000m²
Team
Ove Arup & Partners
Bovis Construction
Edinburgh University
Hulley and Kirkwood
Northcroft
Sandy Brown Associates

The Faculty of Management marks the first phase in a twenty-year masterplan to restructure Robert Gordon University, uniting its facilities within a new campus in rolling wooded countryside on the banks of the River Dee. The masterplan preserves the site's natural setting by dividing it into three zones, with car-parking to the north, a central zone of buildings, and parkland to the south. New buildings are planned around a central 'street', which connects the individual faculties, strengthening their interrelationship.

The point at which the street passes through the new Faculty of Management is marked by a four-storey atrium; this is the heart of the building, from where all teaching, library and office areas are accessed. It is flooded with light and echoes the traditional college quad in offering an ideal place for social interaction between students and staff.

The sweeping profile of the building is a response to the undulating topography and the existing tree canopy. The concrete frame forms terraces down the natural slope of the site, oversailed by a curving roof. The roof beams project beyond the building envelope into the landscape at the southern end, where student common rooms overlook a winter garden, opening onto riverside terraces. Cladding of New Kemnay granite – the stone traditionally used in Aberdeen – alternates with infill panels of aluminium and glass, emphasising the building's structure.

This is a low-cost, low-energy project which minimises maintenance and replacement costs and maximises natural light and ventilation: only lecture theatres and studios in the lower levels require mechanical ventilation, while natural temperature control is enhanced by the building's thermal mass.

1. Exterior view at night showing the terraced concrete structure.
2. Model of the campus masterplan with its central zone of buildings.
3. View of the interior.

151

Products

NF 95 Door Furniture
1994–1995
Client
Fusital (Valli & Valli)

Tray for Alessi
1994–1998
Client
Alessi spa, Italy

**Helit Foster Series
Desktop Furniture**
1997–2000
Client
Helit

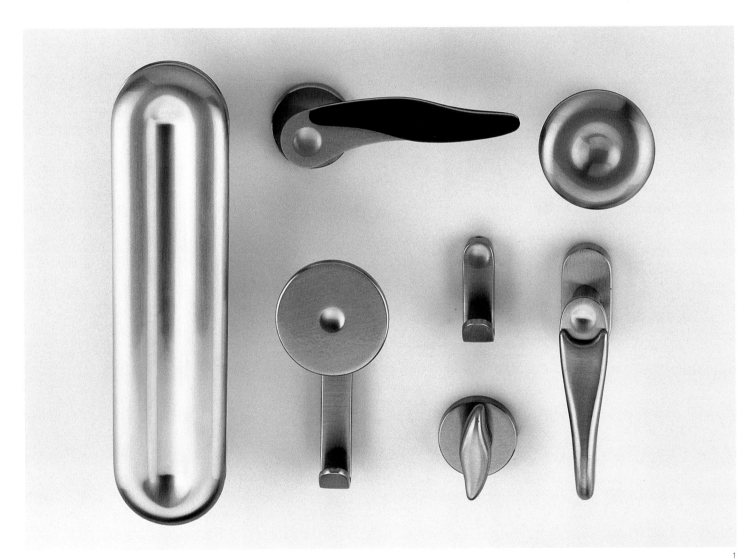

1

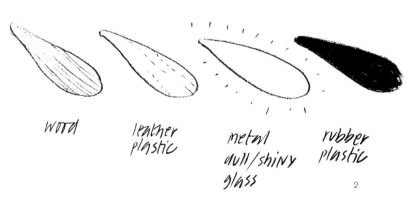

wood
leather
plastic
metal
dull/shiny
glass
rubber
plastic

2

3

4

5

The smallest details of daily life, from the shape of a door handle to the finish of a breakfast tray, are often taken for granted, but it is with these small elements that we have the most direct contact. These objects are like architecture in miniature: they must be functional but also pleasing to use, possessing good ergonomic, aesthetic and tactile qualities. The practice has a team of industrial designers, working on items ranging from tableware to electronic goods, both for specific building projects and for manufacture.

The NF 95 Door Handle for the Italian manufacturer Fusital was partly inspired by the bird-shaped form of a mediaeval door handle in Magdeburg Cathedral, and also by the design of penknives, in which blades and mechanism are sandwiched between grips in a variety of materials. The door handle consists of a metal plate held between grips contoured to the shape of the hand. The handles are available in a range of finishes: metal, plastic, wood, rubber or leather. This system combines the economic benefits of mass production with the flexibility of customising fittings to suit individual projects.

The Italian manufacturer Alessi has brought innovative design to a popular audience and is renowned for its investment in new manufacturing processes. Laser-cutting technology was the starting point for a family of breakfast objects made from folded aluminium sheet. Because their design avoids machine finishing, the pieces can be manufactured with great economy. The 'breakfast landscape' consists of egg cups, salt and pepper dispensers, a toast rack and a tray – currently the only piece in production.

A family of desktop accessories for the German manufacturer Helit is also themed, each object taking the form of an extruded aluminium box with a black lid. These lids create an element of mystery but when they are removed and attached to the base of the boxes they reveal one of the boxes to be a clock, another a pen holder and so on. Other pieces include boxes for computer diskettes and business cards. The contrasting materials – smooth aluminium and 'soft-touch' plastic – add a tactile quality and give the range a coherent identity.

6

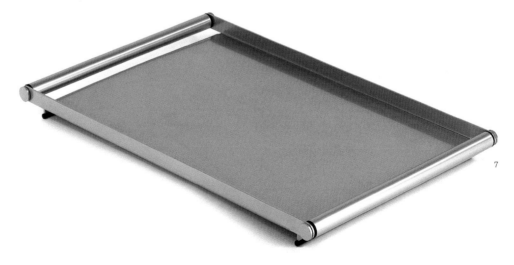

7

1–3. The NF 95 Door Handle shown with its family of related objects, in Norman Foster's sketch, and in some of its many 'sandwiched' finishes.
4, 5. The Helit Foster Series of desktop furniture.
6, 7. Prototype and production version of the Alessi Tray.

Imperial College, Sir Alexander Fleming Building
London, England 1994–1998

Client
Imperial College and South Kensington Millennium Commission
Area
25,000m²
Team
Schal Construction Management

Claude and Danielle
Engle Lighting
Research Facilities Design
Sandy Brown Associates
Warrington Fire
WSP
Waterman Partnership

The demolition of a large number of Imperial College's buildings after World War II left a poorly coordinated campus. In response, the practice has formulated a masterplan that identifies key sites for redevelopment, including environmental improvements, and establishes guidelines for buildings to be designed by others.

The practice's first building within the masterplan is the Sir Alexander Fleming Building, which represents a major advance in medical research facilities, encouraging social and intellectual interaction to an unprecedented degree.

At its heart is a research forum on five levels, where research work not directly associated with the laboratory takes place. It provides an open arena where researchers can meet their colleagues from all disciplines and all levels, and forms the hub of the building's primary circulation system. Standard and specialist laboratories are wrapped around the forum, as are undergraduate teaching spaces, administration and a café.

The forum widens as it rises, forming open-plan terraces for research students on the second and fourth floors, where the perimeter is lined with study carrels. Sculpted rooflights introduce a combination of north light for optimum working conditions and controlled sunlight to bring sparkle into the building. Fully glazed at its northern end – the site's only open aspect – the forum looks onto the Queen's Lawn and Queen's Tower, the last fragment of the 1890s campus.

Modular laboratories are designed to be used by any microbiologist and are flexible enough to allow changes in use or to adapt to new techniques. Alongside these are specialist facilities, which need to be close to the building's service risers. These risers are configured at the edges of the site, leaving the central space free and flexible. This is essential to allow for the rapid pace of change in the research world. Even as the building was being constructed, the requirements of its users were changing – and the design was able to adapt to their evolving needs.

The next buildings to be completed by the practice will be a Management School and the Flowers Building, which will provide bioscience laboratories for interdisciplinary research at postgraduate level.

1. Looking into the research forum.
2. The glazed exterior, reflecting the historical Queen's Tower.
Facing page The upper floors of the forum, looking towards an installation on the south wall by Danish artist Per Arnoldi.

The Great Court at the British Museum

London, England 1994–2000

Client
British Museum
Area
19,000m²
Team
Buro Happold
Northcroft
Mace Ltd
Giles Quarme Associates
Claude R Engle Lighting
EPP
FEDRA
Sandy Brown Associates

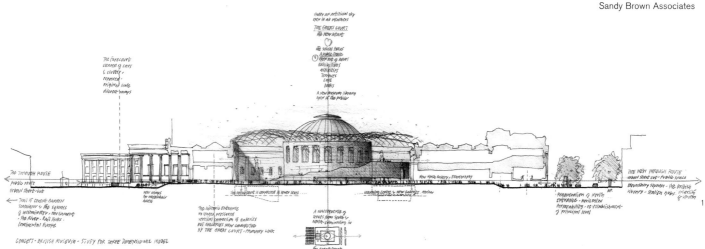

The courtyard at the centre of the British Museum was one of London's long-lost spaces. Originally an open garden, soon after its completion in the nineteenth century it was filled by the round Reading Room and its associated bookstacks. Without this space the Museum was like a city without a park. This project is about its reinvention.

In terms of visitor numbers – over five million annually – the British Museum is as popular as the Louvre in Paris or the Metropolitan Museum of Art in New York. In the absence of a centralised circulation system this degree of popularity caused a critical level of congestion throughout the building and created a frustrating experience for the visitor.

The departure of the British Library to St Pancras in March 1998 provided the opportunity to recapture the courtyard and greatly enhance the Museum's facilities for coming generations. The clutter of book-stacks that filled the courtyard has been cleared away to give the building a new public heart, while the Reading Room has been restored and put to new use as an information centre and library of world cultures. For the first time in its history this magnificent space – its dome larger than that of St Paul's – is open to all.

The Great Court is entered from the Museum's principal level, and connects all the surrounding galleries. Within the space there are information points, a book shop and a café. Two broad staircases encircling the Reading Room lead to two mezzanine levels, which provide a gallery for temporary exhibitions with a restaurant above. Below the level of the Court are the Sainsbury African Galleries, an education centre and facilities for school-children.

The glazed canopy that makes all this possible is a fusion of state-of-the-art engineering and economy of form. Its unique triangulated geometry is designed to span the irregular gap between the drum of the Reading Room and the restored courtyard facades. The lattice steel shell forms both the primary structure and the framing for the glazing system, which is designed to maximise daylight and reduce solar gain.

The Great Court is the largest enclosed public space in Europe. As a cultural square, it lies on a new pedestrian route from the British Library in the north to Covent Garden and the river in the south. To complement the Great Court, the Museum's forecourt has been freed from cars and restored to form a new public space. Both are open to the public from early in the morning to late at night, creating a major amenity for London.

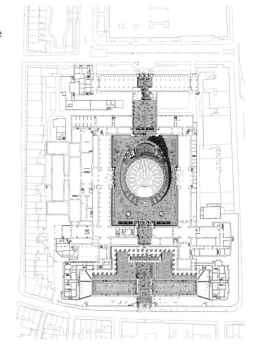

156

3

4

5

6

1. Norman Foster's
sectional drawing
explaining the genesis
of the Great Court within
the British Museum.
2. A plan highlighting the
new public route that
has been created
through the Museum.
3–6. Views of the Great
Court at principal level.
Overleaf A detail of the
glazed roof canopy.

Scottish Exhibition and Conference Centre
Glasgow, Scotland 1995–1997

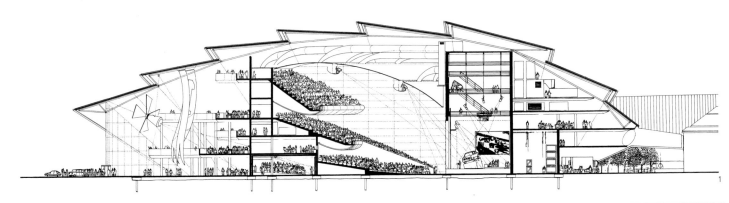

1

World-class corporate events increasingly demand venues that can stage presentations on an epic scale. Few facilities offer a flexible mix of spaces for conferences, exhibitions, live performances, concerts and corporate functions at every level from the intimate to the vast. The Scottish Exhibition and Conference Centre is the first venue of its kind on this scale in the UK and one of only four in Europe capable of seating more than 3,000 delegates.

Within the context of a very tight budget, the challenge was to create the most economic enclosure for all the components of a complex brief – auditorium, exhibition halls, concourses – which form the setting for what might be thought of as 'industrial theatre'. The solution is in the spirit of the shipbuilding traditions of the Clyde and the site on Queen's Dock. It takes a flat sheet material and employs it to clad a series of framed 'hulls', which wrap around the disparate elements, including the auditorium fly-tower. These overlapping, aluminium-clad shells – reflective by day and floodlit at night – create a distinctive profile on the skyline.

Industrial theatre requires a neutral, highly serviced environment, which can be transformed to accommodate a wide variety of events. Accordingly, the conference hall is technically state-of-the-art – complete with wings and full back-stage facilities – but is flexible enough to allow large trucks to be driven directly onto the stage. The main theatre provides electronic delegate voting systems, simultaneous translation, projection facilities and sound control booths.

Visitors approach from the east, entering beneath a canopy formed by the arc of the roof. From the registration area they may enter a 300-seat conference room or go up to the first-floor foyer, which connects with the auditorium and an associated network of break-out and exhibition spaces.

The building provides a symbolic form, which brings a focus to its location and represents the city. This has helped to strengthen Glasgow's reputation as an international business destination, enabling it to compete with conference and exhibition facilities around the world.

2

Client
Glasgow City Council
Area
20,050m²
Team
Ove Arup & Partners
Gardiner & Theobald
SECC
Sandy Brown Associates
Eric Marchant

3

4

1. Cross-section
through the building.
2. Exterior view
from the Clyde.
3. The Centre seen
from the east: overlapping
shells project to form a
canopy over the entrance.
4. The interior of the
3,000-seat auditorium.

ASPIRE National Training Centre

Stanmore, England 1995–1998

Client
ASPIRE/Mike Heaffey
Leisure Ltd
Area
1,700m²
Team
Per Arnoldi
Buchanan

Claude R Engle Lighting
Davis Langdon & Everest
Laing Managment Ltd
LTG Geotechnical and
Environmental
Michael Gallie & Partners
Roger Preston & Partners
Sandy Brown Associates
Waterman Partnership

The ASPIRE Centre provides training and rehabilitation for people with a wide range of disabilities. All of its facilities are fully accessible to users with mobility, hearing and visual impairments, as well as those with learning difficulties. Embedded in the design philosophy is the idea that architects need to explore comprehensive access as a matter of course, and the architects on the team consulted widely with institutions and individuals.

The Centre is located on the campus of the Royal National Orthopaedic Hospital in Stanmore. One of its central concerns is to provide courses to reintegrate patients from the hospital's Spinal Injury Unit into everyday life and work. It also offers specific courses for people with disabilities who wish to become sports centre managers and trainers.

A new, two-storey, steel, glass and timber pavilion provides a competition-standard swimming pool, a café, a computer-training suite for the development of vocational skills, and a studio space for the mixed-mobility CandoCo dance company.

The pavilion is linked by a central reception area to the refurbished Mike Heaffey Sports and Rehabilitation Centre, which is noted for promoting the integration of able-bodied and disabled people. This building contains an enlarged fitness studio, a sports hall and administrative offices.

The swimming pool allows disabled users to enter the water unaided in specially designed wheelchairs. Pool activities include rehabilitative training, life-saving classes, water-confidence lessons and sporting events. There is space for full supervision and for the professional coaching of supervisors, managers and trainers.

The Centre has tactile signage and maps and coding on handrails, while hearing induction loops are fitted throughout. The design of the door thresholds, the widespread use of ramps and the location of all features – from the reception desk to signage – at an appropriate height, make the Centre fully accessible to wheelchair users.

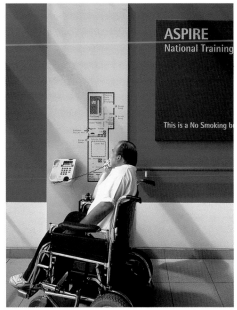

1. View of the competition-standard swimming pool.
2. Cross-section through the Centre.
3. All facilities are located at a suitable height for wheelchair users.

North Greenwich Transport Interchange
London, England 1995–1998

Client
London Underground Ltd
London Transport Property
Area
6,500m²
Team
Max Fordham & Partners
Anthony Hunt Associates
Capital Project Consultancy
MDA Group UK

1

2

North Greenwich Transport Interchange is a vital element in London's transport strategy. A key gateway to the capital, it serves commuters from the South-East and acts as a hub for public transport alternatives for their onward journey. It also plays a significant role in the regeneration of the North Greenwich peninsular, home to the Millennium Dome and the site of a wholly new quarter of London.

Positioned directly above the entrance to North Greenwich Underground station, part of the Jubilee Line extension, the interchange is signalled by its dramatic curving roof. This vast canopy, 160 metres wide, shelters arriving and departing passengers. Supported on tree-like steel columns, its aerodynamic shape is evocative of a bird's wings in flight.

Under one side of the canopy, cars and taxis drop off passengers. Beneath the other, buses arrive and depart. Sandwiched between these two areas, and within sight of both, is a waiting room. Although complex, the structure ensures an experience of openness, simplicity and clarity of form. It is designed to help passengers orient themselves, whether they are boarding buses or descending to the Jubilee Line Underground station.

The roof canopy is perforated to allow daylight to illuminate the deepest spaces, while specially designed lighting units suspended from the ceiling can both project light up to the reflective aluminium ceiling panels and spotlight the area immediately below. Suspended glass panels along the edges of the canopy provide weather protection but allow natural ventilation.

As London grows steadily eastwards and the Greenwich peninsular is redeveloped, the interchange will ensure that thousands of new residents and workers can travel locally and across London without recourse to their cars.

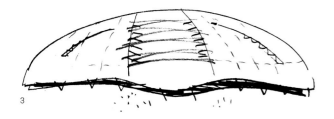

4

5

1. Aerial view.
2. Site plan of the North Greenwich peninsular.
3. Norman Foster's sketch of the aerodynamic roof.
4. The interchange at dusk with its aluminium ceiling lit from below.
5. Detail of the triangular rooflights that punctuate the canopy.

Multimedia Centre
Hamburg, Germany 1995–1999

Client
Hanseatica
Area
13,500m²
Team
Kuehn Bauer und Partner
Dröge Kelemen & Partner
Taubert und Ruhe GmbH
Falcke und Korff

1

2

Hamburg is traditionally a shipping city. Today its communication is less by sea than by satellite: it is one of the main centres of the media industry in Germany, a position that this complex helps to reinforce.

The Multimedia Centre provides offices and studios for multimedia companies, together with shops and restaurants, and is currently let to a large magazine publisher. It connects with an existing Media Centre via a triple-height Media Circus, which forms a circulation hub between the two buildings.

The building is designed to reduce a reliance on mechanical systems. The five office levels are focused on an 8-metre-wide atrium which runs the full length of the block. Perimeter offices are naturally ventilated, while those lining the atrium are ventilated with displacement air, introduced through floor outlets. The atrium itself is ventilated by return air from the offices. As all services are integrated within raised floors, suspended ceilings are not required; this allows the thermal mass of the concrete floor-slabs to contribute to the building's passive temperature control.

A louvred roof shades the atrium, Media Circus and the upper levels, terminating in a canopy above the main entrance. Solar shading to the west facade is provided by adjustable glass louvres – controlled individually for each office – that form a second skin, their animation creating changing patterns of light and shade.

1. Detail of the glass louvres on the west facade.
2. A view of the principal street facade; the louvred roof shades the atrium and forms a canopy above the entrance.
3. Cross-section through the central atrium.

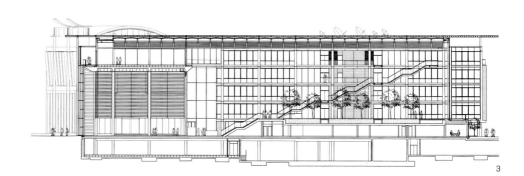

3

Gerling Ring
Cologne, Germany 1995–2001

Client
Baugemeinschaft Gerling Ring GbR
Area
59,000m²
Team
Höhler & Partner
Dr Ing Naumann
IPP
Schmidt Reuter Partner
Emmer Pfenninger Partner AG
Atelier Dreiseitl
Desvigne & Dalnoky
Dipl-Ing D Karlsch

This project brings together the concepts of sustainability and mixed-use inner-city development to maximise the potential of both. It not only combines apartments, offices, shops and restaurants within a single complex, but also provides a structure that allows individual units to be easily adapted from offices to apartments should demand for office space in Cologne fall.

Germany's enlightened legislation on working conditions promotes the individual's right to daylight and thus the design of office buildings with relatively shallow floor-plates. There need be little difference, therefore, between the basic configuration of an apartment or an office building, except for the provision of bathrooms and kitchens. All the offices are naturally ventilated and have raised floors, which means that they can be easily converted into apartments, avoiding the environmentally wasteful alternative of demolition.

The prefabricated concrete elements that form the ceilings perform a variety of roles: their vaulted profile creates a deep void at the centre of the plan for the incorporation of kitchen and bathroom services, and a shallow space for heating and electrical installations along the facade. The ceilings also reflect natural light into the interiors and, combined with fresh air intake, their high thermal mass helps to maintain comfortable temperature levels in summer. The building's double-skinned facades, with black and white adjustable louvres, provide further passive environmental control.

1. Exterior view of the development: all the accommodation housed in the three towers can be converted from office to residential space.

Center for Clinical Science Research, Stanford University

Stanford, USA 1995–2000

1

1. Looking into the central
courtyard – the social hub
of the building.
2. View of the exterior.
3. A detail of the louvres
that shade the courtyard.
4. The bay windows of the
offices, shielded by bamboo.
5. A meeting room.
6. Cross-section showing
the close connection
between laboratory, office
and support spaces.

2

3

Client
Stanford University School
of Medicine
Area
21,000m²
Team
Fong & Chan Architects
Ove Arup & Partners
Research Facilities Design
Peter Walker and Partners
Davis Langdon & Everest
Claude R Engle Lighting
Brian Kangas Foulk

Stanford University has long been recognised as a centre for clinical excellence. The new Center for Clinical Science Research provides the School of Medicine with state-of-the-art laboratory and office space for its ongoing programme of research into cancer and other diseases. Its design responds to emerging trends for interdisciplinary biomedical research and provides flexible, light-filled working spaces in which research teams can expand and contract with ease.

The brief called for close proximity between laboratories, core support areas and offices. Another important stipulation was natural lighting in the laboratory and office spaces. These requirements led to the development of a modular design, which allows intercommunication between functional areas and research groups.

The 21,000-square-metre building consists of two symmetrical wings united around a central courtyard. The wings are connected at roof level by a screen of louvres. Shading the courtyard from direct sunlight, the louvres create a comfortable environment for social interaction, and this space has become the social heart of the building. Offices overlook the courtyard through bay windows. A screen of bamboo at ground level offsets the crisp lines of this space and affords greater privacy for office occupants.

Environmental systems take advantage of Palo Alto's climate, which is among the best in the United States. The offices are naturally ventilated for most of the year, with mechanical assistance only on extremely hot days. Horizontal louvres on the exterior facades provide shade and correspond with a third-story cornice line established by neighbouring buildings.

Seismic performance was another key concern: the campus lies close to the San Andreas Fault and the laboratories contain highly sensitive equipment. Extensive computer simulations were conducted, including real-time animations based on previous earthquakes. In response, the building employs a concrete shear-wall structural system. Bridges spanning the courtyard rely on friction pendulum bearings to allow up to 0.5 metres of seismic movement between the wings.

The practice is designing a second building on the campus. Named after one of the inventors of the Internet, the James H Clark Center provides highly flexible laboratories for interdisciplinary research. These will be shared by the biochemical, biomechanical, biocomputational and biophysical faculties. At its centre will be an open-air amphitheatre, a restaurant and an exhibition space.

4

5

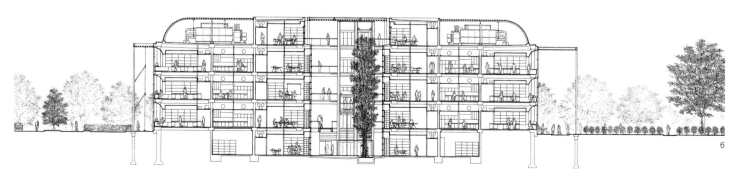

6

Daewoo Electronics Headquarters
Seoul, Korea 1995

Client
Daewoo Electronics
Area
155,000m²
Team
Davis Langdon & Everest
Dewhurst Macfarlane
Han-il
I & S Consortium
Lerch Bates & Associates Ltd
Ove Arup & Partners
Roger Preston & Partners
SAC International
Sandy Brown Associates
Seoul IB

The design of this new headquarters building, commissioned by the technology company Daewoo Electronics, was an opportunity to provide an appropriate landmark for Seoul.

The tower's distinctive, 166-metre, tapered profile optimised the planning envelope permissible within strict shadow regulations to create a curving form, evocative of a leaf or a traditional Korean sailing ship. The steel frame comprised two inner and two outer columns, which followed the curved facades. A slender concrete-and-steel central core fulfilled heavy servicing requirements for long, column-free office floors. Outrigger trusses provided lateral stability, corresponding with triple-height sky gardens with sheltered outside terraces. Glazed high-speed lifts with spectacular views of the city stopped at the garden levels, where escalators linked to intermediate floors.

The south facade was scalloped to provide sunshading and articulate the mast that ran the full height of the building, culminating in a dramatic cantilevered helipad. The climate-responsive facade incorporated adjustable blinds, which could collect or reject solar gain. Openable windows allowed partial natural ventilation. This low-energy system was complemented by a ceiling-mounted radiant cooling system to reduce running costs dramatically.

1. View of the model showing the tower's leaf-shaped form.
2, 3. Visualisation of the entrance hall staircase, and a mock-up of the staircase, constructed in the courtyard of the Foster studio.

Jiushi Corporation Headquarters
Shanghai, China 1995–2001

Client
Jiushi Corporation
Area
62,000m²
Team
Obayashi Corporation
Design Department
East China Architectural
Design Institute (ECADI)
Claude R Engle Lighting

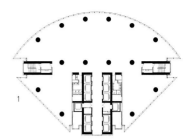

1

Shanghai has undergone a dramatic transformation over the last ten years. Large areas that previously contained only traditional low-rise buildings now feature thickets of office towers.

This 40-storey tower is the headquarters of the Jiushi Corporation, a Chinese company that is providing the inward investment for the next wave of development in the South Bund area of the city. The competition-winning scheme is the practice's first on the Chinese mainland.

Occupying one of the most significant sites in Shanghai, the tower looks over the Huangpu River to the historical Bund and Pudong – the new business district. These views govern the structure of the building – its concrete core is positioned away from the river to create flexible curved floor-plates on the riverside, free of internal columns.

A triple-skin ventilated glazing system allows the tower to enjoy maximum daylight penetration without any attendant build-up of solar gain in the internal spaces. It is the first building in the city to employ such a system.

The floor-plates step back at three points over the height of the tower to form terraces, which animate the facade and are ideally suited to conferences. At the top is a six-storey glazed winter garden – unique in a city where most towers are capped by services installations.

Adjacent to the tower, a six-storey block containing shops, restaurants and bars follows the line of the street, responding to its historical context with a double-height colonnade, reminiscent of traditional Shanghai shopping arcades.

1. The tower's distinctive plan, designed to maximise views across the old city.
2. The 40-storey tower rises from the historical South Bund area of Shanghai.

2

171

Great Glasshouse, National Botanic Garden of Wales
Llanarthne, Wales 1995–2000

Client
National Botanic Garden
of Wales
Area
5,800m²
Team
Gustafson Porter
Anthony Hunt Associates
Max Fordham & Partners
Symonds Ltd
Colvin and Moggridge
Schal International

1

The Great Glasshouse at the National Botanic Garden of Wales reinvents the glasshouse for the twenty-first century, offering a model for sustainability. The largest single-span glasshouse in the world, it contains more than a thousand plant species – many endangered – and conserves specimens from Mediterranean climates around the globe.

Set in hills overlooking the Tywi Valley in Carmarthenshire, the building forms the centrepiece of the 230-hectare park of the former Middleton Hall. Elliptical in plan, it is tilted at its northern edge, forming a toroidal roof, measuring 99 by 55 metres, which swells from the ground like a glassy hillock, echoing the undulations of the surrounding landscape.

The aluminium glazing system and its tubular-steel supporting structure are designed to minimise materials and maximise light transmission. Twenty-four arches spring from a concrete ring beam, rising to 15 metres at the apex of the dome. Because the roof curves in two directions, only the central arches rise perpendicular to the base; the outer arches lean inwards at progressively steep angles.

To optimise energy usage, conditions inside and outside are monitored by a computer-controlled system. This adjusts the supply of heat and opens glazing panels in the roof to achieve desired levels of temperature, humidity and air movement.

The building's concrete substructure is banked to the north to provide protection from cold northerly winds. It is concealed by a covering of turf so that the three entrances on the northern side appear to be cut discreetly into the hillside. Within this base are a public concourse, a café, educational spaces and service installations.

The principal heat source is a biomass boiler, located in the park's Energy Centre, which burns timber trimmings. This method is remarkably clean when compared with fossil fuels, and because the plants absorb as much carbon dioxide during their lifetime as they release during combustion, the carbon dioxide cycle is broadly neutral. Rain water collected from the roof supplies 'grey water' for irrigation and flushing lavatories while waste from the lavatories is treated in reed beds before release into a watercourse.

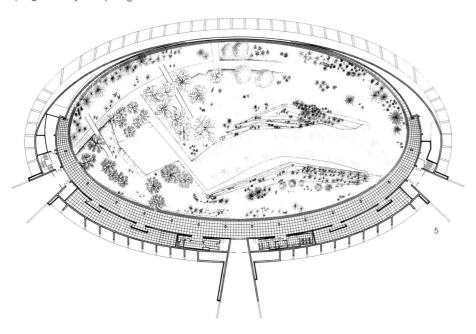

1. Interior view of the overarching toroidal roof.
2. Norman Foster's sketch showing the banking of the Glasshouse to the north.
3. The building in the landscape.
4. Opening roof panels release exhaust air.
5. Plan at entrance level.

Prado Museum Extension
Madrid, Spain 1996

Client
Ministry of Culture for Spain
Board of Trustees, Prado
Museum
Area
18,000m²
Team
Ove Arup & Partners
Claude R Engle Lighting
Davis Langdon & Everest

1, 2. Visualisations of
the exhibition spaces in
the new perimeter wing
and the rooftop plaza
at ground level.
3. Aerial view of the model
showing the rooflights of
the extension at plaza level.

If the nineteenth century was the great era for museum founding, the late twentieth and early twenty-first centuries are proving to be the epoch of museum expansion. In recent years, virtually all the major art institutions have either built themselves new galleries or initiated plans to do so.

The Prado is home to one of the world's greatest art collections. It occupies a fine building in Madrid, but its capacity is severely limited, allowing only eleven per cent of the collection to be displayed at any one time. Consequently, in 1996, the Museum launched an international competition to extend its facilities. The competition brief suggested the creation of underground links between the historical Villanueva building and others around the site; but the practice's proposal challenged that strategy and explored an alternative approach.

The scheme opened up the entire perimeter of the Villanueva building as public space with a sculpture garden, terraces, cafés and a substantial entrance area on the northern side, at present a car-park. By removing a nineteenth-century exterior staircase and exploiting the natural slope of the site, the entrance was configured to allow access on two levels.

A new wing, respecting the historical facades, was proposed around the perimeter to the north and east, utilising the higher level of the street along the eastern side, so that much of the rooftop became a ground-level plaza, punctuated by strips of glazing to bring daylight down into the building. The extension was designed to contain permanent and temporary exhibition spaces, together with administration, ticketing, a restaurant, a library, storage and restoration facilities. The entire Villanueva building was to be restored and freed to play its traditional role of displaying works of art.

174

Her Majesty's Treasury Redevelopment
London, England 1996–2002

Client
Exchequer Partnership
(Stanhope Bovis and
Chesterton
Area
50,000m²
Team
Waterman Partnership

JBB
Hanscomb Partnership
BDSP
Speirs & Major
Gustafson Porter
Ove Aurp & Partners
Fielden and Mawson
Per Arnoldi

Most office buildings dating from the late-nineteenth and early-twentieth centuries are not naturally suited to modern working practices. Externally, however, they add to the architectural wealth of our cities, and many can be restructured to fit contemporary needs.

Her Majesty's Treasury is such a building. Situated between Parliament Square and Horse Guards Parade, it was completed in 1917 and is now Grade II listed. The existing building has a roughly symmetrical plan, with two halves linked by a circular drum-shaped courtyard. Each half is punctuated by smaller courtyards and lightwells. Radical reorganisation of the building will enable the staff who currently work there to be accommodated in its western half, allowing the eastern half to be renovated for occupation by another government department. This rationalisation is being achieved by breaking down the exclusively cellular structure of the office floors to introduce open-plan spaces, and by making use of previously inaccessible spaces.

The courtyards and lightwells will be capped with translucent roofs, creating five-storey-high spaces to house a library, café, training rooms and a new entrance atrium. The circular courtyard at the heart of the building, hitherto used for parking, will be emptied of cars and landscaped to form a new public space for London.

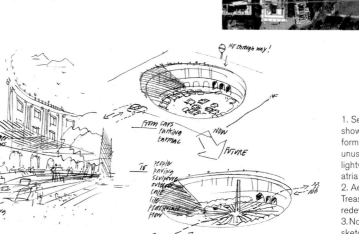

1. Sectional model showing the transformation of currently unused courtyards and lightwells into glazed atria and internal gardens.
2. Aerial view of the Treasury before redevelopment.
3. Norman Foster's sketches describing the transformation of the central drum-shaped courtyard.

175

Technical Parks
England

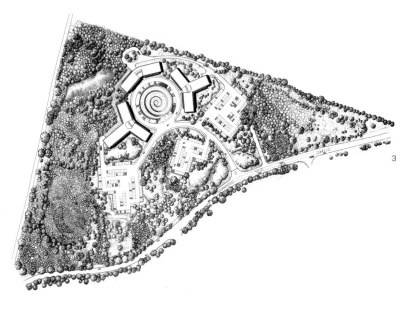

1–3. Kingswood Park: exterior views and site plan showing the clustering of the office buildings around a central green.
4. Green Park: exterior view of the first completed building, which provides office space and a social focus for the campus.
5, 6. British Gas Offices at Thames Valley Park: exterior view and site plan.

British Gas Offices
Thames Valley Park,
Reading 1992–1998
Client
British Gas Properties
Area
7,850m²
Team
Mace Ltd
Roger Preston & Partners
Waterman Partnership

Kingswood Park
Ascot 1996–1998
Client
Slough Estates Plc
Area
12,500m²
Team
Barton Willmore Partnership
Bovis Construction
Derek Lovejoy Partnership
McBains Cooper
Oscar Faber
Peter Brett Associates

Green Park
Reading 1996–1999
Client
Prudential Portfolio
Managers Ltd
Site Area
210,000m²
Area, Office Building
7,500m²
Team
Gardiner & Theobald
HBG Construction
Hoare Lea & Partners
Whitby Bird and Partners

Business or technical parks for new, clean industries provide opportunities to create environmentally friendly solutions to the design of the workplace. They can also be catalysts for the renewal of neglected landscapes, to the benefit of the wider community.

Kingswood Park is an interesting model. It occupies a clearing in mature woodland, touching only on areas left by the demolition of earlier structures, and enhances the existing setting with new strategic planting. Sheltered among the trees, three flexible office buildings are clustered around a circular 'village green' which forms the focal point of a new working community. The buildings rely on natural lighting and ventilating systems and solar-shading devices. They can be let as a single unit or subdivided, and they allow for a variety of environmental systems depending on tenant demand.

Green Park – close to the M4 motorway south-west of Reading – is an example of the next generation of technical parks, providing the most advanced working environment for clean industries. The site lies on a flood plain. One key to the development, therefore, was the implementation of flood alleviation works.

This generated a landscape in which a central ribbon of water is surrounded by buildings. In contrast to other business parks, with manicured gardens often reminiscent of golf courses, it provides a natural wetland landscape with reeds, marsh grasses and indigenous species of trees and bushes.

The environmental design of individual buildings within such parks is exemplified by the office building for British Gas at Thames Valley Park in Reading. At the time of its completion it was one of only four buildings to be awarded a certificate of excellence by BREEAM, the organisation that monitors 'green' building in Britain.

The key to its energy efficiency is the use of mixed-mode natural ventilation, which exploits the thermal mass of the exposed-concrete structure to alleviate the need for summer cooling. Fresh air is supplied at low level and extracted via ductwork in the concrete soffit. Excess heat is absorbed by the soffit, re-radiated at night and flushed away through high-level automatically opening windows. This arrangement makes air-conditioning virtually redundant.

4

5

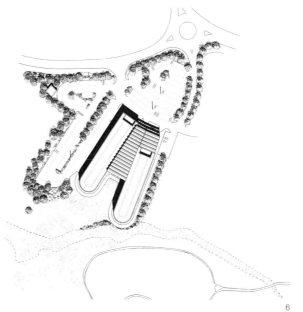

6

Bathroom Foster
1996–2001

Bathroom Foster
1996–2001
Client
Duravit and Hoesch

Taps for Stella
1995–1999
Client
Rubinetterie Stella

1

2

3

4

Bathroom suites normally consist only of 'ceramic' items – bath, shower unit, washbasin, toilet and bidet – requiring people to match taps, accessories and other bathroom furniture as best they can. The practice has a holistic and integrated approach to the design of interiors and believes this separation to be artificial. It has collaborated with two German companies – Duravit and Hoesch – to design a bathroom suite with a fully complementary range of sanitaryware, furniture, taps and accessories, which provides cohesive interiors for domestic and commercial bathrooms.

There are more than thirty elements in the Duravit series, ranging from baths, shower units and basins to towel rails and liquid soap dispensers. Each of these elements is generated by a consistent geometry based on two adjacent circles. All the sanitary elements are made from high-quality acrylic, and the showers and baths are made from vacuum-formed acrylic.

The bath has an optional whirlpool system and is available in free-standing and built-in versions or with a wall attachment. Both the basins and baths are generous in capacity but have a light appearance because of the extremely fine profile of their rims, which also aids easy access to the bathtub. The shower unit has a transparent surround and optional side-jets for hydromassage. The range also includes one and two-person steam baths.

The storage units – wall-mounted mirrored cabinets and larger free-standing cupboards for storing towels and bathrobes – follow the geometry of the sanitary elements. The curved doors of the cabinets have a wide opening angle, allowing especially easy access to their contents.

The series can be used in conjunction with a family of taps designed by the practice for Rubinetterie Stella. This Italian company has been manufacturing taps since 1882 and has a reputation for innovation and quality. The taps are available in a variety of forms and finishes suitable for a wide range of interiors. Exploiting a unique mechanism, the taps allow the user to control both water flow and temperature with unprecedented ease. The first five products in the range are a mono-command basin tap, a bidet tap, a kitchen tap, a bath tap and a thermostatic control.

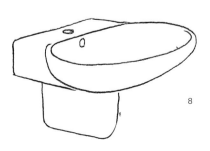

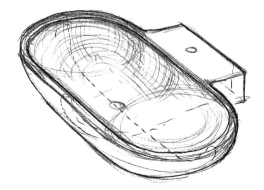

1–4. Some of the elements of the Bathroom Foster series: basin, shower unit, bidet, toilet and bath.
5, 6. The Stella Tap.
7. Norman Foster's definition of the bathroom – far more than just a place to wash.
8. Design sketches by Norman Foster: all of the bathroom elements are generated by a simple geometry of two adjacent circles.

Millennium Bridge
London, England 1996–2000

Client
Millennium Bridge Trust
London Borough of
Southwark
Length
320m
Team
Ove Arup & Partners
Sir Anthony Caro
Davis Langdon & Everest
Claude R Engle Lighting
Monberg & Thorsen/
McAlpine

1

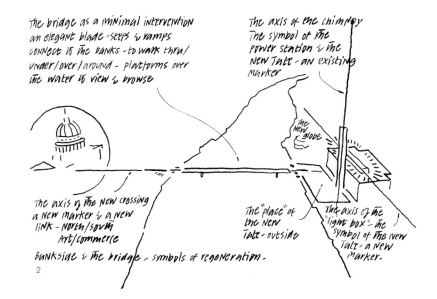

2

1. View of the
bridge at night.
2. Norman Foster's
drawing exploring the
symbolism of the bridge.
3, 4. Views showing the
shallow suspension system.
Overleaf The low-slung
cables and arms allow
pedestrians to enjoy
uninterrupted views.

180

3

4

The Millennium Bridge springs from a creative collaboration between architecture, art and engineering. Developed with sculptor Anthony Caro and engineers Ove Arup & Partners, the commission resulted from one of the most popular international competitions ever held. It is London's only bridge solely for pedestrians, and the first new Thames crossing since Tower Bridge in 1894.

The bridge links the City and St Paul's Cathedral to the north with the Globe Theatre and Tate Modern on Bankside to the south. A new element in London's pedestrian infrastructure, it has a social and economic impact on both sides of the river, creating new routes into Southwark – contributing to its regeneration – and encouraging new life on the embankment alongside St Paul's.

The paramount concern in designing the bridge was the experience that it offers the user. Those crossing can pause comfortably and enjoy London from a new vantage point, free from traffic and fumes.

Structurally, the bridge pushed the boundaries of technology. Spanning 320 metres, it is a very shallow suspension bridge. Two Y-shaped armatures support eight cables which run along the sides of the 4-metre-wide deck. Steel transverse arms clamp onto the cables at 8-metre intervals to support the deck itself. This groundbreaking structure means that the cables never rise more than 2.3 metres above the deck – one-tenth of the height of any other suspension bridge – allowing pedestrians uninterrupted panoramic views of London and preserving sight lines from the surrounding buildings.

As a result, the bridge has a uniquely thin profile, forming a slender arc across the water. It spans the greatest possible distance with the minimum means. By day it appears as a thin ribbon of steel and aluminium. At night it forms a glowing blade of light.

The bridge opened in June 2000 and an astonishing 100,000 people crossed it during the first weekend. However, because of greater than expected movement the bridge had to be closed. Extensive research and testing involving the international engineering profession revealed that the movement was caused by synchronised pedestrian footfall – a phenomenon of which little was previously known in the engineering world. The solution to this problem was to fit dampers below the deck to mitigate movement.

Faculty of Social Studies, University of Oxford

Oxford, England 1996–2000

1. Exterior view of
the building amidst its
historical neighbours.
2. View of the grand
staircase in the atrium.
3. Looking out of the
atrium through the
glazed end-wall.
4. South elevation.

Client
University of Oxford
Area
3,500m²
Team
Andrew Kent & Stone
Roger Preston & Partners
Turner and Townsend
Claude R Engle Lighting
Sandy Brown Associates
Heery International Ltd

Building within a historical city such as Oxford requires great contextual sensitivity. The proximity of the University's new building for the Social Studies Faculty to a number of listed buildings made these considerations all the more meaningful. The design attempts to emulate the enduring quality of much of the city's traditional architecture through its simplicity and integrity.

The three-storey building provides a new focus for the Faculty, replacing accommodation previously scattered throughout Oxford. The ground floor contains a library and IT training rooms. Faculty offices, seminar rooms and a staff common room are located on the upper two floors. The commission extended to the design of low-cost flexible furniture systems, including reception desks, meeting tables and occasional tables.

The building's concrete structure, cast in situ, is clearly expressed both internally and externally. The column grid accommodates both the dimensions of the standardised book stacks in the ground-floor library and the cellular offices on the upper floors. The layout of the building anticipates change and growth within the Faculty, allowing for linear extension in the future.

The entrance is positioned prominently at one corner of the plan to take advantage of views over a neighbouring stream. All the peripheral spaces are naturally ventilated and daylight is brought into the centre of the building via an atrium that runs almost the full length of the plan. Within this space a processional staircase rises through all the floors and offers spectacular views back out through the atrium's glazed end-wall.

The atrium is toplit by means of a clerestory that sits a full storey higher than the adjacent accommodation. Light is admitted through translucent panels, which consist of fibrous insulation material sandwiched between double-glazing units. Similar panels are used in the main facades, alternating with clear glazed units to allow filtered daylight into the spaces, where solar shading is provided by full-height fabric screens.

3

4

Millennium Tower
London, England 1996

Client
Trafalgar House Property Ltd
Area
140,000m²
Team
Ove Arup & Partners
BH2
Emmer Pfenninger
Partner AG

F C Foreman & Partners
Franklin & Andrews
G V A Grimley
Jones Lang Wootton
Lerch Bates & Associates Ltd
Roger Preston & Partners
Schatunowski Brooks
Trollope & Colls Ltd

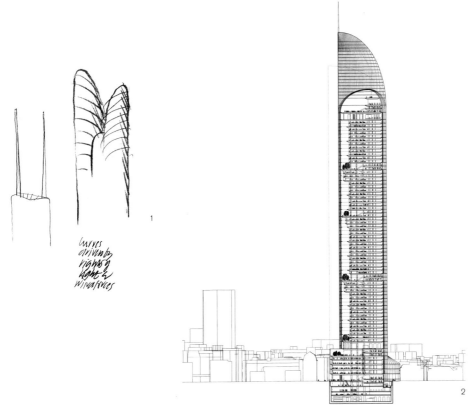

1

curves
driven by
rights of
light &
wind forces

2

Tall buildings can be expressive of the energy and aspirations of modern cities. The Millennium Tower project was rooted in the needs of the City of London and responded to an influx of people returning from the suburbs to enjoy a new quality of urban life.

Located in the heart of the City, on the site of the former Baltic Exchange, the Tower was designed to provide 140,000 square metres of accommodation, including dealing floors, apartments, shops, restaurants and gardens. At 92 storeys and rising 385 metres, it remains Europe's tallest projected building.

Its curving plan and varied massing were developed to provide unique views from every angle, with reflective glass facades designed to dematerialise its form. Its bifurcated top articulated a shift from deep-planned commercial floors to domestic space, resulting in two streamlined 'mini-towers' of different heights on the skyline. Public facilities were planned at the junction between the offices and residential floors, and at ground level. A viewing gallery offered panoramic views across London and beyond.

When the client decided not to develop the project, the site was bought by Swiss Re. They commissioned the practice to create a new building which, while not as tall as the Millennium Tower, takes an equally radical approach in its form and ecology.

1. Norman Foster's sketch of the tower's bifurcated summit.
2. Cross-section through the tower.
3. Visualisation showing the tower on the London skyline.

3

126 Phillip Street

Sydney, Australia 1996–2005

Client
BT funds Management
Area
67,370m²
Team
Hassell
Ove Arup & Partners
Roger Preston & Partners
Lincoln Scott Australia
Rider Hunt Sydney
Norman Disney & Young

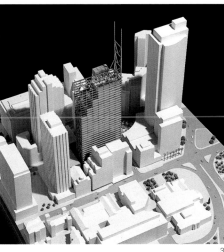

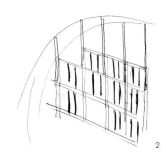

This 31-storey office tower occupies a prominent site on the edge of Sydney's main business district, overlooking the harbour. Its distinctive stepped profile is the result of planning rules protecting the amount of sunlight falling onto two nearby public spaces.

The tower has a highly innovative design which takes advantage of views over the harbour and maximises the amount of flexible floorspace. Its main structural core is offset to the western edge of the site and consists of two aluminium-clad concrete towers, which provide the main stiffening elements and act as solar buffers.

Daylight is drawn into the office levels and the mall below via an atrium which runs the full height of the building between the core and the office floor-plates.

To permit greater flexibility in planning internal divisions, curtain walling on the three glazed facades has been turned 'inside out' – mullions and transoms are placed externally, where they support shading devices.

Because of a steep slope across the site, the entrance foyer to the east, opposite the Parliament buildings on Macquarie Street, is a full storey higher than the entrance on Phillip Street to the west. This has allowed the creation of a retail mall, which runs from the Phillip Street entrance to form a new public route through the city block. Escalators connect the lower level to the Macquarie Street entrance foyer, which contains a public café.

1. Photomontage of the tower at night.
2. Norman Foster's development sketch showing an alternative treatment for the top of the tower.
3. Site model showing the tower's stepped profile and open framework.

World Squares for All Masterplan
London, England 1996–2002

World Squares for All
1996–2002
Client
City of Westminster
Department for Culture,
Media and Sport
English Heritage
Government Office
for London
The Houses of Parliament
London Transport
The Royal Parks Agency
Area
19,000m²

Masterplan Team
Halcrow Fox
Civic Design Partnership
Davis Langdon & Everest
Space Syntax Laboratory
W S Atkins
Feilden and Mawson
Schal Construction
Management
Speirs & Major
GMJ
Ricky Burdett

National Police Memorial
1993–2002
Client
The Police Memorial Trust
Area
50m²
Team
Ove Arup & Partners
Per Arnoldi
Francis Golding

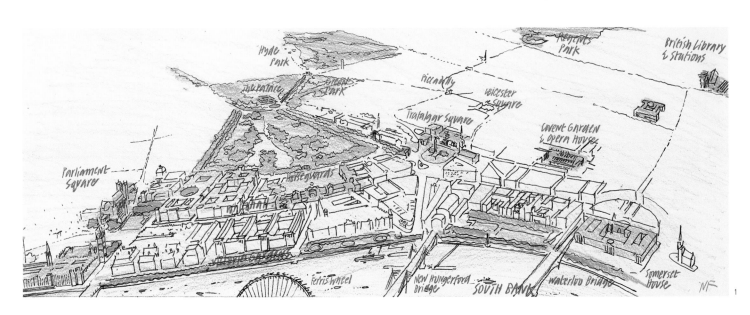

'World Squares for All' provides a detailed masterplan for the environmental improvement of Trafalgar Square, Parliament Square and Whitehall in Central London. It aims to improve pedestrian access and enjoyment of the area while enhancing the settings of its buildings, monuments and spaces. The masterplan area is familiar the world over. It contains a World Heritage Site – the Palace of Westminster and Westminster Abbey – and such national emblems as Nelson's Column and the Cenotaph.

Yet the area is a largely unfriendly environment, dominated by motor vehicles, its squares reduced to traffic gyratories. It provides few facilities for Londoners and the thousands of people who visit each year.

Extensive research involved two major studies of traffic and pedestrian movement and consultations with more than 180 public bodies and thousands of individuals.

One of the tools utilised was a plan model of London developed by Space Syntax at University College, London, which demonstrates the potential for connectivity and pedestrian access. This research led to the development of two possible strategies, which were launched at a public exhibition in Whitehall in November 1997. The response was an overwhelming support for change.

A project of this kind is a balancing act, which must promote genuinely integrated solutions to cater for the many needs of our cities. This holds true for any historical urban environment attempting to sustain contemporary activities.

Cities such as Amsterdam, Barcelona and Paris have shown how the containment of traffic can contribute to the economic and cultural vitality of city centres, and these proposals help to redress the balance between pedestrians and vehicles.

The first phase to be implemented focuses on Trafalgar Square. As part of a comprehensive programme of detailed improvements, the northern side of the square will be closed to traffic and the National Gallery reconnected with the main body of the square, creating a broad pedestrian plaza in front of the building.

Within the masterplan area the practice is designing the National Police Memorial, which honours police officers killed whilst on duty. It will be located at Cambridge Green at the junction of The Mall and Horse Guards Parade, directly on the state ceremonial route.

1. Norman Foster's drawing of the masterplan area.
2. Visualisation of the new National Police Memorial on The Mall.

Site photographs, left, and visualisations, right, before and after implementation of the masterplan…
3, 4. Looking from Trafalgar Square towards the National Gallery.

3

4

5, 6. The north side of Trafalgar Square.

5

6

7, 8. Whitehall.

7

8

9, 10. Parliament Square.

9

10

Wembley Stadium
London, England 1996–2003

Client
Wembley National
Stadium Limited
Area
170,000m²
Team
HOK/LOBB
Mott Stadium Consortium
Franklin & Andrews
Nathanial Lichfield & Partners
Steer Davies Gleeve

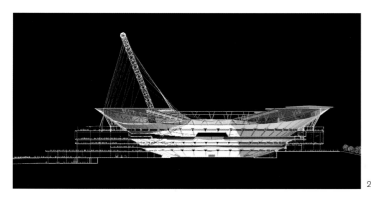

Since it was built for the British Empire Exhibition of 1924, Wembley Stadium has become the most important sports venue in Britain. Home to the England national football team, it was the site of the Olympic Games in 1948 and the football World Cup Final in 1966. It has also acted as a venue for major rock concerts and other popular events.

The new Wembley Stadium will be the first of a new generation of sports stadia, with facilities unparalleled anywhere in the world, including a hotel, offices, a banquet hall, pre-function gathering spaces and facilities for media coverage. The design builds upon the heritage of the old stadium to provide future generations of sports and music fans with a venue equipped for the twenty-first century. When completed in 2003 it will form a new home for English football.

The key feature of the new stadium is its partly retractable roof. When fully open it allows sunlight to reach the whole pitch – an essential element in maintaining the world-standard quality of the turf. In poor weather, the roof can be closed within 15 minutes, providing cover for all 90,000 seats.

The roof is supported structurally by a spectacular 133-metre-high arch that soars over the stadium, providing an iconic replacement for the old building's landmark twin towers. Dramatically illuminated at night, the arch will be visible from vantage points across London.

Facilities are designed to maximise spectator comfort and enjoyment of events: the stadium's geometry and its steeply raked seating tiers ensure that everyone has an unobstructed view; seats are larger than at present with more leg-room; the highest tiers are easily accessed via escalators; and a new concourse wrapping around the building allows easy circulation and provides catering for up to 40,000 spectators at any one time.

To create an intimate atmosphere during football and rugby games, the stadium has been designed with seats as close to the pitch as possible. Yet it also has the potential to host track and field competitions, for which an elevated running track and athletics field can be installed above the pitch and the first few rows of seats, supported by pillars. Acoustic studies have been undertaken to ensure that the new stadium will recreate the distinctive 'Wembley roar'.

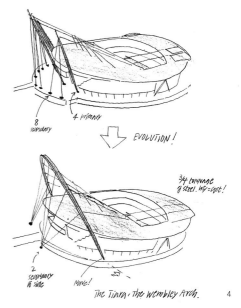

1, 3. Visualisations of the interior of the stadium and Olympic Way as it will look when complete.
2. Cross-section.
4, 5. Sketches by Norman Foster outlining the structural principles of the new arch and its symbolic role.
Overleaf The new arch will form a beacon across London.

Citibank Headquarters
London, England 1996–2000

Client
Canary Wharf Contractor
(DS-6) Ltd
Citibank
Area
90,000m²
Team
Ove Arup & Partners
Roger Preston & Partners
Lerch Bates & Associates Ltd
Gardiner & Theobald
Claude R Engle Lighting

Located alongside the new Jubilee Line station at Canary Wharf, Citibank's new headquarters occupies a key position in this emerging financial quarter of London and heralds the next phase in the area's continuing expansion.

Following a very rapid development programme, which included the study of an alternative location in the City, the site was developed to meet a complex brief, providing 90,000 square metres of accommodation, including two 3,000-square-metre trading floors. Organisationally the new building comprises two distinct parts: an office building to the west and a service core to the east. The latter rises higher than the former in response to different height restrictions across the site. As well as preserving views to the west this allows the building to be opened up around a central atrium, fulfilling the client's request for broad open spaces to encourage social interaction, and maintaining a key north-south pedestrian route across the site.

The western building rises seventeen floors above plaza level. Liberated from services, it is able to contain all the Bank's activities, including the two trading floors, a staff restaurant, an auditorium and a gymnasium. The four floors below plaza level contain car-parking and IT support facilities. The lofty main atrium is flanked by secondary atria, which step back to allow daylight and fresh air into the depths of the office floors.

1. Aerial view of the Citibank headquarters from the east showing the articulated frames of its two towers. The emerging form of the HSBC headquarters is visible beyond; the glazed canopies of the Jubilee Line Station can be seen in the foreground.

HSBC Headquarters
London, England 1997–2002

Client
Canary Wharf Contractor
(DS-2) Ltd
HSBC Holdings plc
Area
160,000m²
Team
Ove Arup & Partners
Lerch Bates & Associates Ltd
Davis Langdon & Everest
Claude R Engle Lighting

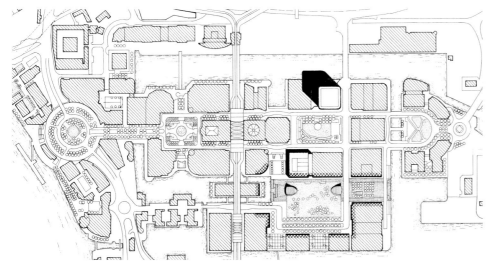

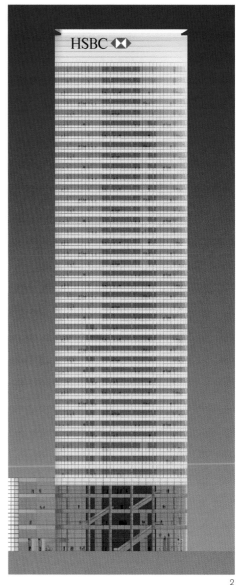

In 1979 the Hongkong and Shanghai Bank (HSBC) presented a brief for its Hong Kong headquarters that allowed the practice to rewrite the rules of tall office building design. Twenty-eight years later the Bank offered a very different challenge: to design a London headquarters in Canary Wharf.

As the owner-occupier of the Hong Kong building, the Bank was able to encourage formal and technical experimentation to an unprecedented degree. In London, however, the Bank decided to follow a commercially led path: although it has initially leased the entire building, later it may wish to sublet part or all of the accommodation. The developer-led solution therefore had to work within tight cost limits and meet market expectations for high-quality, flexible office space.

This meant providing an air-conditioned building with a central core, to maximise the development potential of the site and optimise net to gross floor ratios. The challenge was not simply to meet market expectations, however, but to raise values in every area, from materials to ecological performance, thereby setting new standards.

All main facilities are configured within the core, allowing open-plan floors throughout. Rapid transit to the 39 office floors is provided by a sophisticated multi-tier elevator system. Three interchange levels allow easy movement between elevator groups and contain meeting rooms, shops, cafés, catering and medical facilities. From the entrance lobby there is escalator access to three double-height trading halls. Below ground there is a direct link to Canary Wharf Underground station, together with three levels of car-parking.

The 200-metre-high tower is given elegant, minimal expression through its sheer glass surface treatment. Curved corners soften the form and the tower's transparent shaft is capped with an illuminated 'halo'.

1. Site plan of Canary Wharf including the HSBC Headquarters, Citibank and the new Jubilee Line Underground station.
2, 3. Visualisations of the fully glazed shaft of the HSBC tower and the 28-metre-high entrance lobby.

195

Repsol Service Stations
Spain 1997

Client
Repsol
Height
8m
Team
Ove Arup & Partners
Davis Langdon & Everest
Roger Preston & Partners
Claude R Engle Lighting

1

When the Spanish oil company Repsol commissioned a new service station system, the challenge was to update its roadside identity while delivering a highly flexible solution capable of adaptation to 200 sites planned around Spain.

The result is a modular canopy system in the Repsol signature colours of red, white and orange. Clusters of these structures form overlapping 'umbrellas' sheltering each station forecourt. The canopy head is an inverted pyramid, its crisp edges balanced by the less emphatic lines of the cladding.

The umbrellas vary in number, height and in the degree of overlap between them, according to the specifics of each site. The associated shop unit, car wash, petrol pumps and signage elements belong to a related family of pure, box-like forms. Together, they provide maximum flexibility in planning and accommodate numerous variations in site configuration. All these elements are factory made and easily transported and installed on site, providing cost benefits while ensuring high quality standards and rapid delivery.

The canopies are arranged in a pre-determined sequence which ensures that a red one is always the tallest. This brightly coloured combination creates a strong three-dimensional image. Even from the air Repsol's identity is clearly announced. On the road the stations are identifiable from a distance and are vivid and inviting when approached.

1. Norman Foster's sketch of the modular station system.
2. A typical station forecourt at night.
3. The brightly coloured umbrellas are executed in Repsol's signature colours.

196

2

3

J C Decaux International Headquarters
Brentford, England 1997–2000

1, 2. Photograph and
Norman Foster's concept
sketch for the central
canopied 'street'.
3. Elements of J C
Decaux's street
furniture on display.
4. Elevation showing
how the three different
parts of the building
are linked.
5. The refurbished
Art Deco building.
6. The new storage
warehouse.

Client
J C Decaux
Area
5,030m²
Team
Anthony Hunt Associates
BDSP
David Langdon & Everest
Mott McDonald
Heery International Ltd

4

The quality of a city's street furniture is an indicator of its self-esteem: it can be a source of delight or dismay. J C Decaux is one of the world's leading suppliers of street furniture and advertising space. The company emphasises design excellence and has commissioned some of the world's leading architects to design bus shelters and advertising structures.

The practice has worked with J C Decaux to develop a range of items, including advertising billboards, a bus shelter system, a city boundary sign and an updated version of the Colonne Morris – an advertising drum incorporating grit bins, benches, lavatories, a roof canopy and electronic information systems. These can be found worldwide in cities such as London, Paris, Prague, New York and San Francisco.

The company's international headquarters in West London has three distinct parts: an Art Deco building, which forms the street frontage; a new storage warehouse; and a 'street' with a vaulted glazed canopy, which links the two and provides exhibition space for Decaux's extensive range of street furniture.

The Grade II-listed Art Deco building – built in 1936 for Currys Cycles and Radios – has been restored in accordance with English Heritage's advice. In addition to offices it provides a gymnasium and café.

The warehouse is a fully integrated structure, designed for maximum economy and efficiency. It employs an American system of pre-cast, thermally insulated concrete panels, known as 'hardwall construction', which allowed the columns and walls to be erected in only twelve days. Wall panels were simply craned into position, one on top of another, and secured with steel dowels. This system has significant benefits beyond its ease of construction: internal walls require no lining; and the panels are 97 per cent thermally efficient, leading to long-term energy savings.

Circular glazed apertures cut into the aluminium roof admit sufficient daylight to light the warehouse interior on bright days. Light fittings are installed directly below these apertures so that light-pools are cast on the floor whether the space is naturally or artificially lit. The bright yellow epoxy-resin flooring reflects light back up, bathing the space in a warm glow.

5

6

Expo Station

Singapore 1997–2001

Client
Land Transport Authority
Area
7,164m²

Team
Ove Arup & Partners
Cicada Private Ltd
Claude R Engle Lighting
Davis Langdon & Seah
Singapore Pte Ltd
Land Transport Authority
PWD Consultants Pte Ltd

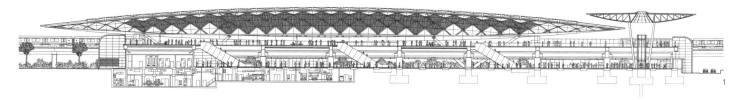

1

Like airports, railway stations have great symbolic value as urban gateways – they are often the first buildings that people experience when arriving in a city. The vast number of passengers using these structures defines their scale and their key design criteria: they must be easy to negotiate and they must employ durable, low-maintenance materials.

The Expo Station on the new Changi Airport Line serves the new Singapore Exhibition Centre. Two dramatic roof structures announce the station: a 40-metre-diameter stainless-steel disc covering the ticket hall, and a 130-metre-long ellipse – clad in titanium that will last a hundred years – which shelters the passenger concourse. These shapes overlap to dynamic visual effect.

In one of the warmest climates in the world the choice of roof materials also has an environmental significance. The stainless-steel soffit reflects daylight into the concourse, while the titanium cladding deflects the sun's rays, thus helping to create a microclimate on the platforms that is up to four degrees cooler than the outside temperature.

1. Cross-section through the station.
2. View of the main concourse: the stainless-steel underside of the roof reflects daylight into the space.

2

Dresden Station Redevelopment
Germany 1997–2003

Client
Deutsche Bahn AG
Area
30,000m²
Team
Buro Happold
Homola AYH AG
Schmidt Reuter Partner
Schmidt Stumpf Fruehauf
und Partner

Dresden's main railway terminus, built between 1892 and 1898 to a design by Ernst Giese and Paul Weidner, is the third largest in eastern Germany after Berlin and Leipzig. It is also one of the most impressive late-nineteenth-century railway stations in Europe. Linking Dresden with Berlin and Prague, the railway played a significant role in the city's industrial and economic growth in the first half of the twentieth century. During World War II the station was badly damaged in Allied bombing raids, which destroyed 80 per cent of the city. In the post-war period it was poorly maintained and finally reached a state where remedial conservation was required.

The practice has devised a masterplan for the renovation and expansion of the station, as part of a wider project to revive the surrounding area. The scheme removes various additions and alterations made to the building over the last hundred years in order to restore the integrity of the original design. Circulation within and through the station is improved by creating additional openings in the walls leading to the outer platforms.

The barrel-vaulted roofs over the outer platforms are extended by 200 metres to provide cover for new high-speed trains, which are almost twice the length of the station. The central tracks are pulled back in order to create a large open space at the heart of the building, which can be used as a market place or for cultural events.

Currently only the most urgent element of the masterplan is to be carried out – the reconstruction of the 30,000-square-metre roof. Much of the steelwork is so degraded that it is unsafe. The entire structure will be restored to its original condition and covered with a translucent skin of Teflon-coated glass fibre. Originally the roof was partially glazed, but since the war it has been covered with timber, admitting no daylight. The new roof will transmit 13 per cent of daylight and significantly reduce the station's reliance on artificial lighting. At night, light will reflect off the underside of the roof, creating an even wash of illumination inside and announcing the station from without by a silvery glow.

1

2

1. Computer-generated image of the translucent glass-fibre roof.
2. Perspective drawing of the station after redevelopment.

Music Centre

Gateshead, England 1997–2002

Client
Gateshead Metropolitan
Borough Council
Folkworks
Northern Arts
Northern Sinfonia
Arts Council of England
Area
17,500m²
Team
Ove Arup & Partners
Mott MacDonald
Buro Happold

Davis Langdon & Everest
Theatre Projects
Consultants
Equation Lighting
Design Ltd
Lerch Bates &
Associates Ltd
Burdus Access
Management
Winton Nightingale
Desvigne & Dalnoky
WSP
Laing Ltd
Space Syntax Laboratory

1

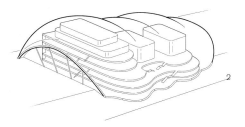

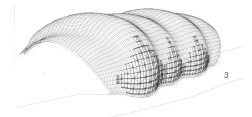

The new Music Centre in Gateshead will be a landmark on Tyneside, forming the heart of an exciting project to regenerate the area's river frontage. It will be a regional centre of international standing with an expected half-million visitors each year. The site is adjacent to the new Baltic Millennium Bridge – a pedestrian and cycle bridge linking Gateshead and Newcastle – and the Tyne Bridge with its great arch, which is echoed in the shell-like form of the Music Centre's roof.

The Centre provides accommodation for three auditoria and the Regional Music School and also acts as a base for the Northern Sinfonia and Folkworks, which promotes folk, jazz and blues performances. The largest of the three main performance spaces is acoustically state-of-the-art and seats up to 1,650 people. The second hall caters for folk, jazz and chamber music, with an informal and flexible seating arrangement for up to 400 people. The third space is a large rehearsal hall for the Northern Sinfonia and also forms the focus of the Music School. The School will be accessible to children, schools and people of all ages, raising the profile of the region as a provider of musical education.

Each auditorium was conceived as a separate enclosure but the windswept nature of the site suggested a covered concourse along the waterfront to link them. As a result the entire complex is sheltered beneath a broad, enveloping roof that is 'shrink-wrapped' around the buildings beneath and extends over the concourse.

With cafés, bars, shops, an information centre and the box office, the concourse is a major public space. It acts as a foyer for the auditoria and a common room for the Music School – which is located beneath it – as well as offering views out onto the Tyne. An atmosphere of informality is encouraged by reducing back-of-house hospitality areas so that performers mix with their audience and with students in the concourse bars.

The Music Centre has taken ten years of planning by the client and has been designed after extensive consultation with audiences and musicians. Geographically it fills the 'gap on the map' for music venues, the nearest alternatives being more than three hours away. It also complements the redevelopment of the neighbouring Baltic Flour Mills as a centre for contemporary art, consolidating Tyneside's position as an arts destination.

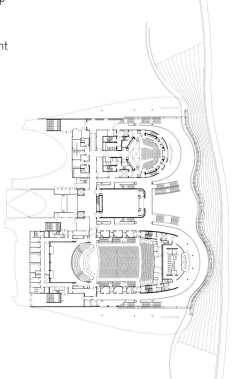

1. Visualisation of
the completed Centre.
2, 3. Design studies
for the free-form roof,
which is 'shrink-wrapped'
around the auditoria.
4. Visualisation of
the concourse linking
the auditoria.
5. Site plan.

Swiss Re Headquarters
London, England 1997–2004

Client
Swiss Reinsurance
Company (Swiss Re)
Area
76,400m²
Team
Ove Arup & Partners
Gardiner & Theobald
Hilson Moran
Partnership Ltd
RWG Associates
Van Densen & Associates

Swiss Re is one of the world's leading reinsurance companies. This new building will bring together all the company's London-based staff. Located on the site of the former Baltic Exchange in the City, the tower rises 41 storeys and provides 76,400 square metres of accommodation, including offices and a shopping arcade accessed from a new public plaza.

The project takes a radical approach – technically, architecturally, socially and spatially – to create the capital's first ecological tall building. Conceptually it develops ideas first explored in the Climatroffice design with Buckminster Fuller. Climatroffice suggested a new rapport between nature and workspace. Its garden setting created a microclimate within an energy-conscious enclosure which resolved walls and roof into a continuous triangulated skin.

The tower has a radial plan with a circular perimeter. In profile it widens as it rises and tapers towards its apex. This form responds to the constraints of the site: the building appears more slender than a rectangular block of equivalent size; reflections are reduced and transparency is improved; and the slimming of its profile towards the base maximises the public realm at ground level. A diagonally braced structure supports the building at its perimeter, allowing column-free floorspace and a fully glazed envelope which opens up the building to daylight.

Each of the floor-plates is rotated with respect to the one below it. This allows the spaces between the radiating fingers of each floor to combine to form spiralling 'gardens in the sky'. Socially these spaces break down the scale of the building. Environmentally they help to regulate the internal climate, becoming the building's 'lungs'. Fresh air is drawn in at each floor via slots in the cladding. Exhaust air can be recycled to provide heating to the building, or vented to the outside.

The spiral form of the atria generates pressure differentials that greatly assist this natural flow. The system is so effective that air conditioning will not be required for a significant proportion of the year. As a result, energy consumption is dramatically reduced in comparison with conventional office buildings.

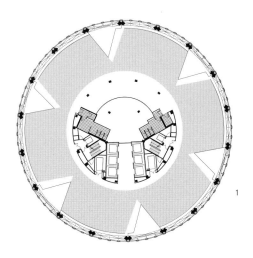

1

1. Typical floor plan.
2, 3. Norman Foster's sketch studies for the layered structure and cladding system and for a club on the top level. *Facing page* Visualisation of the completed tower – London's first ecological tall building.

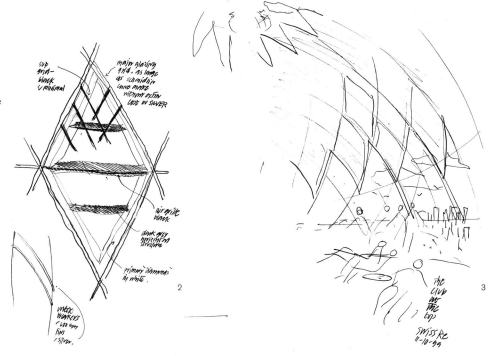

2

3

Electronic Arts European Headquarters
Chertsey, England 1997–2000

Client
Electronic Arts
P+O Developments
Area
24,000m²
Team
Whitby Bird and Partners
Oscar Faber
Wheelers
Land Use Consultants

Mark Johnson Consultants
Recording Architecture
Tricon
Jeremy Gardner
Partnership
Claude R Engle Lighting
Schumann Smith Ltd
Rowney Sharman
Exterior International Ltd

The practice has consistently encouraged companies to adopt flexible, non-hierarchical working environments. In the design of their European Headquarters, Electronic Arts – a leading computer-game software development company – wholly embraced this philosophy. The headquarters sets new standards in this fast-moving industry, providing high-quality workspace, a state-of-the-art media centre for presentations, and an extensive range of on-site facilities.

The two-phase development provides 24,000 square metres of accommodation. Bound to the north by an eighteenth-century lake, the building comprises a group of three-storey office blocks arranged as five 'fingers', projecting into the landscape. The fingers are linked by a sweeping glass wall which encloses a street-like atrium. This is an animated showcase for Electronic Arts' work and the social focus of the campus; it provides primary circulation at ground level and forms an environmental buffer between the offices and the landscape beyond.

In offices equipped with large amounts of hardware, cooling and ventilation are the chief environmental concerns. The building employs a low-energy environmental strategy and a range of new-technology building systems. Comfortable conditions are maintained by combining displacement ventilation with natural cooling from the high thermal mass of the building's exposed structure. When supplementary ventilation and cooling are required the building management system can simply open the windows or, on the very hottest days, switch on the air conditioning. Heat gain is minimised by extensive use of brise-soleil as part of the low-energy facade design.

Electronic Arts' staff take pride in working as a family with common values. In keeping with this ethos, a huge range of facilities is provided, including games arcades, a gym and sports pitch, a library, a bar and a 140-seat restaurant. With this wealth of leisure options, staff members have joked that the experience is like 'homing from work'.

1

2

1. 'Homing from work'.
2. The restaurant, which opens onto the lakeside.
3. Norman Foster's concept sketch of the building and its landscaped setting.
4. View along the internal 'street'.
5. The restaurant interior.
Overleaf The building viewed across the lake.

5

Interior Design

Willis Faber & Dumas 1971–1975 **Client** Willis Faber & Dumas Ltd **Area** 21,000m²	**Hongkong and Shanghai Bank Headquarters** 1979–1986 **Client** Hongkong and Shanghai Banking Corporation **Area** 99,000m²	**Imperial College, Sir Alexander Fleming Building** 1994–1998 **Client** Imperial College and South Kensington Millennium Commission **Area** 25,000m²

1

OPTIONS are considered JOINTLY & IN-DEPTH

with the aim of finding the target

Electronic Arts
European Headquarters
1997–2000
Client
Electronic Arts
Area
24,000m²

4

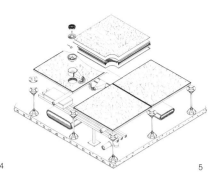

5

From its earliest days, the practice has never seen a division between the design of the shell of a building and that of its interiors. All the projects illustrated in this book have benefited from continuity of design process and a consistent philosophical approach, which means working with the client and asking the right questions. Recently the practice has taken a step forward by forming a specialist interior design team that offers consultation with clients on every aspect of a building's interiors, from space planning to commissioning works of art.

In the context of the workplace, flexibility is at the heart of the practice's approach. A client's requirements may change over time and if a building is to respond to these needs it must be able to adapt quickly and economically. Two of the practice's early projects – for Willis Faber & Dumas and the Hongkong and Shanghai Bank (HSBC) – were pioneers in this regard.

As a result of a detailed consultation with the building's future users, it was possible at Willis Faber to anticipate how working patterns might change. In fact the building was to prove more flexible than anyone could have foreseen. When the company introduced computerisation in the1980s, more than a decade after its completion, raised floors in the offices allowed the changeover to be made without disruption.

The Bank took the concept of flexibility a stage further: it was created to previously unheard-of performance criteria. Interestingly, HSBC acknowledges the way in which the building has been able to adapt over the years as a factor in its continuing strong world rating.

Flexibility is also of crucial importance in the realm of scientific and biomedical research. The Sir Alexander Fleming Building for Imperial College in London is designed to encourage social and intellectual interaction. The provision of a purpose-designed, modular workstation in the central 'forum' allows postgraduate students and research leaders to regroup easily, thus encouraging dynamic working relationships. A similar module is used in the laboratories, which can be configured to suit any microbiologist.

Similarly, in the headquarters for Electronic Arts – a computer games development company with a young, highly motivated staff – everybody, even the managing director, has the same standardised workstation, which staff are encouraged to personalise. This informal working environment reflects the company's non-hierarchical management structure and supports creativity and communication.

6

PROGRAMMING & MODELLING STUDIES

RESEARCH

ALLOW FOR TESTING OF MOCK-UPS & PROTOTYPES

7

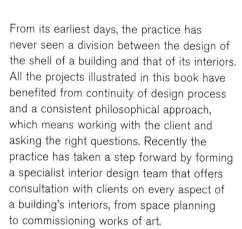

8

9

1. Electronic Arts: an informal meeting space.
2, 3, 7. Norman Foster's sketches highlighting the collaborative nature of the design process.
4, 5. Hongkong and Shanghai Bank: looking into the open-plan office spaces, and detail of the raised-floor system.
6. Imperial College: view down into the 'forum' with its modular workstations.
8, 9. Willis, Faber & Dumas: comparative views in the era of the typewriter and after computerisation: a change-over that was made without disruption.

Free University of Berlin
Berlin, Germany 1997–2004

Since the end of World War II the Free University has occupied a central role in the intellectual life of Berlin. It is one of the city's most symbolically important institutions, its foundation marking the rebirth of liberal education there after the war. Today, with more than 60,000 students, it is the largest of Berlin's three universities. This redevelopment scheme includes the restoration of its Modernist buildings and the design of a new library on the campus.

The University was founded in 1949 in Dahlem, West Berlin, by the Western Allied Powers to compensate for the loss of the Humboldt University – historically Germany's premier seat of learning – which was isolated in the Soviet Sector following the division of Berlin. The University's web-like campus was designed in 1963 by the architects Candilis Josic Woods Schiedhelm, and the first buildings were completed in 1973.

The facade, designed by Jean Prouvé, followed Le Corbusier's Modulor proportional system and consisted of framed panels in Corten steel, which has self-protecting corrosive qualities. Its rusty appearance led to the affectionate nickname of 'die Rostlaube' – 'the rust bucket'. In the thin sections used here, however, the Corten steel was prone to decay, which by the late 1990s had become extensive.

As part of a comprehensive process of renovation the steel panels and framing have been replaced with patinated bronze elements. While these are faithful to the original architects' intentions some details have been sensitively altered to meet contemporary technical requirements and energy standards. The roof will be covered with vegetation to add insulation and improve microclimatic conditions.

Six of the University's courtyards have been united to form the site of a new library for the Faculty of Philology. The five-storey building is housed within a free-form skin consisting of aluminium panels, ventilation elements and double-layered glass panels, supported on steel frames with radial geometry. The library's curved form and its double skin create pressure differentials in the cavity between the skins, which assist a natural ventilation system. An inner membrane of glass fibre allows soft sunlight to penetrate the space while creating an atmosphere of concentration. Scattered transparent openings punctuate this membrane at strategic points to allow glimpses of the courtyard.

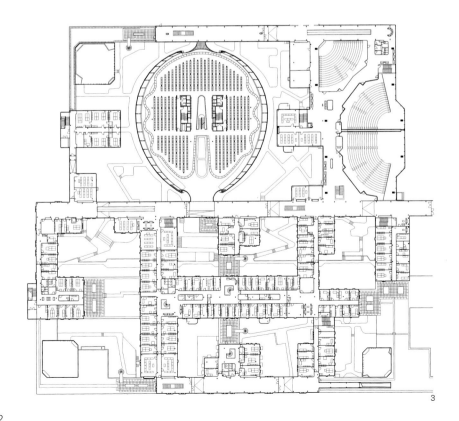

Client
Free University of Berlin
Berlin Senat Administration
for Urban Development
Area
46,200m²
Team
Schmidt Reuter Partner
Pichler Ingenieure
Institut für Fassadentechnik
Schott

Höhler & Partner
Büro Peters
Büro Noack
Kappes & Scholtz
Hosser Hass & Partner
Ingenieur Büro Langkau
Moers
Akustik-Ingenieurbüro
Moll GmbH

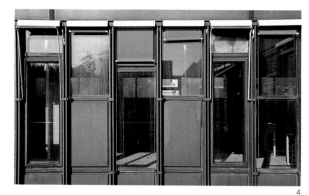

4

5

1. Interior view of one of
the restored lecture halls
with acoustic panelling.
2. Aerial view of the
campus before restoration.
3. Plan showing how the
curved form of the new
library has been inserted
into the existing campus.
4, 5. Details of the
cladding before and after
renovation, respectively.

Cultural Centre
Dubai 1998

Client
Confidential
Area
100,000m²
Length
1km
Team
Ove Arup & Partners
Davis Langdon & Everest

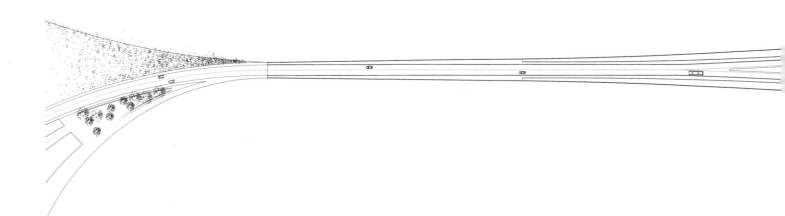

1. Plan of the Centre.
2. Model showing the curving roof that shades the entire complex.
3. Perspective drawing of the central 'oasis', with travelators carrying the public past the perimeter music school.

2

214

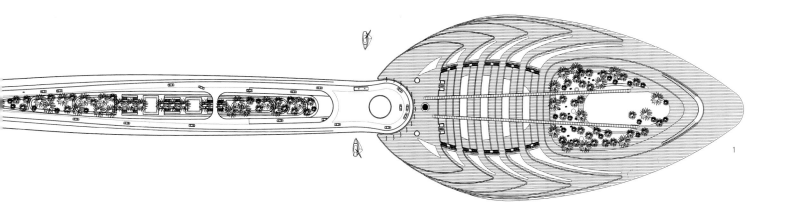

The design of this Cultural Centre in Dubai draws upon vernacular architectural traditions from the Gulf region. Its plan echoes the layout of a traditional Arabic house, with a communal space at the centre, surrounded by a layer of private or semi-public accommodation and an outer layer of gardens and social spaces. These spatial arrangements reflect the importance within Arab culture of private family life and the primacy of the public gathering space and the spoken word. The centre also draws upon local typologies such as the oasis, the tent and the covered bazaar.

The proposed complex is located just off the coast of Dubai. Its dramatic form projects into the sea and is linked to the coast by an inhabited bridge. Apartments, with gardens at their centres, are suspended beneath the road deck, within the supporting structure of the bridge.

The road both provides natural shading for the apartments and maintains their privacy, since they cannot be seen from above. The building forms a jetty around which boats can be moored, and an opening in the bridge structure allows small craft to sail through.

The Cultural Centre houses a residential music school, two concert halls and an exhibition centre with galleries for temporary exhibitions and a permanent collection. At the heart of the complex is an oasis and gathering space. This public area, with its shops, sports club and business centre is reached by travelators that swoop dramatically down from the main drop-off point. By this means a distinct separation is maintained from the private areas of the music school, which are wrapped around the central area and reached by a separate entrance.

The Centre relies upon environmental controls traditional within the region. A vast permeable roof shades the entire complex. This provides protection against the sun and encourages cooling air currents to flow through the public spaces. Consisting of aluminium louvres on a curvilinear steel ring beam, the structure is light enough to be supported at only two points.

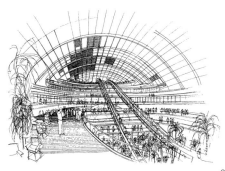

Greater London Authority Headquarters
London, England 1998–2002

The Greater London Authority Headquarters is one of the capital's most symbolically important new projects. The new building expresses the transparency of the democratic process and demonstrates the potential for a wholly sustainable, virtually non-polluting public building.

The headquarters occupies a prominent site on the Thames beside Tower Bridge. It houses an Assembly chamber, committee rooms and public facilities, together with offices for the Mayor, Assembly members, the Mayor's cabinet and support staff, providing 18,000 square metres of accommodation on ten levels.

The Assembly chamber faces north across the river to the Tower of London, its glass enclosure allowing Londoners to watch the Assembly at work. Members of the public are also invited to share the building: a flexible space on the top floor – 'London's Living Room' – can be used for exhibitions or functions, and the public commands the rooftop, where a terrace offers unparalleled views across London. At the base is a piazza with a café, from which the riverside can be enjoyed. Lifts and gentle ramps allow universal access throughout the building.

The building has been designed so that it has no front or back in conventional terms. Its shape is derived from a geometrically modified sphere, developed using computer modelling techniques.

This form achieves optimum energy performance by minimising the surface area exposed to direct sunlight. Analysis of sunlight patterns throughout the year produced a thermal map of the building's surface, which is expressed in its cladding.

A range of active and passive shading devices is employed: to the south the building leans back so that its floor-plates step inwards to provide shading for the naturally ventilated offices; and the building's cooling systems utilise ground water pumped up via boreholes from the water table. These energy-saving techniques mean that chillers will not be needed and that for most of the year the building will require no additional heating. Overall, it will use only a quarter of the energy consumed by a typical air-conditioned office building.

The building is located within the Southwark Riverside Masterplan, which covers a 5.5-hectare area between London Bridge and Tower Bridge. The practice is designing all nine buildings in what is the largest commercial development in London in the last fifteen years. The masterplan establishes a streetscape with two major new public squares for London and provides amenities including shops, restaurants, cafés and a hotel. It includes five large office buildings, which together comprise 93,000 square metres of high-quality lettable space.

1. Visualisation of the completed Southwark Riverside Masterplan.
2, 3. Visualisations of the Greater London Authority Headquarters: the exterior seen from the south bank of the Thames, looking towards Tower Bridge, and the flask-shaped Assembly chamber, with spiralling public ramp.

1

2

GLA Headquarters
1998–2002
Client
CIT Group
Area
18,000m²
Team
Ove Arup & Partners
Davis Langdon & Everest
Mott Green & Wall
Claude R Engle Lighting

Southwark Riverside Masterplan
1998–2007
Client
CIT Group
Site Area
5.5 hectares
Team
Ove Arup & Partners
Davis Langdon & Everest
Townshend Landscape Architects
Equation Lighting Design
Fountain Workshop

Paragon Research and Development Centre
Woking, England 1998–2002

Client
TAG McLaren Holdings
Area
60,000m²
Team
Arlington Securities
Ove Arup & Partners
Schmidt Reuter Partner
Davis Langdon & Everest
Terence O'Rourke
WSP
Intec Management
Claude R Engle Lighting
Atelier Dreiseitl

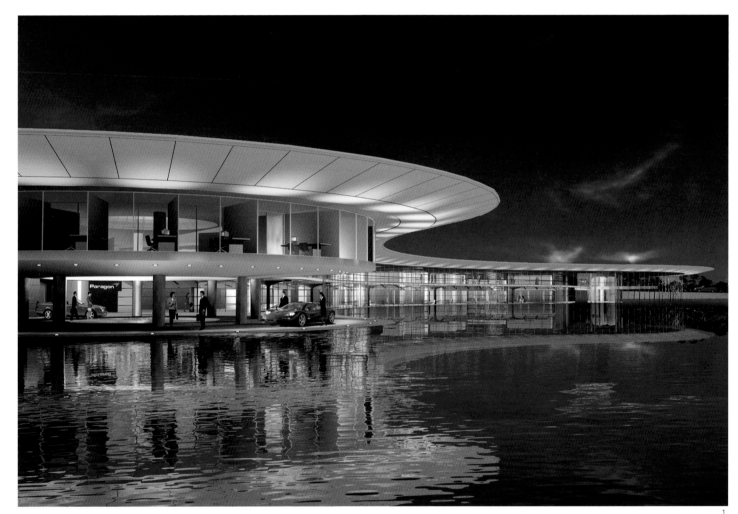

1

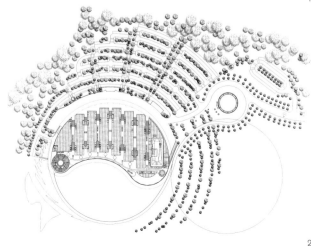

2

The TAG McLaren Group is a collection of high-tech companies involved in the design and development of Formula One cars, high-performance road cars, electronic systems and composite materials. Since McLaren began competing in Formula One in 1966, it has established a global reputation as one of the most successful teams in the history of the sport.

The Paragon Research and Development Centre provides a headquarters for the group's 850 staff. It includes design studios, laboratories and testing and production facilities for Formula One and road cars, including the Mercedes-Benz SLR McLaren.

Internally, the building is organised around double-height linear 'streets', which form circulation routes and articulate 'fingers' of flexible accommodation. These house production and storage areas on the lower levels, with design studios, offices and meeting rooms above.

Viewed on plan, the building is roughly semi-circular, the circle being completed by a formal lake, which forms an integral part of the building's cooling system. The principal lakeside facade is a continuous curved glass wall, shaded by a cantilevered roof. Directly behind the facade a circulation 'boulevard' leads to areas for hospitality and to the staff restaurant, both of which look out across the landscape beyond. Other social facilities include shopping galleries, a swimming pool and a fitness centre.

A Visitor Centre with educational facilities is located in a separate building at the entrance to the complex. This two-storey structure is buried underground – like the rest of the Research Centre it is designed to make a minimal intervention in the landscape – and is visible only by its circular rooflight. It houses a temporary exhibition space and lecture theatre and is linked to the main centre by a subterranean building with a permanent display of McLaren's historical racing and road cars.

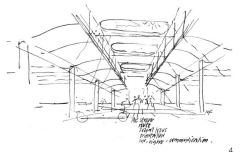

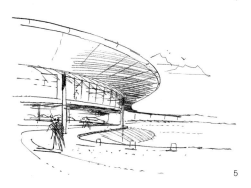

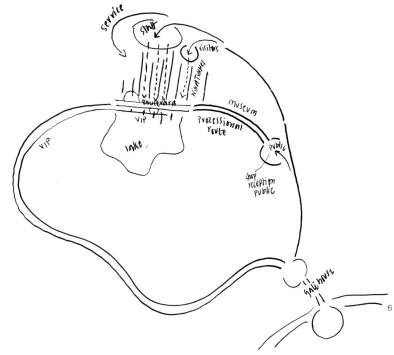

1, 3. Visualisations of the curving glass facade overlooking the lake, and of the circulation boulevard.
2. Site plan.
4–6. Concept sketches by Norman Foster exploring the form of the internal street and the building's siting with respect to the lake.

Petronas University of Technology
Malaysia 1998–2004

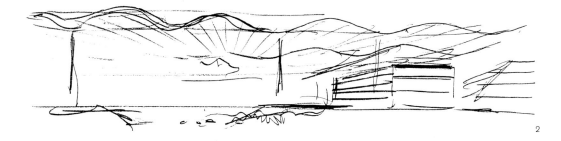

1. Aerial view of
the site model.
2. Concept sketch
by Norman Foster.
3, 4. Views of the model,
showing the arrangement
of the accommodation
beneath a curving canopy.
5. Panorama of the site
under construction.

Client
Universiti Teknologi
Petronas
Site Area
450 hectares
Team
GDP Architects
Ove Arup & Partners
Roger Preston & Partners
Majutek Perunding
Research Facilities Design
Schumann Smith Ltd

Sandy Brown Associates
Majid & Associates
BDG McColl
HSS Integrated
Jurukur Bahan Malaysia
KPK
KLCCB
Ranhill Bersekutu
Shah P K & Associates
Vision Design
Marshall Day Acoustics

This new technological university in Malaysia will be the region's largest academic centre for the study of civil, mechanical, chemical and electrical engineering. Most of the funding for the project comes from the Malaysian oil company Petronas.

The complex emerges from a dense jungle some 300 kilometres north of the capital, Kuala Lumpur. The 450-hectare site is characterised by steep hills and lakes formed by flooded disused tin mines. In the monsoon season the skies open every afternoon to flood the place with torrential rain; yet it can also be intensely hot in the sun. The design responds to the physical landscape of the site and to this cycle of alternate scorching and soaking by the elements.

Pedestrian routes meander along the edge of the jungle, protected by a soaring curved roof – held aloft by tall columns – which encircles a central landscaped park. Students will be able to stroll through shaded gardens or contemplate heavy downpours from the protection of this great canopy.

Around the park, a perimeter deck gives access to laboratories, lecture theatres, shops and communal facilities. These are contained in four-storey blocks, tucked under the edges of the canopy. Decking extends from this accommodation out of the park, leading to blocks of housing and other student facilities.

A resource centre in the form of a large drum marks the entrance to the campus. This building houses the University library, containing half a million books, and the main hall – a multi-purpose theatre capable of seating 3,000 people. The resource centre forms the chief social hub of the University, with cafés spilling out onto the circular plaza at its centre.

Future expansion will provide a large sports stadium and a mosque – amenities that will be shared with the residents of a new town planned adjacent to the campus.

3

4

5

Grandstand, Newbury Racecourse
Newbury, England 1999–2000

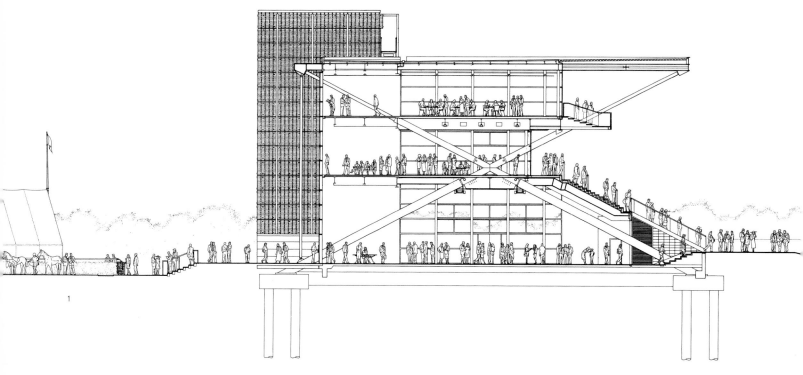

1

The new grandstand at Newbury Racecourse replaces two outdated early-twentieth-century stands located in the Tattersall's enclosure. It provides Newbury with the range and quality of amenities expected by modern race-goers.

The building has a simple, highly efficient and economical structure based on six X-shaped frames. These support three sets of terraces facing the racecourse, with tiered balconies above. The structure is freely expressed and serves as a striking symbol of Newbury's process of regeneration.

Unlike its predecessors, the new building offers excellent views of both the racecourse and paddock and provides clear circulation and wheelchair access. Movement between the parade ring and the racecourse has been considerably improved to ease the passage of up to 25,000 spectators from one area to the other between races, which typically take place every 30 minutes.

The grandstand offers extensive facilities, including a restaurant, a bar and a flexible ground-floor betting hall. These can all be used on non-race days for exhibitions, conferences and corporate entertainment.

The restaurant can accommodate up to 600 people, who can move easily onto the adjacent tiered balconies to view races without changing level. The bar also enjoys a broad panoramic view of the course.

Entrances to the ground floor are located on all four sides of the building to ensure maximum permeability in an extremely busy environment. To avoid congestion in the betting hall and in the bar and restaurant on the upper floors, all core elements – lifts, stairs, lavatories and services – have been compressed into a single spine running along the northern edge of the building. One bay in the spine is articulated to mark the main entrance and reception area.

Maximum use is made of natural light in the public spaces, aiding user orientation and minimising energy consumption. A canopy over the south-facing terraces, bar and restaurant shades spectators from the sun and prevents the risk of glare from the building's glazing, which might otherwise distract horses and jockeys.

1. Cross-section showing the X-shaped structural frames.
2–4. Views of the grandstand on race days.

Client
Newbury Racecourse Plc
Area
6,900m²
Team
Whitby Bird and Partners
Roger Preston & Partners
Montagu Evans
Davis Langdon & Everest
Heery International Ltd

2

3

4

Albion Wharf Development
London, England 1999–2003

The development of Albion Wharf reinforces a growing new community on the south bank of the Thames, alongside the Foster studio between Battersea and Albert bridges. A mixed-use development, its ingredients are designed to promote a lively urban quarter where people can live, work and enjoy life in the city.

The scheme comprises three separate buildings linked by new public spaces and routes. Shops, business spaces, cafés and leisure facilities are grouped at ground level, with parking below and residences, including low-cost housing, above.

The principal building on the waterfront is eleven storeys high. Its massing is designed to respect the heights of neighbouring buildings and to frame the view of the river from the opposite bank. The building arcs back from the river's edge in an asymmetrical crescent to create a public space alongside the river walk.

The facades are principally of glass, used in a range of translucency to create elevations which vary in appearance and sparkle according to prevailing light conditions and changing viewpoints. On the river facade, curved balconies with clear glass balustrades are accessed through full-height sliding glazed panels, which allow the apartments to open out onto the water. The strong horizontal line of the balconies reinforces a sense of visual order, allowing the clutter of inhabitation to proliferate but not dominate.

The southern facade is expressed as a veil of aluminium rods, which forms a rain-screen in front of a metal and glass weathering layer. The roof continues the building's curving form, appearing to wrap over and around in a single sweep.

2

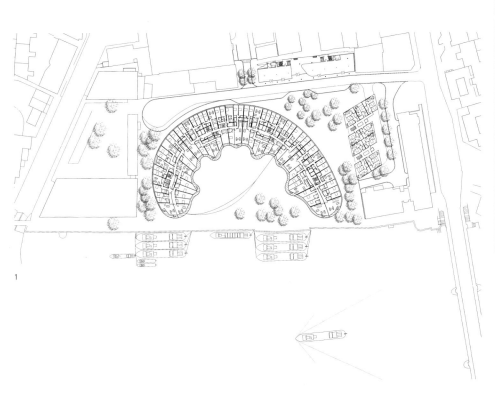

1

Client
Hutchison Whampoa
Property
Area
30,000m²
Team
Ove Arup & Partners
Davis Langdon & Everest
Exterior International Plc
CM International
Jolyon Drury Consultancy
Townshend Landscape
Architects

1. Site plan.
2. Visualisation from
Chelsea Embankment
showing the completed
buildings alongside
Foster and Partners'
studio to the left.

Chesa Futura
St Moritz, Switzerland 2000–2002

Client
Sisa AG
Area
4,650m²
Team
Ove Arup & Partners
Davis Langdon & Everest
Edy Toscano AG
Peter Walker & Partners
Emmer Pfenninger
Partner AG
EN/ES/TE AG
R & B Engineering GmbH

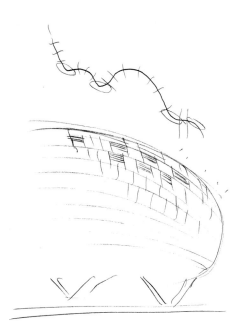

The Chesa Futura apartment building in the Engadin Valley fuses state-of-the-art computer design tools and traditional, indigenous building techniques to create an environmentally sensitive building. Although its form is novel, it utilises timber construction – one of the oldest, most environmentally benign and sustainable forms of building.

In Switzerland, building in timber is particularly appropriate: it follows indigenous architectural traditions and contributes to a local foresting practice of harvesting older trees to encourage regeneration. Furthermore, timber is a renewable resource, it absorbs carbon dioxide as it is growing and, if local wood is used, little energy is consumed in transporting it. The larch shingles that make up the building's skin will respond to weather, changing colour over time, and appear as an organic part of the landscape.

The building consists of three storeys of apartments and an underground level for car-parking, plant and storage. Its bubble-like form responds to its location and local weather conditions. The site is small but is spectacularly located on the edge of a slope, looking down over the village towards a lake. The curved form allows windows to wrap around the facade, providing panoramic views of the lake and surrounding mountains. On the south facade are balconies which benefit from sunlight, while the colder north facade facing the mountain is closed, providing insulation through its thermal mass.

To maximise views the building has been lifted above the ground on eight pilotis. In Switzerland, where snow lies on the ground for many months of the year, there is a long tradition of elevating buildings clear of the ground to avoid the danger of wood rotting due to prolonged exposure to moisture. This light footprint is expressed in the landscaping concept which will reinstate the rocky texture and scale of the mountain terrain beneath the building.

2

3

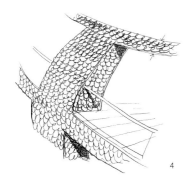

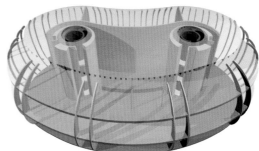

1. Facade study
by Norman Foster.
2, 3. Visualisations
of the Chesa Futura
on its mountainside site.
4, 5. Norman Foster's
sketches of the building's
larch-shingle skin.
6, 7. Visualisation showing
the building's bubble form.

Cisco Systems Office Campus
Munich, Germany 2000–2003

The concept of highly flexible, tray-like office floors contained within an independent skin – first explored in the Climatroffice project with Buckminster Fuller in the 1970s – has found an echo in this masterplan for a German office campus for Cisco Systems. It is a response to the volatile nature of the Internet industries, for which Cisco Systems is the world's largest supplier of hardware.

The masterplan is designed to allow Cisco to develop the site in four to ten separate phases and to occupy all the resulting spaces, or let any of them to other companies. The planning of individual buildings allows for separate entrances, security arrangements and identities to facilitate the multi-tenancy scenario, or for a unified identity if Cisco is the sole occupant. Four buildings will be completed in the first phase, for which the practice is designing the complete environment, from the buildings and their interiors to the landscaping.

The campus is designed around a central garden that acts like a village green – a focus for social activities. All the offices are accessed via an encircling road and all car-parking is underground, leaving the centre of the campus free for pedestrians.

The landscaping exploits the high water table, with lakes in the central garden and canals parallel to the buildings, which are bridged with wooden decking. Social facilities include a canteen, gymnasium, café and crèche.

Each three-storey building has two or three fingers of office accommodation linked by glazed atria, which bring natural light to all levels. Solar gain is avoided through the use of external shading devices. The buildings are naturally ventilated with openable windows located above head height; this ensures that air can circulate freely throughout the offices without disturbing those seated closest to the windows. The thermal mass of the concrete structure is used to cool the buildings, working in combination with ground water, which is pumped through pipes embedded in the floor-slabs. These passive energy-saving features will result in carbon dioxide emissions one-third lower than a German-standard office building, and running costs half those of a conventional air-conditioned building.

1, 3. Two views of the model, showing a single unit of accommodation and a group of ten potential units arranged around a central green.
2. Perspective drawing showing the 'fingers' of accommodation with open tray-like floors, linked by glazed atria.

2

3

Client
Cisco Systems
Masterplan Area
115,000m²
Team
Bovis Lend Lease
Davis Langdon & Everest
Sailer Stepan & Partner
Schmidt Reuter Partner
Emmer Pfenninger
Partner AG
Brandschutzplanung
Klingsch
Ove Arup & Partners
Höhler & Partner

London City Racecourse
London, England 2000–2004

Client
Wiggins Group Plc
Area
70,000m²
Team
Adams Kara Taylor
The Landscape Partnership
Cyril Sweett
WSP Environmental
Ecological Services Ltd
Buchanan

1, 2. Views of the
model, showing the
grandstand as seen
from the racecourse.
3. Site plan of the
racecourse.

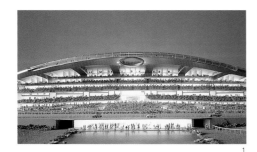

The establishment in the north-east of London of England's first new racecourse since 1927 provided the opportunity for a comprehensive rethink of the layout and design of contemporary racecourse facilities.

Many racecourses have grown up over time, usually with buildings added and distributed in a haphazard fashion. Typically, an ad hoc placement of stables, saddling boxes and the winners' enclosure at a distance from the main grandstand has led to a frustrating experience for both participants and race-goers. This new race-course, by contrast, sets out to fulfil the needs and expectations of the racing fraternity.

The form of the grandstand is generated by the logical concentration of spectators around the home stretch and the finishing line. It will be possible to watch every aspect of the racing ritual from within the building – either from one of the stepped terraces or from the comfort of a table in one of the restaurants on the upper levels.

The stables are positioned directly opposite the grandstand to allow spectators to see the horses' route to the parade ring, which is sunk into the ground in front of the terraces, forming a natural amphitheatre.

The grandstand accommodates half of the course's 20,000 capacity. The organic, curving form of its metallic roof swells and tapers along its length. This cantilevered structure shelters the spectators and the parade ring. The curve of the roof also reflects sound into the interior, allowing spectators in the restaurants and bars to share the excitement of the racing experience. The other buildings on the site – stables, a crèche and a fitness club – share the roof's curved form.

Visitors will also be able to watch races from a viewing area within the roof, reached by lifts in the building's structural cores. This space will be open to all members of the public, inverting the hierarchy of spectator accommodation found at most racecourses.

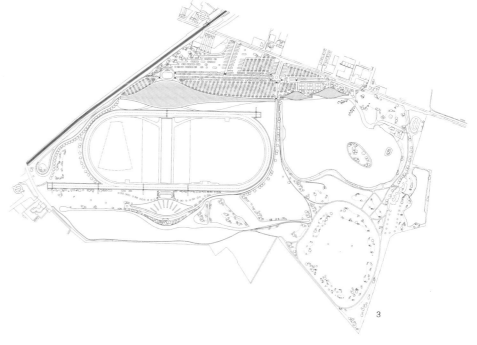

The Studio

Norman Foster:

'The tempo of the studio changes by the week, the day and the hour. The bar is a lively meeting place from early breakfast-time, through lunch to evening drinks. Smaller groups might gather in the early hours, as the office is open twenty-four hours a day, seven days a week…'

'…From the very beginning, our studio has been open to scrutiny. Meetings, whether formal or informal, take place in the midst of the creative process itself…'

232

'…Riverside is virtually a self-contained world with its own printing shop and photographic studio…'

'…In the main studio almost everyone has a place at one of the long benches – directors, students, partners, model-makers, computer operators, secretaries and architects.'

'…There are no pressures or rewards for working antisocial hours; preferences and attitudes vary between individuals and this is reflected in a degree of choice – the important thing is that people are together when they need to be…'

'Two crucial
characteristics of
the studio and the
way that we work
are the democracy
and freedom of
communication
that we enjoy…'

'…It is a very young
office – the average
age is around thirty,
and you can hear as
many languages
spoken. It is so
cosmopolitan that I
sometimes joke that
it is another country.
You do not need a
passport to visit us
but we do have our
own currency – the
"Foster dollars" that
we exchange at our
long bar…'

'…The essence of
the spaces has
always been about
lifestyle and
communication…'

'…For me, Riverside
is a rare combination
of a wonderful team
and a great place
to work.'

'…Although design
is centralised in the
London studio and
management flows
out from there, it is
impossible to think
of the practice in
isolation from the
network of project
offices around the
world. The dynamic
of Riverside is rooted
in the interaction
between different
places and cultures…'

Biographies

Norman Foster graduated from Manchester University School of Architecture and City Planning in 1961 and won a Fellowship to Yale University where he gained a Master's degree in architecture.

In 1963 he co-founded Team 4 with Richard Rogers and in 1967 he established Foster Associates, now known as Foster and Partners. The practice has project offices worldwide with its main studio in London. It has received over 220 awards and citations for excellence and won over 50 national and international competitions.

He was awarded the RIBA Royal Gold Medal for Architecture in 1983, the Gold Medal of the French Academy of Architecture in 1991 and the American Institute of Architects Gold Medal in 1994. Also in 1994, he was appointed Officer of the Order of Arts and Letters by the Ministry of Culture in France. In 1999 he became the 21st Pritzker Architecture Prize Laureate. He was granted a knighthood in the Queen's Birthday Honours of 1990, appointed by the Queen to the Order of Merit in 1997 and in 1999 was honoured with a life peerage, taking the title Lord Foster of Thames Bank.

He has lectured throughout the world and taught architecture in the United Sates and the United Kingdom. He has been vice president of the Architectural Association in London, council member of the Royal College of Art, a member of the Board of Education and visiting examiner for the Royal Institute of British Architects, and is a trustee of the Architecture Foundation of London.

Spencer de Grey studied architecture at Cambridge University. As a student he worked on a competition entry for a new city at Espoo in Finland that was highly placed in a large entry. On leaving Cambridge in 1969, he worked for the London Borough of Merton on one of the first middle schools in the country.

He joined Foster Associates in 1973, continuing his work in education on the Palmerston Special School in Liverpool. He then worked on the Hammersmith Centre before, in 1979, setting up Foster Associates' office in Hong Kong to build the Hongkong and Shanghai Bank. In 1981 he returned to London to become the director in charge of Stansted Airport, which he saw through to completion in 1991. During this period, he also worked on the BBC Radio Centre and was responsible for the Sackler Galleries at the Royal Academy of Arts in London.

Since becoming a partner in 1991, he has overseen a wide range of projects, including Cambridge Law Faculty, the Commerzbank Headquarters in Frankfurt, the Great Court at the British Museum, the Great Glasshouse at the National Botanic Garden of Wales, the World Squares for All Masterplan for London and Boston Museum of Fine Arts Masterplan.

He lectures widely at locations such as the Louvre in Paris and the RIBA in London, is a trustee for the Royal Botanical Gardens in Kew and a governor of the Building Centre Trust, and is also on the board of London First. He was made a CBE in the Queen's Birthday Honours of 1997.

David Nelson studied three-dimensional design at Loughborough College of Art and Hornsey College of Art, specialising in furniture and industrial design, before gaining a Master's degree at the Royal College of Art Environmental Design School. In 1974 he received a travelling scholarship to study town planning in northern Italy.

He began working at Foster Associates in 1976, and some of his most important early projects included the Sainsbury Centre for Visual Arts and the Hammersmith Centre. In 1979 he joined the Hongkong and Shanghai Bank team, initially taking responsibility for internal systems design, then acting as design coordinator and finally sharing joint responsibility for the project. He was made a director of Foster Associates in 1984.

He returned to London in 1986 and was the director responsible for the American Air Museum at Duxford, Century Tower in Tokyo and many other projects in Asia, Europe, Australia and the United States. Becoming a partner in 1991, he has worked on several projects in Germany and was the partner responsible for the New German Parliament in the Reichstag, Berlin. He has also overseen a number of transport projects, including Bilbao Metro in Spain, and North Greenwich Transport Interchange and Canary Wharf Underground Station in London. Recent work includes the Center for Clinical Science Research at Stanford University, Petronas University of Technology in Malaysia and the Paragon Research Centre for TAG McLaren.

Graham Phillips studied architecture at Liverpool University. As a student he received an RIBA Award for the best Part 1 work countrywide. He spent his year out working in Toronto, Canada, and graduated with first class honours in 1971. After leaving Liverpool he joined Ove Arup & Partners in London as part of a multi-disciplinary team.

He began work at Foster Associates in 1975, taking charge of IBM Technical Park at Greenford and developing special skills in the field of project management, cost control and contract administration. He was involved at the inception of the Hongkong and Shanghai Bank project in 1979 and became a resident director in Hong Kong in 1980, playing a key role in the management of the project and the practice's Hong Kong office. Whilst in Hong Kong he qualified as an Authorised Person.

On his return to London in 1986 he became involved in the overall management of the practice and was also responsible for the design of projects for Sir Robert and Lady Sainsbury at the University of East Anglia. He was made a partner in 1991 and returned to Hong Kong as part of the Hong Kong International Airport competition team.

Since returning from Hong Kong in 1993 he has continued as managing director of the practice, involved not only in its worldwide business and management aspects but also in maintaining the highest design standards.

His own house, 'Skywood', won an RIBA Award in 1999 and was nominated for a Mies van der Rohe Foundation Award in 2000.

Ken Shuttleworth studied at the City of Leicester Polytechnic School of Architecture, where he received a diploma in architecture with distinction in 1977. He first worked at Foster Associates in 1974 as a team member on the Willis Faber & Dumas project. After an architectural study tour of the United States and Canada, he returned to the practice in 1977 to work on the IBM Technical Park at Greenford and the Hammersmith Centre.

In 1979 he began work on the Hongkong and Shanghai Bank, moving to Hong Kong and taking responsibility for all aspects of design from inception to completion. He was appointed a director of Foster and Partners in 1984 and became a partner in 1991.

Since his return from Hong Kong in 1986 he has worked on the design of many projects including the Torre de Collserola telecommunications tower in Barcelona, the ITN Headquarters in London, King's Cross Masterplan in London, the Carré d'Art in Nîmes, Valencia Congress Centre in Spain and Cranfield University Library in Bedfordshire. Recent projects include the new international airport in Hong Kong and the Al Faisaliah Complex in Riyadh and, in London, the Millennium Bridge, Citibank Headquarters in Canary Wharf and the London Bridge City development.

In 1994 he received an honorary doctorate at De Montfort University. He has also written a column for 'New Builder' magazine and is a member of the editorial board of 'Building' magazine.

Stefan Behling received his diploma from the University of Aachen in Germany. He joined Foster Associates in 1987, became a director in 1996 and is also joint managing director of the practice's German offices. An expert in ecology and energy conservation, he has worked on a number of projects that have pioneered new techniques for energy management, including the Microelectronic Park and the Inner Harbour Masterplan at Duisburg, the New German Parliament in the Reichstag, Berlin and the Commerzbank Headquarters in Frankfurt. Recent projects include the Greater London Authority Head-quarters in London, the Free University of Berlin, the Headquarters for Cisco Systems in Munich and the Paragon Research Centre for TAG McLaren in Woking.

Since 1995 he has been a professor of Building Construction at the University of Stuttgart. He has led several research projects funded by the European Commission in the field of solar energy, and published two books: 'Sol Power', written with his wife Sophia, which deals with solar energy in architecture; and 'Glass: Structure and Technology'.

Grant Brooker studied architecture at Canterbury in England and joined Foster Associates in 1987. He was the project architect responsible for the award-winning ITN Headquarters in London and went on to work on numerous projects and competitions in Europe, including the Musée de Préhistoire at Verdon, a masterplan for Edinburgh and projects for rail stations in Bilbao and Helsinki.

In 1992 he moved to Hong Kong to establish and lead the design team for the new airport at Chek Lap Kok. From 1992 to 1997 he was resident director in Hong Kong, where he also held regional responsibilities and was involved in the Kowloon-Canton Railway Terminal, the HACTL Superterminal and Ground Transportation Centre at Hong Kong Airport and office projects in Malaysia, Singapore, and Guangzhou in China.

On returning to London in 1997 he became a director of the practice. Since then he has overseen Foster and Partners' first two completed buildings in the City of London at Finsbury Square and Wood Street, and continues to develop the practice's portfolio of office, commercial and masterplanning work.

Iain Godwin was educated as a town planner in Liverpool and went on to work in CAD and IT management on a variety of masterplanning projects in Manchester, as well as becoming project leader for the 1996 and 2000 Manchester Olympic bid documents.

He joined Foster and Partners in 1995 and became a director in 2000. He is responsible for all the practice's IT systems worldwide, including CAD, Internet and Intranet, and the establishment of a global area network. He has set up a specialist visualisation group to create high-quality presentation images and animations and has instigated a specialist modelling group to develop methodologies for the use of complex 3D geometry from design through to fabrication and construction.

He has lectured on a range of IT-based subjects relevant to the construction industry and sat on a number of construction industry committees, including the Construction Industry Gateway Steering Committee. He is currently vice chairman of the VR Centre for the Built Environment at the Bartlett School of Architecture, London, and chairman of the SER Document Management User Group.

Brandon Haw graduated from London University in 1982, going on to live and work in New York, where he gained a Master's degree at Princeton while undertaking freelance design and construction work in Manhattan. He later worked for Skidmore, Owings and Merrill and HOK. In 1987 he joined Foster Associates in London, working on a number of projects, including the King's Cross Masterplan, the award-winning ITN Headquarters and an office development at London Wall, as well as the competition-winning entry for Hong Kong International Airport and a masterplan project in Barcelona.

In 1992 he began work on Commerzbank Headquarters in Frankfurt, becoming one of the resident directors in charge of delivering construction documentation for tender. Returning to London in 1994, he became a director of the practice in 1995 and has been responsible for a number of skyscrapers, including the Al Faisaliah Complex in Riyadh, Saudi Arabia, and the Citibank and HSBC World Headquarters, both at Canary Wharf in London. He is currently working on major office developments in New York and Chicago.

Paul Kalkhoven studied architecture and town planning at the Technical University of Delft in The Netherlands and went on to join MacCormac, Jamieson and Prichard in London in 1980, where he was involved in projects for student residences at Worcester College, Oxford, and the extension of the Arts Faculty at the University of Bristol.

He joined Foster and Partners in 1985, working on the Katharine Hamnett shop and on Stansted Airport. Becoming project director in 1991 and then director in 1995, he worked on a number of transport projects, including an international railway terminal and concourse building at St Pancras in London and competition entries for Shanghai and Guangzhou international airports, both in China.

His many projects in Northern Europe include the Commerzbank Headquarters in Frankfurt, Essen Design Centre, the Agiplan Headquarters extension in Mülheim, the World Port Centre in Rotterdam, various projects in Duisburg and the competition-winning design for the Gerling Ring mixed-use development in Cologne.

Mouzhan Majidi studied architecture at Strathclyde University, receiving an RIBA Part 1 Design Award in 1985 and the RIBA Silver Medal for the best diploma project countrywide in 1987. After graduating with first class honours in 1987 he joined Foster Associates and took charge of fit-out contracts and planning coordination for Stansted Airport. He went on to become project architect of two competition-winning schemes – Cambridge University Law Faculty and the Lycée Albert Camus in Fréjus.

Following his involvement in the successful competition entry for Hong Kong International Airport he moved to Hong Kong at the start of the project in April 1992, becoming a director of Foster Asia and one of the directors responsible for designing the airport terminal. He also oversaw other buildings on the airport site, including the HACTL Super-terminal and Ground Transportation Centre.

Since his return to London, Mouzhan has been working on Wembley Stadium and is a member of the Joint Venture Board of the World Stadium Team. He became a director of the practice in 1998.

Andrew Miller studied at the environmental department of Gloucestershire College of Art and Design. On graduating in 1981 he worked at Yorke Rosenberg Mardall in Hong Kong, before joining Foster Associates in 1983 to work on the Hongkong and Shanghai Bank.

He moved to the London office in 1987 and began work on Century Tower in Tokyo, leading to his relocation in 1988 to the new Tokyo office, where he oversaw the design and on-site coordination of the tower from commencement to completion. He became resident director of Foster Japan in 1992 and a board member of Foster Asia in 1993 and has worked on many East Asian projects, including a masterplan for Yokohama Basin, the Tokyo Millennium Tower project, Oita Stadium in Japan and the Jiushi Corporation Headquarters in Shanghai.

On his return to London in July 1996 he became a director of the practice. Since then he has been responsible for the design development of the London Millennium Tower and continues to oversee projects in Asia including the Supreme Court, Singapore and Petronas University of Technology in Malaysia.

Robin Partington studied architecture at Liverpool University before joining Foster Associates in 1984. He has worked on an extremely broad range of projects, including communications – the Torre de Collserola in Barcelona, the Santiago de Compostela telecommunications facility, also in Spain, the ITN Headquarters in London and Televisa Headquarters in Mexico City; and cultural projects – the Carré d'Art in Nîmes and the American Air Museum at Duxford. They have ranged in scale from private houses in Japan, London and Corsica to the new international airport at Chek Lap Kok in Hong Kong.

As a director of the practice since 1992 he has continued to work on a variety of projects. These have included a number of skyscrapers – he shared responsibility for the Commerzbank Headquarters in Frankfurt, oversaw the ARAG Headquarters in Düsseldorf, where he was in charge of the Foster Düsseldorf office, and is director in charge of the Swiss Re Headquarters in London, with responsibility for the design development of the project.

John Silver studied at the Bartlett School of Architecture, University College London, graduating with first class honours in 1982 and gaining his postgraduate diploma in 1984. In 1982 he joined Yorke Rosenberg Mardall as an assistant designer on various projects at Gatwick Airport and spent six months working for building contractors McLaughlin and Harvey as a site engineer. His entry for the RIBA Sinclair Research Centre Student Competition was exhibited at the Royal Academy of Arts in London in 1984.

He joined Foster and Partners in the same year and has worked on numerous projects, acting as project director on Stansted Airport, the Lycée Albert Camus in Fréjus, Cambridge Law Faculty, the Commerzbank Headquarters in Frankfurt and the Sackler Galleries at the Royal Academy of Arts in London. As a director of the practice since 1994, he has been responsible, amongst other projects, for the ASPIRE National Training Centre in North London, the Electronic Arts European Headquarters in Chertsey, private residential projects and City of London office buildings at Holborn Place and Tower Place.

Mark Sutcliffe studied architecture at London Polytechnic before joining Team 4 in 1963, working on Reliance Controls in Swindon. After completing his studies and a period with Albert Kahn Associates in Detroit he worked at the Greater London Council and London Borough of Camden on residential and education projects. He returned to Foster Associates in 1969 as project architect for the IBM Pilot Head Office, Cosham and went on to lead the Willis Faber & Dumas project.

In 1976 he became a freelance architect specialising in project management. He rejoined Foster Associates in 1983 as the director responsible for BBC Radio Centre.

From 1987 he worked in private practice for clients including Marks & Spencer, before rejoining Foster and Partners in 1992 as a resident director on the Commerzbank Headquarters in Frankfurt. In the same year he became a director of the practice. Following a management role on the Valencia Congress Centre, he divided his time between London and Berlin, providing management support to the Reichstag team. He directs a number of projects, including offices for Hines in Warsaw.

Complete Works

Banks
HSBC Headquarters, London,
England 1997–2002, *195*
Citibank Headquarters, London
England 1996–2000, *194*
Emirates Bank Headquarters,
Dubai 1995
Credit du Nord Headquarters,
Paris, France 1993
World Trade Centre, Berlin, Germany 1992
Commerzbank Headquarters,
Frankfurt, Germany 1991–1997, *102*
Hongkong and Shanghai Bank
Headquarters, Hong Kong 1979–1986, *42*

Bridges
Millennium Bridge, London,
England 1996–2000, *180*
Arsta Bridge, Stockholm,
Sweden 1995–2003
Millau Viaduct, Gorge du Tarn,
France 1993–2005, *139*
Oresund Bridge, Sweden-Denmark 1993
Spandau Bridge, Berlin, Germany 1992
Viaduct, Rennes, France 1991–2000
Pont du Medoc, Bordeaux, France 1991
Pont de la Fourvière, Lyon, France 1991
Pont d'Austerlitz, Paris, France 1988

Civic Realm
World Squares for All, London,
England 1996–2002, *188*
National Police Memorial, London,
England 1993–2002
Porte Maillot Masterplan, Paris,
France 1993
Masterplan, Lüdenscheid, Germany 1992
Masterplan, Berlin, Germany 1990
Masterplan, Nîmes, France 1990
Statue Square Masterplan,
Hong Kong 1980

Communication
NTT Broadcasting Centre,
Nagano, Japan 1995
Multimedia Centre, Hamburg,
Germany 1995–1999, *166*
Telecommunications Facility, Santiago
de Compostela, Spain 1994, *84*
Torre de Collserola, Barcelona,
Spain 1988–1992, *84*
ITN Headquarters, London,
England 1988–1990, *78*
Bunka Radio Station, Tokyo, Japan 1987
Televisa Headquarters, Mexico City,
Mexico 1986, *62*
BBC Radio Centre, London,
England 1982–1985, *52*

Conference
Convention Centre, Perth, Australia 2000
Scottish Exhibition and Conference Centre,
Glasgow, Scotland 1995–1997, *160*

Congress Centre, Valencia, Spain
1993–1998, *142*
Villepinte Exhibition Halls, Paris,
France 1993
Convention and Exhibition Centre,
Hong Kong 1993
Congress Hall, San Sebastian, Spain 1990
Trade Fair Centre, Berlin, Germany 1990
Congress Hall, Toulouse, France 1989
Knoxville Energy Expo, USA 1978, *28*

Culture
Museum of Fine Arts, Boston
Masterplan, USA 2000–2012

Musée Quai Branly, Paris, France 1999
'Modern Britain 1929–1939' Exhibition,
Design Museum, London, England 1999
Anthony D'Offay Gallery Redevelopment,
London, England 1998–2001
Uffizi Redevelopment, Florence, Italy 1998
Cultural Centre, Dubai 1998, *214*
Music Centre, Gateshead,
England 1997–2002, *202*
Feasibility Study for the Roundhouse,
London, England 1997
Prado Museum Extension,
Madrid, Spain 1996, *174*
The Great Court at the British Museum,
London, England 1994–2000, *156*
Cardiff Bay Opera House, Cardiff, Wales 1994
Centre de la Mémoire, Oradour sur
Glanes, France 1994

National Gallery of Scottish Art,
Glasgow, Scotland 1993
Imperial War Museum, Hartlepool,
England 1993
Musée de Préhistoire des Gorges
du Verdon, Quinson, France
1992–2001, *138*
Design Centre, Essen, Germany
1992–1997, *122*
Addition to Joslyn Art Museum,
Omaha, USA 1992–1994, *118*
Clore Theatre, Imperial College,
London, England 1992
Houston Museum of Fine Arts
Redevelopment, Houston, USA 1992
Crescent Wing, Sainsbury Centre
for Visual Arts, Norwich, England
1988–1991, *82*
Sackler Galleries, Jerusalem,
Israel 1988
American Air Museum, Duxford,
England 1987–1997, *74*
Salle de Spectacles, Nancy,
France 1986
Sackler Galleries, Royal Academy of
Arts, London, England 1985–1991, *60*
Carré d'Art, Nîmes, France
1984–1993, *54*
Whitney Museum Development
Project, New York, USA 1978

Sainsbury Centre for Visual Arts,
Norwich, England 1974–1978, *30*
Floating Theatre, London, England 1972
Samuel Beckett Theatre, St Peter's
College, Oxford, England 1971, *28*

Education and Health
Petronas University of Technology,
Malaysia 1998–2004, *220*
Free University of Berlin,
Germany 1997–2004, *212*
Faculty of Social Studies, University
of Oxford, England 1996–2000, *184*
Faculty of Management, Robert
Gordon University, Aberdeen,
Scotland 1994–1998, *151*
British Library of Political and
Economic Science, London School of
Economics, England 1993–2001, *144*
Forth Valley Community Care Village,
Larbert, Scotland 1993–1995, *150*
School of Physiotherapy, Southampton,
England 1992–1994

Marine Simulator Centre, Rotterdam,
The Netherlands 1992–1993, *114*
Lycée Albert Camus, Fréjus,
France 1991–1993, *100*
Institute of Criminology, University
of Cambridge, England 1991
Faculty of Law, University of
Cambridge, England 1990–1995, *96*
Cranfield University Library,
Cranfield, England 1989–1992, *92*
Students' Union Building,
University College, London,
England 1980

Palmerston Special School,
Liverpool, England 1974–1975
Special Care Unit, Hackney,
London, England 1971–1973
Newport School, Wales 1967, *24*

Government
New Supreme Court, Singapore
2000–2004
Greater London Authority Headquarters,
London, England 1998–2002, *216*
Her Majesty's Treasury Redevelopment,
London, England 1996–2002, *175*
New German Parliament, Reichstag,
Berlin, Germany 1992–1999, *132*
Police Academy, New York, USA 1992
EEC Parliament, Brussels, Belgium 1991
Hôtel du Département, Marseilles,
France 1990

Housing
Chesa Futura, St Moritz, Switzerland
2000–2002, *226*
Housing Development for Rialto,
London, England 1997
Private House, USA 1995
Private House, Germany 1992–1994, *66*
Refurbishment of Mendelsohn
and Chermayeff House, London,
England 1992–1993

Private Houses, Japan 1991
Private House, Corsica 1990–1993, *66*
2nd Avenue Apartments, New York,
USA 1989
Private Houses, Japan 1987–1992, *66*

Autonomous House for Buckminster
Fuller, Los Angeles, USA 1982–1983, *28*
Foster Residence, London,
England 1978–1979
Bean Hill Housing, Milton Keynes,
England 1973–1975
Housing for Wates, Coulsdon,
England 1965 (with Team 4)
Skybreak House and High-Density
Housing, Radlett, England
1965–1966 (with Team 4), *66*
Creek Vean House and Retreat, Feock,
England 1964–1966 (with Team 4), *18*
Forest Road Annexe, East Horsley,
England 1966 (with Team 4)
Murray Mews Houses, London,
England 1965 (with Team 4)
Waterfront Housing, Feock,
England 1964 (with Team 4)

Industrial
Tecno Headquarters Factory,
Valencia, Spain 1992
High Bay Warehouse,
Lüdenscheid, Germany 1992
Billingsgate Fish Market,
London, England 1981
Renault Distribution Centre,
Swindon, England 1980–1982, *44*
IBM Technical Park, Greenford,
England 1975–1980, *34*
Cincinnatti Milacron, USA 1974
German Car Centre, Milton
Keynes, England 1973–1974
Modern Art Glass Warehouse,
Thamesmead, Kent 1972–1973

Factory for SAPA, Tibshelf,
England 1972–1973
Computer Technology Factory, Hemel
Hempstead, England 1970–1971
Pirelli Warehouse 1970
Factory Systems Study 1969, *34*
Reliance Controls Electronics Factory,
Swindon, England 1965–1966
(with Team 4), *20*

Leisure and Sport
London City Racecourse,
London, England 2000–2004, *230*
Sitooterie, Belsay Hall, England 2000

Grandstand, Newbury Racecourse,
Newbury, England 1999–2000, *222*
Wembley Stadium, London,
England 1996–2003, *190*
Great Glasshouse, National Botanic
Garden of Wales, Llanarthne,
Wales 1995–2000, *172*
ASPIRE National Training Centre,
Stanmore, England 1995–1998, *162*
Science World, Bristol, England 1995–1996
Clubhouse, Silverstone Racetrack,
Silverstone, England 1995
Stadium, Oita, Japan 1995
Sealife Centre, Birmingham,
England 1994–1996
Sealife Centre, Blankenberge,
Belgium 1994–1995
Space Discovery Museum, Japan 1994
Grand Stade, Paris, France 1994

Casino-Kursaal, Oostende, Belgium 1994
Tennis Centre, Manchester, England 1993
Mediaeval Centre, Chartres, France 1993
Volcano Theme Park 1992
Stage Set for Paul McCartney 1988
Holiday Inn, The Hague,
The Netherlands 1988
Royal Thames Yacht Club, London,
England 1987
Hotel for La Fondiaria, Florence, Italy 1987
Marina, Battery Park, New York, USA 1986
Athletics Stadium, Frankfurt,
Germany 1981–1986, *50*
Granada Entertainment Centre,
Milton Keynes, England 1979
London Gliding Club, Dunstable
Downs, England 1978
Country Club and Marina for Fred
Olsen, Vestby, Norway 1974
Pavilion Leisure Centres, Knowsley,
England and Badhoevedorp,
The Netherlands 1972

Masterplans
Royal Infirmary, Edinburgh, Scotland 2000
Elephant and Castle, London,
England 2000–2008

Ferensway, Hull, England 1999
Southwark Riverside, London,
England 1998–2007, *216*
Durban, South Africa 1997

Vienna, Austria 1997
Madrid, Spain 1997
Regensburg, Germany 1995
Linz Solar City, Austria 1995
Park BIT Business Park, Mallorca,
Balearic Islands 1994
Lisbon Expo '98, Portugal 1993
Corfu, Greece 1993
Albertopolis, London, England 1993

Gare d'Austerlitz, Paris, France 1993
Brickfields, Kuala Lumpur,
Malaysia 1993
Freising Business Park,
Germany 1992
Atrium Business Park, Berlin,
Germany 1992
Yokohama, Japan 1992
Olympic Bid Masterplan,
Manchester, England 1992
Imperial College, London, England 1992
Wilhelminapier, Rotterdam, The
Netherlands 1991–2010, 114
Inner Harbour, Duisburg,
Germany 1991–2001, 112
Greenwich, London, England 1991
Sagrera, Barcelona, Spain 1991, 98
Neu-Isenburg, Frankfurt,
Germany 1991
Gerland Business Park, Lyon,
France 1990
Bordeaux, France 1990

Cannes, France 1990
City of Cambridge, England 1989
King's Cross, London, England 1987, 68
Paternoster Square, London, England 1987
St Helier Harbour, Jersey,
Channel Islands 1976–1977
Gomera, Canary Islands 1975, 36
Fred Olsen Masterplan, London,
England 1968

Mixed Use
Albion Wharf Development, London,
England 1999–2003, 224
Apartments and Hotel Extension,
Zuoz, Switzerland 1999
Millennium Tower, London,
England 1996, 186
Gerling Ring, Cologne,
Germany 1995–2001, 167
Retail and Office Development,
Zhongshan Guangzhou, China 1994
Al Faisaliah Complex, Riyadh,
Saudi Arabia 1993–2000, 148
Shinagawa Mixed-Use Development,
Tokyo, Japan 1990, 94
Millennium Tower, Tokyo, Japan
1989, 90
Riverside Complex, London, England
1987–1989
Riverside Apartments and Studio,
London, England 1986–1990, 64
Open House Community Project,
Cwmbran, Wales 1978
Fred Olsen Amenity Centre, London,
England 1968–1970, 22

Offices
Demag Headquarters, Düsseldorf,
Germany 2000
Farnborough Business Park Offices,
Farnborough, England 2000–2001
Cisco Systems Office Campus,
Munich, Germany 2000–2003, 228
Walbrook House, London, England 1999
Hines Offices, Warsaw,
Poland 1998–2003

126 Phillip Street, Sydney,
Australia 1996–2005, 187
Swiss Re Headquarters,
London, England 1997–2004, 204
50 Finsbury Square, London,
England 1997–2000, 146
Electronic Arts European Headquarters,
Chertsey, England 1997–2000, 206
J C Decaux International Headquarters,
Brentford, England 1997–2000, 198
100 Wood Street, London, England
1997–2000, 146
Parkview Offices, Singapore 1997
Moor House, London, England 1997
Gresham Street Offices, London,
England 1996–2002
Green Park Offices, Reading,
England 1996–1999, 176
Kingswood Park Offices, Ascot,
England 1996–1998, 176
Bath Road Offices, Slough,
England 1996–1998

Jiushi Corporation Headquarters,
Shanghai, China 1995–2001, 171
World Port Centre, Rotterdam,
The Netherlands 1995–2000, 114
Samsung Motors Office and
Showroom, Korea 1995–1998
Daewoo Electronics Headquarters,
Seoul, Korea 1995, 170
21 Moorfields, London, England 1995
I G Metall Headquarters, Frankfurt,
Germany 1995

Murr Tower, Beirut, Lebanon 1995
LIFFE Offices, London, England 1995
Visions for Europe Offices,
Düsseldorf, Germany 1994
Criterion Place, Leeds, England 1994
ARAG Headquarters, Düsseldorf,
Germany 1993–2001, *145*
Holborn Place, London,
England 1993–2000, *146*
Timex Headquarters, USA 1993
Tower Place, London, England
1992–2002, *136*
British Gas Offices, Thames Valley Park,
Reading, England 1992–1998, *176*
Electricité de France Regional
Headquarters, Bordeaux, France
1992–1996, *121*
Agiplan Headquarters, Mülheim,
Germany 1992–1996, *120*
Obunsha Corporation Headquarters,
Tokyo, Japan 1991–1993

Gateway Building for Spitalfields
Masterplan, London, England 1991
Bosch Headquarters, Frankfurt,
Germany 1991
Sanei Corporation Headquarters,
Makuhari, Japan 1991
St George's Court, London, England 1991
Business Promotion Centre, Duisburg,
Germany 1990–1993, *88*
DS-2 Tower, London, England 1990
Fonta Offices, Toulouse, France 1990

Britannic House Refurbishment,
London, England 1990
Chiswick Park Offices,
London, England 1989
Alpha Building, Isle of Dogs,
London, England 1989
Jacob's Island Offices,
London, England 1989
Microelectronic Centre, Duisburg,
Germany 1988–1996, *88*
Telematic Centre, Duisburg,
Germany 1988–1993, *88*
One London Wall, London,
England 1988
Century Tower, Tokyo,
Japan 1987–1991, *72*
Stockley Park Offices, Uxbridge,
England 1987–1989, *70*
IBM London Computing Centre,
London, England 1985
IBM Pilot Head Office Refit,
Cosham, England 1984–1986
Humana Headquarters,
Louisville, USA 1982
Foster Associates Studio, Great
Portland Street, London, England 1981
Fred Olsen Gate Redevelopment,
Oslo, Norway 1975
Fred Olsen Offices, Vestby, Norway 1974
Willis Faber & Dumas Headquarters,
Ipswich, England 1971–1975, *26*
Foster Associates Studio, Fitzroy
Street, London, England 1971–1972
Climatroffice 1971, *28*
IBM Pilot Head Office, Cosham,
England 1970–1971, *24*
Air-Supported Office for Computer
Technology, Hemel Hempstead,
England 1969–1970
Henrion Studio, London, England
1965 (with Team 4)

Products and Furniture
Saturn Lighting for Iguzzini 2000
Pylons for ENEL, Italy 1999–2000, *140*
NF 98 Door Handles for Fusital 1998

Helit Foster Series Desktop Furniture
1997–2000, *152*

A900 Seating and Table for
Thonet 1997–1999, *80*
Airline Seating System for Vitra
1997–1999, *80*
Oto Track Lighting System for
Artemide 1997–1999
Ra Lighting System for Artemide 1997
Room Control Device for Weidmüller 1997
Bathroom Foster for Duravit and
Hoesch 1996–2001, *178*
Taps for Stella 1995–1999, *178*
Cladding System for Technal 1995
Tray for Alessi 1994–1998, *152*
Library Storage System for Acerbis
1994–1996, *106*
NF 95 Door Furniture for Fusital
1994–1995, *152*
E66 Wind Turbine for Enercon 1993, *140*
Street Lighting for J C Decaux 1993
Tabula Table System for Tecno
1992–1993, *106*
Cladding System for Jansen Vegla
Glass 1991–1992
Airport Desking System 1989–1991, *106*
Street Furniture for J C Decaux 1989
Contract Carpet and Tile Design for
Vorwerk 1988
Kite! Chair for Tecno 1987–1997, *80*
Nomos Desking System for Tecno
1985–1987, *58*
Systems Furniture for Foster
Associates 1981

Research

Clark Center for Biomedical
Research, Stanford University,
Stanford, USA 1999–2003
Paragon Research and
Development Centre, Woking,
England 1998–2002, *218*
Flowers Multi-Disciplinary Research
Building, Imperial College, London,
England 1997–2001
Center for Clinical Science
Research, Stanford University,
Stanford, USA 1995–2000, *168*

Imperial College, Sir Alexander
Fleming Building, London,
England 1994–1998, *154*
Napp Laboratories, Cambridge,
England 1991
Technology Centres, Edinburgh
and Glasgow, Scotland 1989

Retail

Selfridges, London, England 1999–2005
Selfridges, Glasgow, Scotland 1997
Repsol Service Stations, Spain 1997, *196*
Al Faisaliah Shopping Centre, Riyadh,
Saudi Arabia 1993–2000, *128*
Chek Lap Kok Shopping Centre,
Hong Kong International Airport,
Hong Kong 1992–1998, *128*
Cacharel Shops and Franchises,
Europe 1991–1992, *40*

Esprit, London, England 1988, *40*
Savacentre, Southampton, England 1987
Katharine Hamnett, London,
England 1987, *40*
Stansted Airport Shopping Centre,
Stansted, England 1981–1991, *128*
Joseph, London, England 1978, *40*
Fred Olsen Travel Agency, London,
England 1974
Lord's Hill Shopping Centre,
Southampton, England 1973
Orange Hand Boyswear Shops for
Burton Group, England 1972–1973
Pavilion Shopping Centre,
Exeter, England 1971–1972

Transport

Transport Interchange,
Paramatta, Australia 2000
Motorway Signage System 1998
Dresden Station Redevelopment,
Dresden, Germany 1997–2003, *201*
Expo Station, Singapore 1997–2001, *200*
St Pancras International Rail Terminal
and Stratford and Ebbsfleet Channel
Tunnel Stations, England 1996–1997, *68*
North Greenwich Transport
Interchange, London,
England 1995–1998, *164*
Bangkok Airport, Thailand 1994

Ground Transportation Centre, Chek
Lap Kok, Hong Kong 1993–1998
Platform-Edge Screens, Signage and
Furniture for Mass Transit Railway,
Hong Kong 1993–1997
Hong Kong International Airport, Chek
Lap Kok, Hong Kong 1992–1998, *124*
HACTL Superterminal, Chek Lap
Kok, Hong Kong 1992–1998, *130*
Kowloon-Canton Railway Terminal,
Hong Kong 1992–1998, *131*
Solar-Electric Vehicle, London,
England 1992–1994, *117*
Station La Poterie, Rennes, France 1992
Canary Wharf Underground Station,
London, England 1991–1999, *108*
Motoryacht 1991–1993, *116*
British Rail Station, Stansted Airport,
Stansted, England 1989–1991
Heathrow Terminal 5, London, England 1989
Passenger Concourse Building for
British Rail, King's Cross Station,
London, England 1989
Metro System, Bilbao, Spain 1988–1995
and 1997–2004, *86*
City of London Heliport, England 1988

Kansai Airport, Kansai, Japan 1988
Turin Airport, Turin, Italy 1987
Stansted Airport, Stansted,
England 1981–1991, *46*
Hammersmith Centre, London,
England 1977–1979, *38*
Fred Olsen Passenger Terminal,
London, England 1969–1970, *23*

Project Awards

2001

Bathroom Foster for Duravit and Hoesch
Innovationspreis Architektur und Technik,
Sanitaryware Category
Electronic Arts European Headquarters
Civic Trust Award
Great Glasshouse, National Botanic
Garden of Wales
Civic Trust Award
H & V News Awards Environmental
Initiative of the Year
Helit Foster Series Desktop Furniture
Industrie Forum Design Hanover
Product Award Winner
Kingswood Technical Park
Civic Trust Award

2000

A900 Seating for Thonet
Design Innovation Red Dot Award
Baden-Württemberg International Design
Award 2000, Focus Working Environment
American Air Museum, Duxford
Celebrating Construction Achievement
Award
ASPIRE National Training Centre
Civic Trust Commendation
Canary Wharf Underground Station
RIBA Regional Architecture Award
British Construction Industry Awards,
Special Award for the Pursuit of
Engineering and Architectural
Excellence in Public Transport
Civic Trust Award
Railway Forum/Modern Railways Industry
Innovation Award
Royal Fine Art Commission Trust Building
of the Year Award, High Commendation
AIA UK Design Awards, Commendation
Electronic Arts European Headquarters
RIBA Regional Architecture Award
The Times/Gestetner Digital Office
Collection Award, Third Prize
Runnymede Borough Council Design
Award, Commercial Category
Whitby Bird and Partners' Structural Award

Great Glasshouse, National Botanic
Garden of Wales
RIBA Regional Architecture Award
Architecture in Wales Eisteddfod
Gold Medal in Architecture
Structural Steel Award
Royal Institute of Chartered Surveyors
Building Efficiency Award
The Concrete Society Building Award
The 2000 Leisure Property Awards,
Finalist for Best National Scheme
Helit Foster Series Desktop Furniture
Architektur und Office 2000, Architecture
and Industry in Partnership
Imperial College, Sir Alexander
Fleming Building
Civic Trust Commendation
J C Decaux International Headquarters
RIBA Regional Architecture Award
RIBA Crown Estate Conservation
Architecture Award
The Concrete Society and British Precast
Concrete Federation Award for Excellence
in Precast Concrete
New German Parliament, Reichstag
Architekturpreis 2000 des BDA Berlin
Auszeichnung
Preis des Deutschen Stahlbaues 2000
MIPIM Special Jury Prize
The Design Sense Corporate Award
North Greenwich Transport Interchange
Civic Trust Award
National Lighting Design Awards, Distinction
Room Control Device for Weidmüller
Industrie Forum Design Award
Saturn Lighting for Iguzzini
Industrie Forum Design Award
Singapore Expo Station
NRCA Gold Circle Award for Innovation
Metal Roofing and Cladding Association
of Australia Special Achievement Award
Institute of Engineers Australia, High
Commendation
World Port Centre
Corus Construction Award for
the Millennium

1999

American Air Museum, Duxford
Civic Trust Award
FX International Interior Design Award,
Best Museum
Concrete Society Award
Design Council Millennium Product Award
Hong Kong International Airport,
Chek Lap Kok
Construction Quality Awards International
Project of the Year
Structural Steel Design Award
International Lighting Design Award
of Excellence
Travel & Leisure Magazine Critics' Choice
Award for Best Airport
Design Council Millennium Product Award
Best Architecture in Hong Kong, Second
Prize, voted by the people of Hong Kong
Institute of Structural Engineers Structural
Award, Commendation
Hongkong and Shanghai Bank Headquarters
Best Architecture in Hong Kong, First
Prize, voted by the people of Hong Kong
Imperial College, Sir Alexander
Fleming Building
RIBA Regional Architecture Award
R & D Laboratory of the Year, USA,
High Honours
New German Parliament, Reichstag
RIBA Regional Architecture Award
RIBA Conservation Category Award
Deutscher Architekturpreis
ECCS European Award for Steel
Structures
Architects' Journal and Bovis Europe
Grand Award for Architecture at the
Royal Academy Summer Exhibition
Eurosol Preis für Solares Bauen
Design Council Millennium Product Award
Du Pont Benedictus Award,
Special Recognition
North Greenwich Transport Interchange
Aluminium Imagination Awards Winner
Structural Steel Design Award,
Commendation

Repsol Service Stations
  *City Planning, Architecture and
  Public Works Award, Madrid*
Robert Gordon University Faculty of
Management
  RIBA Regional Architecture Award
  Civic Society Award
Room Control Device for Weidmüller
  Design Plus Award
Valencia Congress Centre
  RIBA Regional Architecture Award
Willis Faber & Dumas Headquarters
  *British Council for Offices Test of
  Time Award, Commendation*

1998
Agiplan Headquarters
  *Bund Deutscher Architekten, 'Guter
  Bauten', Ruhr Area*
American Air Museum, Duxford
  RIBA Stirling Prize
  RIBA Regional Architecture Award
  *Royal Fine Art Commission BSkyB
  Building of the Year Award*
ASPIRE National Training Centre
  Harrow Heritage Trust Observer Award
Bath Road Offices
  Business Industry Agents Society Award
Bilbao Metro
  RIBA Regional Architecture Award
  Brunel Award, Madrid
  *Veronica Rudge Green Prize in
  Urban Design*
British Gas Offices, Thames Valley Park
  RIBA Regional Architecture Award
  British Council for Offices Award
Carré d'Art
  *Veronica Rudge Green Prize in
  Urban Design*
Commerzbank Headquarters
  RIBA Regional Achitecture Award
  *Bund Deutscher Architekten,
  Martin-Elsaesser-Plakette Award*
Duisburg Microelectronic Centre
  *Bund Deutscher Architekten Preis,
  Nordrhein Westfalen Area*

Great Glasshouse, National Botanic
Garden of Wales
  BIAT Open Award for Technical Excellence
Hong Kong International Airport,
Chek Lap Kok
  *British Construction Industry
  International Award*
  HKIA Silver Medal
Kingswood Technical Park
  Business Industry Agents Society Award
Kowloon-Canton Railway Terminal
  HKIA Certificate of Merit
Motorway Signage System
  Design Council Millennium Product Award
Wind Turbine for Enercon
  Design Council Millennium Product Award

1997
American Air Museum, Duxford
  *British Construction Industry Awards,
  High Commendation*
  *AIA London Chapter Excellence
  in Design Commendation*
  *British Guild of Travel Writers
  Silver Unicorn Award*
Bilbao Metro
  *Manuel de la Dehesa Award,
  Commendation*
Cambridge University Faculty of Law
  *David Urwin Design Awards,
  Commendation*
Commerzbank Headquarters
  *British Construction Industry
  International Award*
Duisburg Microelectronic Centre
  RIBA Regional Architecture Award

1996
Duisburg Microelectronic Centre
  *Bund Deutscher Architekten, 'Guter
  Bauten', Rechter Niederrhein Area*
Linz Solar City
  *International Academy of Architecture
  Medal and Honorary Diploma*
Solar-Electric Vehicle
  ID Design Distinction Award in Concepts

1995
Bilbao Metro
  Premio Radio Correo Award
Cranfield University Library
  Civic Trust Award
Duisburg Inner Harbour Masterplan
  *Disabled Access Award for Steiger
  Schwanentor*
Joslyn Art Museum Extension
  AIA State Architecture Award
  AIA Regional Architecture Award
  *American Concrete Institute (Nebraska)
  Award of Excellence*
Solar-Electric Vehicle
  Design Week Award for Product Design
  *Design Review Minerva Award,
  Commendation*

1994
Century Tower
  Intelligent Building Promotion Award
  *The Society of Heating, Air Conditioning
  and Sanitary Engineers of Japan Award*
Cranfield University Library
  *British Steel Colourcoat Award,
  Runner Up*
Duisburg Business Promotion Centre
  *Bund Deutsche Architekten
  Bezirksgruppe Ruhr Award*
Marine Simulator Centre
  Interiors (USA) Award
  *Architectural Review Best European
  Lighting Scheme Highlight Award*
Stansted Airport
  BBC Design Award Finalist

1993
Barcelona Telecommunications Tower,
Torre de Collserola
  *The Architecture and Urbanism Award
  of the City of Barcelona*
  The Architecture FAD Award, Barcelona
  The Opinion FAD Award, Barcelona
  Cultural Foundation of Madrid Award
Carré d'Art
  Interiors (USA) Award

Cranfield University Library
  RIBA Regional Architecture Award
  British Construction Industry
  Supreme Award
  British Construction Industry
  Building Award
  Interiors (USA) Award
  Eastern Electricity Commercial Property
  Award, Building of the Year
  Bedfordshire Design Award, Special Award
  Design Review Minerva Award,
  Commendation
  Financial Times Architecture
  Award, Commendation
  Concrete Society Award, Highly
  Commended
  Lighting Design Award, Highly
  Commended
Crescent Wing, Sainsbury Centre
for Visual Arts
  International Association of Lighting
  Designers Awards, Citation
Sackler Galleries, Royal Academy
of Arts
  RIBA Best Building of the Year Award
  Design Review Minerva Award
  Marble Architecture Award
Stansted Airport
  Benedictus Award, USA, for Innovative
  Use of Laminated Glass
  Financial Times Architecture
  Award, Commendation
Stockley Park Offices
  British Council for Offices Award

1992
Barcelona Telcommunications Tower,
Torre de Collserola
  Premio Alcantara Award for Public
  Works in Latin American Countries
Century Tower
  Nikkei Business Publications Award
  for New Technology
  BCS Award Tokyo
  Lightweight Metal Cladding
  Association Award

Crescent Wing, Sainsbury Centre
for Visual Arts
  RIBA Regional Architecture Award
  Civic Trust Award
  Design Review Minerva Award,
  Commendation
ITN Headquarters
  RIBA Regional Architecture Award
  British Council for Offices Best
  Building Award
  Design Review Minerva Award,
  Commendation
Sackler Galleries, Royal Academy
of Arts
  RIBA National Architecture Award
  RIBA Regional Architecture Award
  The Royal Fine Art Commission and
  Sunday Times Building of the Year Award
  Structural Steel Award
  Interiors (USA) Award
  Institution of Civil Engineers Merit Award
  British Construction Industry Award,
  High Commendation
  Mansell Refurbishment Award
  National Dryline Wall Award
  Design Review Minerva Award,
  Commendation
Stansted Airport
  RIBA National Architecture Award
  RIBA Regional Architecture Award
  Civic Trust Award
  Structural Steel Award
  Royal Institute of Chartered Surveyors
  Energy Efficiency Award
  Brunel Award, Madrid for British Rail Station
  Concrete Society Award
  English Tourist Board Car Park Award
  Design Review Minerva Award,
  Commendation
  Architects' Journal Hilight Lighting
  Award, Commendation

1991
Century Tower
  Institute of Structural Engineers
  Special Award

ITN Headquarters
  Aluminium Imagination Architectural Award
Stansted Airport
  Mies van der Rohe Pavilion Award for
  European Architecture
  British Construction Industry Supreme Award
  Aluminium Imagination Architectural Award
  Business and Industry Panel for
  the Environment Award
  Colourcoat Building Award
  British Gas Energy Management Award
  British Association of Landscape
  Industries Award
  Royal Town Planning Institute Silver
  Jubilee Award
  National Childcare Facilities Award
Stockley Park Offices
  Aluminium Imagination Architectural Award

1990
Willis Faber & Dumas Headquarters
  RIBA Trustees Medal

1989
Stockley Park Offices
  British Construction Industry Award

1988
Esprit Shop
  Interiors (USA) Award
Hongkong and Shanghai Bank Headquarters
  Quaternario Award for Innovative
  Technology in Architecture
  PA Innovations Award

1987
Nomos Desking System for Tecno
  Premio Compasso d'Oro Award
  Design Centre Award Stuttgart

1986
Hongkong and Shanghai Bank Headquarters
  Structural Steel Award
  R S Reynolds Memorial Award
  Institute of Structural Engineers
  Special Award

Renault Distribution Centre
First Prize, European Award for Industrial Architecture, Hanover

1984
Renault Distribution Centre
Civic Trust Award
Structural Steel Award
Financial Times Architecture at Work Award

1983
Hongkong and Shanghai Bank Headquarters
Premier Architectural Award at the Royal Academy of Arts, London

1981
IBM Technical Park
Financial Times Industrial Architecture Award
RIBA Commendation

1980
IBM Technical Park
Structural Steel Award
Sainsbury Centre for Visual Arts
Sixth Eternit International Prize for Architecture, Brussels
Ambrose Congreve Award
Museum of the Year Award

1979
Sainsbury Centre for Visual Arts
R S Reynolds Memorial Award
British Tourist Board Award

1978
Sainsbury Centre for Visual Arts
RIBA Award
Structural Steel Finniston Award

1977
Palmerston Special School
RIBA Award
Willis Faber & Dumas Headquarters
RIBA Award

1976
Palmerston Special School
Eternit International Prize for Architecture, Brussels
Willis Faber & Dumas Headquarters
R S Reynolds Memorial Award
Business and Industry Panel for the Environment Award

1974
Modern Art Glass Warehouse
Financial Times Industrial Architecture Award

1972
IBM Pilot Head Office
RIBA Award
Structural Steel Award

1971
Air-Supported Office for Computer Technology
Financial Times Industrial Architecture Award, Commendation

1970
Fred Olsen Amenity Centre
Financial Times Industrial Architecture Award, Commendation

1969
Creek Vean House
RIBA Award
Fred Olsen Amenity Centre
Architectural Design Project Award

1967
Reliance Controls Electronics Factory
Financial Times Industrial Architecture Award

1966
Reliance Controls Electronics Factory
Architectural Design Project Award

1965
Housing for Wates
Architectural Design Project Award

1964
Waterfront Housing
Architectural Design Project Award

Practice and Personal Awards

2001
Norman Foster
  South Bank Show Award for Visual Arts

1999
Norman Foster
  *Laureate of the 1999 Pritzker
  Architecture Prize
  Life Peerage in the Queen's Birthday
  Honours List
  Commander's Cross of the Order of
  Merit of the Federal Republic of Germany
  Le Prix Européen de l'Architecture de la
  Fondation Européenne de la Culture
  Special Prize, 4th Internatonal Biennial
  of Architecture, São Paulo, Brazil*

1998
Foster and Partners
  *The Building Award, Architectural
  Practice of the Year*
Norman Foster
  German-British Forum, Special Prize

1997
Foster and Partners
  *The Building Award, Large Architectural
  Practice of the Year
  British Construction Industry Awards,
  A Decade of Success 1988–1997
  International Association of Lighting
  Designers IALD/Hilight Excellence
  in Lighting Award
  European Aluminium Award
  for Architecture*
Norman Foster
  *Appointed to the Order of Merit
  by the Queen
  Silver Medal of the Chartered Society
  of Designers
  International Academy of Architecture
  Grand Prize '97 Cristal Globe
  Prince Philip Designers Prize,
  Special Commendation
  Premi a la millor tasca de promoció
  international de Barcelona*

1996
Foster and Partners
  *The Building Award, Large Architectural
  Practice of the Year*
Norman Foster
  *American Academy of Arts and
  Sciences Award
  The Building Award, Construction
  Personality of the Year
  MIPIM Man of the Year Award
  Honorary Doctorate, Doctoris Honoris
  Causa, Technical University of Eindhoven
  Honorary Doctorate, Doctor of Letters
  Honoris Causa, University of Oxford
  Honorary Doctorate of Literature,
  University of London*

1995
Foster and Partners
  *The Building Award, Architectural Practice
  of the Year
  Queen's Award for Export Achievement*
Norman Foster
  *Gold Medal, Universidad Internacional
  Menedez Pelayo Santander, Spain*

1994
Foster and Partners
  CICA CAD Drawing Award
Norman Foster
  *American Institute of Architects Gold Medal
  Officer of the Order of Arts and Letters,
  Ministry of Culture, France*

1993
Norman Foster
  Honorary Degree, University of Manchester

1992
Norman Foster
  *Arnold W Brunner Memorial Prize from the
  American Academy and Institute of Arts
  and Letters, New York
  Honorary Degree, University of Valencia,
  Spain
  Honorary Degree, University of Humberside*

1991
Norman Foster
  *Gold Medal of the French Academy
  of Architecture
  Honorary Doctorate, Royal College of Art,
  London*

1990
Norman Foster
  *The Chicago Architecture Award
  Knighthood in the Queen's Birthday
  Honours List*

1989
Norman Foster
  *Grosse Kunstpreis Award, Akademie der
  Kunst, Berlin*

1988
Norman Foster
  Royal Designer for Industry

1987
Norman Foster
  Japan Design Foundation Award

1986
Norman Foster
  Honorary Doctorate, University of Bath

1984
Foster and Partners
  *Honourable Mention, UIA Auguste
  Perret Prize for Applied Technology
  in Architecture*

1983
Norman Foster
  The Royal Gold Medal for Architecture

1980
Norman Foster
  *Honorary Doctorate, University of East
  Anglia*

Practice Details

Partners
Norman Foster
Spencer de Grey
David Nelson
Graham Phillips
Ken Shuttleworth

Directors
Stefan Behling
Grant Brooker
Iain Godwin
Brandon Haw
Paul Kalkhoven
Mouzhan Majidi
Andrew Miller
Robin Partington
John Silver
Mark Sutcliffe

Project Directors
Sean Affleck
Andy Bow
Chris Bubb
Chris Connell
Nigel Dancey
John Drew
Gerard Evenden
Pedro Haberbosch
Christian Hallmann
Katy Harris
Richard Hawkins
Richard Hyams
Mike Jeliffe
David Jenkins
Iwan Jones
Michael Jones
Jan Landolt
Antoinette
Nassopoulos
Max Neal
Sven Ollmann
Jonathan Parr
Tom Politowicz
Tim Quick
Charles Rich
Giles Robinson

Paul Scott
John Small
Huw Thomas
Andrew Thomson
Brian Timmoney
Neil Vandersteen
Chris Windsor
Armstrong Yakubu

Associates
Ewan Anderson
Bob Ashworth
Mark Atkinson
John Ball
Alexander Barry
Gamma Basra
Lee Bennett
Toby Blunt
Etienne Borgos
Simon Bowden
Arthur Branthwaite
Angus Campbell
Kevin Carrucan
Mark Costello
David Crosswaite
Steve Day
Bryn Dyer
Matteo Fantoni
D'Arcy Fenton
Frank Filskow
Lulie Fisher
Jason Flannagan
Mike Gardner
Anna Garreau
Simon Hallett
Ulrich Hamann
Darron Haylock
Ken Hogg
Thouria Istephan
Reinhard Joecks
David Keech
Lester Korzilius
Stuart Latham
Paul Leadbetter
Alistair Lenczner
Neil MacLeod

Nikolai Malsch
Robert McFarlane
Bobbie Michael
Niall Monaghan
Katherine Murphy
Justin Nicholls
Anthony O'Donovan
Ross Palmer
Jason Parker
Divya Patel
Ingo Pott
John Prevc
Tony Price
Catherine Ramsden
Simon Reed
Martin Riese
David Rosenberg
Narinder Sagoo
Paul Smith
Hugh Stewart
David Summerfield
Steve Trstenjak
Nic Underwood
Juan Vieira-Pardo
John Walden
Jeremy Wallis
Colin Ward
Chris West
Miriam White
Hugh Whitehead
Richard Wotton
Michael Wurzel
Edson Yabiku

**Foster and Partners
Architects and Designers**
Riverside Three
22 Hester Road
London SW11 4AN
Tel 020 7738 0455
Fax 020 7738 1107/08
enquiries@fosterandpartners.com
www.fosterandpartners.com

Index

Picture Credits

l = left, m = middle, r = right, t = top, b = bottom.
Thanks are due to the following for permission to reproduce copyright photographs and drawings:

Acerbis: 107(4)
Aerofilms Ltd: 23(2)
Aitor Oritiz: 87(5)
Arcaid/Richard Bryant: 6(1), 40(1,3), 41(6,7), 67(9), 132(1), 200(2), 249(m)
Arcaid/Richard Einzig: 18(2), 19(4–6), 67(4)
Arup: 10(1), 227(7)
Atelier Weidner/Imebisa: 86(1)
Birds Portchmouth Russum Architects: 19(3), 93(4), 96(2), 109(3), 133(5), 169(6), 185(4), 195(1), 200(1), 222–3(1)
Clive Boursnall: 50(2,3)
Broadway Malyan: 71(4)
Robert Canfield: 168(1,2), 169(5)
Mario Carrieri: 208–9
Pietro Carrieri/Tecno spa: 58(1), 59(8)
Martin Charles: 72(1), 73(3,4)
Peter Cook: 83(5)
Richard Davies: 29(5), 35(5), 51(4), 52(1,2), 53, 62(1), 63(4), 65(4), 68(2), 69(3,4), 70(2), 71(3), 83(4), 84(3), 87(4,6), 88(1), 90(1), 94(1), 98(2), 99(3), 112(1), 113(4), 117(1–3), 139(3), 151(2), 160(2), 161(3,4), 170(1), 174(3), 187(3), 189(7), 214(2), 223(2), 230–1(2), 231(1), 247(l),
Spencer de Grey: 54(1)
John Donat: 26(2), 211(7)
Patrick Drickey: 118(1), 119
Duravit/Hoesch: 178(2–4)
Enercon: 140(1)
Essen Design Centre: 122(1)
Georg Fisher: 116(2)
Norman Foster: 16–17, 18(1), 20(2), 21(3,4), 25(2), 26(3), 29(4), 30(1), 35(4), 40(2), 41(4,8), 42(1,2), 45(3,4),

47(4), 50(1), 52(3), 55(3,5), 58(2), 60(3), 63(2), 65(3), 67(5), 73(5), 81(7), 83(3), 84(1,4), 87(3), 95(2), 97(3), 102(2), 107(5), 113(6,7), 118(3), 121(2), 125(5), 132(3), 142(2), 148(1), 150(1), 152(2), 156(1), 165(3), 173(2), 175(3), 179(7,8), 180(2), 186(1), 187(2), 188(1), 191(4,5), 196(1), 198(2), 204(2,3), 207(3), 210(2,3), 213(6), 219(4–6), 220(2), 226(1), 227(4,5)
Ti Foster: 169(3)
Foster and Partners: 7(4), 12(1), 13(3), 20(1), 22(2), 25(4), 28(2), 31(3,5), 34(1,3), 36(1), 37(9,10) 38(1), 39(3), 44(2), 47(5), 51(5), 54(2), 55(4), 63(5), 64(1), 66(2), 67(8), 68(1), 70(1), 75(4), 81(5), 86(2), 89(8), 90(2), 95(3), 98(1), 101(2,4), 107(6), 114(1,3), 116(1,4), 117(4), 120(2), 122(3), 130(1), 137(4), 138(1,2), 139(1), 141(5,6), 144(2–4), 145(3), 146(2), 148(3), 150(4), 156(2), 160(1), 163(2), 164(2), 165(3), 166(3), 171(1), 173(5), 176(3), 177(6), 186(2), 191(2), 197(3), 199(4), 201(1), 203(2,3,5), 204(1), 211(5), 212(3), 213(7), 214(1,3), 217(3), 218(2), 224(1), 228(2), 231(3), 245(r)
Foster Visualisation: 11(3), 13(4), 69(3), 81(4), 139(2), 141(4), 144(1), 146(1) (Nigel Young), 147(5), 167(1) (Nigel Young), 170(2), 174(1,2), 187(1), 188(2), 189(4,6,8,10), 191(3), 192–3 (Nigel Young), 195(2–3), 202(1) (Richard Davies), 203(4), 205 (Richard Davies), 216–17(2) (Richard Davies), 218(1), 219(3), 224–5(2) (Nigel Young), 226(2,3), 227(6), 244(m) (Richard Davies), 249(r) (Richard Davies)
Yukio Futagawa: 238(l)
GDP Architects: 211(5)
Getmapping Plc: 175(2)

GMJ: 180–1(1) (Jeremy Young), 190(1) (Foster Visualisation)
Hayes Davidson: 136–7(1) (Richard Davies), 186(3) (Tom Miller), 161(1), 216(1)
John Hewitt: 10(2)
Birkin Howard: 29(3,6,7), 36(2–4), 37(5–8), 39(2)
Aliastair Hunter: 44(1)
Kerun Ip: 130(2), 131(1), 171(2)
Helmut Jacoby: 63(3), 201(2), 245(l)
Ben Johnson: 82(2), 84(2), 158–9
Joslyn Art Museum: 118(2)
Ken Kirkwood: 24(1), 25(3), 27(5), 30(2), 31(4), 32–3, 34(2), 46(2,3), 107(7)
Holger Knauf: 145(1,3)
Mirko Kritzarovic: 80(2), 248(r)
Ian Lambot: 42(3), 44, 72(2), 102(3), 103, 104–5, 116(3), 211(4), 244(l), 248(l)
John Edward Linden: 85, 96(1), 97(4), 169(4), 249(l)
Satoru Mishima: 66(1,3)
James H Morris: 56–7, 93(3), 121(1,3), 211(6)
Obayashi Corporation: 91
Joe Poon: 128(2), 148(2), 149
Michel Porro: 7(3), 125(4)
Paul Raftery: 41(5), 101(3)
Klaus Ravenstein: 120(1)
Tim Soar: 106(2), 157(4)
Space Syntax: 69(5,6)
Tim Street Porter: 22 (1,3), 23(1,3), 26(1), 27(4), 28(1), 246(l)
Peter Strobel: 58(3), 59(4–7), 80(3), 152(1,3), 153(4–7), 179(5,6)
Tecno spa: 106(1), 157(4)
Don Varney: 244(r)
View/Dennis Gilbert: 14(1), 46(1,2) 60(1,2), 61, 67(6,7), 79(3), 89(7), 92(1,2), 97(5), 100(1), 107(3), 115(4,5), 124(1,2), 125(3), 126–7, 128(1) 128–9(3), 130(3), 132(2), 151(1,3), 154(1,2), 155, 157(5),

Credits

176(1,2), 185(3), 245(m)
Visum/Rudi Meisel: 4, 133(4),
134–5, 211(8), 212(2), 213(4),
232(tl, tr, ml, bl, bm), 233(tl, tr, m,
mr, bm), 234–5, 236, 237, 238(m, r),
241(l), 242(l)
Morley von Steinberg: 150(2,3)
Jens Willebrand: 89(5), 123(5)
Nigel Young: 6(2), 8, 9(1), 12(2),
15, 48–9, 64(2), 74(1), 75(2,3),
76–7, 78(1), 79(4), 80(1), 81(6),
82(1), 88(2–4), 89(6), 102(1),
108(1), 109(2), 110–11, 112(2,3),
113(5), 114(2), 122(2), 123(4,6),
137(2,3), 140(2,3), 142(1), 143(3–5),
147(3,4), 157(3,6), 162–3(1), 163(3),
164(1), 165(4,5), 166(1,2), 170(3),
172(1), 173(3,4), 175(1), 177(4,5),
178(1), 181(3,4), 182–3, 184(1,2),
189(3,5,9), 194(1), 196–7(2),
198(1,3), 199(5,6), 206(1,2),
207(4,5), 210(1), 212(1), 213(5),
220(1), 221(3,4), 223(3,4), 228(1),
228–9(3), 232(m, r), 233(m, l), 239,
240, 241(m, r), 242(m, r), 243,
246(m, r), 247(l)

Every effort has been made to
contact copyright holders and the
publishers apologise for any omissions,
which they will be pleased to rectify at
the earliest opportunity.

Editing: David Jenkins, Philippa Baker,
Gerard Forde, Christine Davis

Picture Research: Kate Stirling, Stephan
Potchatek, Katy Harris, Lois McDowell,
Eleanor Clark

Design: Thomas Manss & Company
with Per Arnoldi, Thomas Manss,
Lisa Sjukur

Research: Matthew Foreman, Janneke Lewis

Book Production: Turner Publicaciones, Madrid